CRISIS IN THE REFORMED CHURCHES

Crisis
IN THE REFORMED CHURCHES

Essays in
Commemoration of
the Great Synod of Dort,
1618-1619

Peter Y.
De Jong,
Editor

Reformed Fellowship, Inc.
3363 Hickory Ridge Ct. SW
Grandville, MI 49418

© 1968, 2008
All rights reserved.

Reformed Fellowship, Inc. is a religious and strictly nonprofit organization composed of a group of Christian believers who hold to the biblical Reformed faith. Its purpose is to advocate and propagate this faith, to nurture those who seek to live in obedience to it, to give sharpened expression to it, to stimulate the doctrinal sensitivities of those who profess it, to promote the spiritual welfare and purity of the Reformed churches, and to encourage Christian action.

www.reformedfellowship.net

Requests for permission to quote from this book should be directed to: Editor, The Reformed Fellowship, 3363 Hickory Ridge Court, Wyoming, MI 49418.

Book design by Jeff Steenholdt.

Printed in the United States of America

ISBN 978-0-9793677-6-2

CONTENTS

INTRODUCTION TO THE SECOND PRINTING *9*
INTRODUCTION TO THE FIRST PRINTING *11*
CONTRIBUTORS *14*

ONE
The Rise of the Reformed Churches in the Netherlands *17*
Peter Y. De Jong

TWO
The Background of the Arminian Controversy (1586–1618) *39*
Louis Praamsma

THREE
Leading Figures at the Synod of Dort *57*
Simon Kistemaker

FOUR
The Doctrinal Deliverances of Dort *73*
Fred H. Klooster

FIVE
The Synod and Bible Translation *121*
Marten H. Woudstra

SIX
Preaching and the Synod of Dort *143*
Peter Y. De Jong

SEVEN
The Significance of the Canons for Pastoral Work *169*
Edwin H. Palmer

EIGHT
Calvin, Dort and Westminster on Predestination—
A Comparative Study *183*
John Murray

NINE
Recent Reformed Criticisms of the Canons *195*
Klaas Runia

TEN
The Significance of Dort for Today *215*
Cornelius Van Til

APPENDIX A
Chronological Table *233*

APPENDIX B
Biographical Notes *235*

APPENDIX C
The Remonstrance of 1610 *243*

APPENDIX D
The Counter Remonstrance of 1611 *247*

APPENDIX E
Political Commissioners Assigned by the States-General *251*

APPENDIX F
Delegates to the Synod of Dort *253*

APPENDIX G
Remonstrants Cited to Appear at Synod *259*

APPENDIX H
The Opinions of the Remonstrants *261*

APPENDIX I
The Canons of Dort *269*

INDEX *307*

ENDNOTES *315*

INTRODUCTION TO THE SECOND PRINTING

Forty years ago the Board of Reformed Fellowship commissioned nine men, who today would be considered a "Who's Who" in Reformed theology, to commemorate the 350th anniversary of the Synod of Dort. Under the leadership of the editor, Dr. Peter Y. De Jong, these giants in the faith wrote on a variety of topics regarding this great event in Reformed history. Their contributions brought to the Christian community a greater understanding of the history and necessity of the Synod of Dort, the key figures involved in the Synod, and the application of the decisions made at the Synod to the tumultuous times within the church during the sixties. Each article reflected not only the expertise of the writer, but also his love for the Reformed faith.

In the ensuing years, serious discussions of the Synod of Dort always included references to *Crisis in the Reformed Faith*. Historians, theologians, seminary students, and ministers alike, shared an appreciation for the work of the remarkable defenders of the faith that made their case at the Synod of Dort; and also, for the faithful servants of God who diligently defended the Reformed faith as it was challenged in the twentieth century.

Four decades after its original publication, the Board of Reformed Fellowship is honored to be able to present a second printing of *Crisis in the Reformed Churches*. As the church enters a new millennium, those who hold to the Reformed faith see the crisis within the church is not limited to the seventeenth century nor the twentieth century. The church militant must always be ready to give an account of what she believes, defending her faith rooted in the Word of God.

By understanding our history, may the church move forward until the sovereign God who rules over the church brings us into the church victorious through his Son, Jesus Christ.

On behalf of the Board
and in service to the King,

Rev. Wybren H. Oord
Editor of *The Outlook*

INTRODUCTION TO THE FIRST PRINTING

This coming November marks the passing of three hundred fifty years since the great Synod of Dort convened. Under the aegis of the States-General of the United Republic of the Netherlands, delegates from Reformed churches throughout that land gathered with accredited representatives of several branches of Reformed Christendom in Europe. The aim of the assembly was not theological dialogue but ecclesiastical deliberation and decision. It constituted, therefore, a significant landmark in the story of early Protestantism.

Synod met to resolve a crisis that had plagued the Dutch church and nation for more than two decades. Here Reformation insights were consolidated to achieve a more effective and unified ministry by Christ's church in an age of change and challenge. Too often the catholicity of its concerns has been obscured by a preoccupation with the dismissal and eventual deposition of the Arminians whose views were deemed at variance with the confessional declarations of the churches. Although this matter was of immediate and central interest to Synod, it sought to regulate the totality of the church's life and labors in accordance with "the doctrine which is according to godliness." In this way a serious, Scripturally-based attempt was made to meet the challenge of its own time. And the influence of Dort in and far beyond the confines of the Netherlands continues to our day.

The configurations of today's crisis in church and world differ, indeed, from those of the days of Dort. Yet the underlying issues remain remarkably similar. They concern the church and its calling in God's world that is experiencing a crisis to which the only satisfactory solution is the gospel of our Lord Jesus Christ. Christian doctrine, so much misunderstood and even maligned, sustains an inescapable connection with human perplexities and probings. Men are and live by what at the deepest levels of their existence they believe. Thus ineluctably, even though often unwittingly, they help to shape the society in which they live.

This significance of Christian doctrine for the crisis of our years has been signalized by J.S. Whale in *The Christian Tradition,* who reminds us that,

> Without a similar transcending faith [i.e. like that of the children of the Reformation] liberalism is wistful and lost. It complains that a Hitler, a Stalin, or any dictator typical of the modern age has no sense of the sanctity of individual personality. This is true. It is the most ghastly truth of our time. But if there be no living God, the sovereign Creator, and Redeemer, in whose image man is made, why should the individual take precedence over the mass; over the Party or Nation or Race? . . .

It is precisely in those countries where they care nothing for Christ's death that in a very short space of time they come to care nothing for a man's life . . . It has become increasingly evident to us that the sacred right of the individual human person is *a sacred* right, but only because it presupposes a dogmatic faith in a revelation from on high . . .

This Calvinists in the early seventeenth century sensed. Theological issues were their food and drink. They felt they could not carry on in home and society and state, they could not build schools and pay taxes and wage war against Spanish tyranny and sail their ships across the seas, unless in their hearts these issues were resolved. Hence they discussed what God said to them in his Word—about the world in which they lived, the deep need of all men, the grace revealed in Christ, God's plan for man's redemption and reconciliation and renewal, the call to live in obedience to the divine will. With such matters Dort concerned itself. And with such matters the church today must concern itself daily and deeply, if it is to meet the crisis of this age.

In commemoration of that Synod, which has so signally influenced the course of Reformed Christendom ever since, this symposium is presented. By no means all aspects of its contributions to the life of the churches could be considered. Only an introduction has been attempted to what requires far broader and more basic treatment than a single volume could offer. Yet it is hoped that in the light of these pages about the past, the confessing church today may with greater clarity and conviction warn against all deviation in doctrine and duty as it proclaims by words and deeds the glorious gospel of God's free grace in Christ Jesus.

Deep appreciation is expressed to the contributors whose willingness to write has made this book possible. Thanks are also due to Prof. Dr. Anthony A. Hoekema of Calvin Theological Seminary for his translation of the *Sententia Remonstrantium*, as well as to Prof. Merle Meeter of Dordt College for assistance in gathering material for the third chapter. For financial arrangements in connection with the publication we are indebted to the business committee of Reformed Fellowship, Inc. The editor assumes responsibility for preparing most of the Appendices and for the Index that, although by no means exhaustive, may provide some assistance to the readers.

May the Lord who "gathers, defends, and preserves for himself, by his Spirit and Word, in the unity of the true faith, a Church chosen to everlasting life" employ these pages for a truer understanding of and a deeper commitment to the gospel of God's sovereign grace as defended by the fathers of Dort.

Peter Y. De Jong
June 1968

CONTRIBUTORS

Peter Y. De Jong (1915–2005) served as pastor for several churches in the Christian Reformed denomination and as professor of Practical Theology at Calvin Theological Seminary, Grand Rapids, MI. He was one of the founders of Mid-America Reformed Seminary in Dyer, IN. He was the author of several books, including *The Covenant Idea in New England Theology, Taking Heed to the Flock, The Ministry of Mercy for Today,* and *The Church's Witness to the World* (2 vol.).

Simon Kistemaker is Professor of New Testament Emeritus at Reformed Theological Seminary. His major work, the seven-volume *New Testament Commentary,* was initiated by Dr. William Hendriksen. He is also author of several other books, including *The Psalm-citations in the Epistle to the Hebrews, The Parables of Jesus, The Gospels in Current Study, The Conversations of Jesus,* and *Miracles of Jesus.* A past president of the Evangelical Theological Society, he also served as its secretary-treasurer from 1976 to 1992.

Fred H. Klooster (1922–2003) served for many years as professor of Systematic Theology at Calvin Theological Seminary, Grand Rapids, MI. He was the author of *The Incomprehensibility of God in the Orthodox Presbyterian Conflict, Calvin's Doctrine of Predestination, The Significance of Barth's Theology: an Appraisal,* and *Our Only Comfort,* a comprehensive commentary on the Heidelberg Catechism in two volumes.

John Murray (1898–1975) was born in Scotland. He taught at Princeton Seminary, and was one of the founders of Westminster Theological Seminary, Philadelphia, PA, where he served for many years as professor of Systematic Theology. He was the author of *Conduct: Aspects of Biblical Ethics, Divorce, Christian Baptism, Calvin on Scripture and Divine Sovereignty, Principles of Redemption Accomplished and Applied,* and *The Epistle to the Romans* (2 vol.).

Contributors

Edwin H. Palmer (1922–1980) A minister of the Christian Reformed Church, he also served as professor at Westminster Theological Seminary from 1960–64. He served as executive secretary of the Committee on Bible Translation that produced the New International Version. He was the author of *Scheeben's Doctrine of Divine Adoption*, *The Holy Spirit*, and *The Five points of Calvinism*, and general publisher of the *Encyclopedia of Christianity*.

Louis Praamsma (1910–1984) was professor of Church History at Calvin Theological Seminary, Grand Rapids, MI, from 1962 to 1963, and minister in the Christian Reformed Church in Canada. He was the author of *Abraham Kuyper als Kerkhistoricus, Calvijn, Het dwaze Gods, De Belijdenis in de Crisis*, and *Kerkenordening en Geschiedenis*, and *Let Christ Be King: Reflections on the Life and Times of Abraham Kuyper*.

Klaas Runia (1926–2006) was professor of Systematic Theology at the Reformed Theological College, Geelong (Victoria), Australia, and later professor of Practical Theology in the Theological Seminary in Kampen, the Netherlands. He was the author of *De Theologische Tijd bij Karl Barth met Name in zijn Anthropologie, I Believe in God, Karl Barth's Doctrine of Holy Scriptures*, and *Op zoek naar de Geest*.

Cornelius Van Til (1895–1987) was professor of Apologetics at Westminster Theological Seminary, Philadelphia, PA, and author of *The New Modernism, The Case for Calvinism, Common Grace, Christianity and Barthianism, The Defense of the Faith*, and *A Christian Theory of Knowledge*.

Marten H. Woudstra (1922–1991) was professor of Old Testament at Calvin Theological Seminary, Grand Rapids, MI, and author of *Calvin's Dying Bequest to the Church, The Ark of the Covenant from Conquest to Kingship*, and *The Book of Joshua*. He was one of the translators of the *New International Version* of the Bible.

1 THE RISE OF THE REFORMED CHURCHES IN THE NETHERLANDS

Peter Y. De Jong

That the great Synod of Dort (1618–19) deserves to be remembered as one of the two or three decisive events in the history of the Netherlands has been widely recognized by historians. The subsequent history of neither the Dutch nation or the Dutch churches can be rightly understood apart from it.

Here the threshold was crossed from the growing pains of adolescence to that maturity that ushered in "the Golden Age of the Dutch Republic"—a period of some fifty years in which a small nation established on mist-enshrouded marshlands enjoyed a living standard second to none in that age, developed a rich culture in which all ranks of society could share, demonstrated military prowess that held at bay mighty monarchs and their armies, and sent ships across the seven seas to establish a colonial empire that survived the vicissitudes of the centuries until most recent times. Not until a scion of the house of Orange, William the Third, who married the daughter of Charles II, became joint-sovereign of Great Britain did the leadership among the nations of northern Europe pass from the Dutch to the English. By this time the temper of the Dutch people had been tested in a series of struggles and successes to become what it has largely remained until today. And in this process Dort also played its role.

This may seem a strange judgment, since ecclesiastical assemblies are usually accounted as of small significance. Especially among more recent historians the role of the church in the evolution of a people and a nation has often been obscured by an excessive preoccupation with economic, political, and sociological factors. Yet important as all these are in the story of the Netherlands, they cannot be correctly assessed apart from the religious and ecclesiastical development that culminated in Dort. That Synod has been evaluated so differently by so many. Some regard it as little more than a passing phenomenon on the crowded stage of Dutch history. To others it signalizes the triumph for a season of a harsh, iron-clad theological system over the minds of a liberty-loving people, compelling a conformity that threatened to stifle all that is unique in the Dutch national temperament. To still others it remains the crowning act wherein the Lord of all history showed favor to the land by safeguarding both the political unity of the people and the confessional integrity of the church. Dort, indeed, was not a political assembly. It did not even discuss political issues. Yet it could not meet without political sanction, and its decisions could not be implemented without the subsequent approval and action of the State.

This intertwining of ecclesiastical and political concerns makes an inquiry into what Dort did both fascinating and frustrating. In a very real sense church and state grew up together to shape the Dutch nation. Since the Synod can be understood only against this background, it becomes essential to trace the rise of the Reformed churches in that land as contemporaneous with the struggle for national independence.

The Land and Its People

During the late medieval and early modern period the Netherlands did not constitute the relatively homogeneous ethnic and political unit that we know today. By the beginning of the fifteenth century, however, there were signs of that development that was to make it great for a season.[1]

By then these territories lying along the English Channel and the North Sea were, with the exception of Renaissance Italy, the most influential in all Europe. Older historians have described in glowing terms the industry, intelligence, and prosperity of the people. Agriculture, manufacturing, and commerce were equally lucrative. More than three hundred cities, some of them among the largest on the Continent, were sustained by what flowed into the marketplaces, coffers, and kitchens of the inhabitants. With hinterlands and foreign ports an exciting and expanding trade was conducted to the advantage of the Dutch. And with almost every land- or sea-borne carrier came new ideas. All this stimulated the people. Their ingenuity was demonstrated in the invention of implements and machines of all kinds, as well as in the acquisition of the new learning that was to shake the foundations of the whole western world.

"God created the world, but the Dutch made Netherlands," so runs the well-worn adage. And in so far as the people had wrested much of the land on which they lived and labored from the ever-encroaching sea, this was true. But in an even deeper sense the sea made the Dutch. Without its trackless paths, restlessly explored and charted and controlled, the story of church and nation would have been quite different. The sea expanded the horizons of the people. It challenged them to meet all odds, no matter how formidable. It put strength and stubbornness in their souls. It compelled them, while clinging tenaciously to an innate love for personal freedom and privilege, to cooperate in seeking an even greater strength in unity. These are among the basic, although elusive and indefinable, ingredients that also go into telling the story of Dort. That assembly, because of its peculiar relationships to the social and cultural and political orders, marks the time when the Dutch began to come of age.

By the time of the Reformation there were ties of several kinds without a corresponding political and religious unity. These territories were linked to both the Roman Catholic Church and the Holy Roman Empire, yet these ties were loose and to a large extent imposed from without. Here, then, was a unity that could be easily shattered into a thousand antagonistic pieces by the individualistic and fiercely independent spirit of a people who refused to submit to imprudent rigor.

What political unity did obtain was of a strange sort. The territory consisted of a large number of provinces, duchies, bishoprics, and quasi-independent cities, each jealous of their rights inherited from the past. Much of the area had belonged to the patrimony of the Burgundian princes. By marriage, purchase and force of arms they had acquired this rich and powerful domain. Ruling over lands so strategically located at the mouths of several large rivers, they possessed peculiar political and military advantages that enabled them to withstand successfully the overweening ambitions of the rulers of France, England, and the neighboring German lands. When the line of Burgundian princes became extinct at the death of Charles the Bold (1433–1477), all these territories were under his control except the duchy of Guelders, the bishoprics of Liege and Utrecht, and some extensive tracts in the remote northeast.

Now the story of the Netherlands becomes intertwined with that of the larger European powers, notably Austria and Spain. This set the stage for the tumultuous and trying events of the sixteenth century.

Louis IX of France at once seized Burgundy together with Charolais and Artois and attempted to annex by force the prosperous province of Flanders.[2] This was viewed with envious eyes by the English who depended largely on a flourishing wool-trade with the Lowlands. Meanwhile Mary, as heiress of Charles the Bold, married Maximilian I of the house of Hapsburg. Thus was the strong link forged between Austria and the Netherlands that continued for some centuries. Their son in turn married Joanna, daughter of Ferdinand and Isabella of Spain. From this union was born Charles V whose name is inextricably bound up with the story of the Dutch church and nation. In his day he was Europe's most powerful ruler.[3]

Control over the Netherlands with its advantageous location on the sea and its vast financial resources enabled him to dominate the political scene and thereby also succor the Roman Catholic Church, which was losing its hold on many nations. By the time he bequeathed his far-flung empire to his son Philip II in 1555, all that today belongs to the kingdoms of the Netherlands and Belgium together with some regions of northern France, the dependencies of the bishop of Liege excepted, was politically consolidated. To obtain this he pledged to maintain the rights and privileges that local areas had enjoyed for centuries. Thus a balance was struck between a strongly centralized monarchy and a large measure of local self-government. In the provinces he appointed lieutenants (called "Stadholders") from among the princes. They were to promote the authority of the king as well as to defend the rights of people. So long as both objectives could be reasonably attained, the stability of the political order was assured.

Much of this political consolidation took place when Europe was in ferment because of the rising tide of the Reformation. As devoted son of the Roman Catholic Church and champion of absolute monarchy Charles V took measures early in his reign to stifle every inclination to tolerate or propagate the heresy of Protestantism.[4] This might have had some hope of success among his Austrian or Spanish subjects; it could only end in bitter and protracted opposition among the liberty-loving Netherlanders. To them his edicts against heresy constituted not only an attack on personal rights; they violated those civic and political privileges that had been solemnly guaranteed to them.

For several reasons no open rebellion leading to independence flared during his reign. Charles was always regarded by many of the people as more a Netherlander than a Spaniard. In addition, many of his edicts were not too strictly enforced.[5] Protestantism during the first years also was not a movement with strong leadership. And the king was not above taking a pragmatic view of the situation from time to time. It cannot be denied that he was always deeply interested in the prosperity of those lands, the more so when his many military involvements required the huge sums that could be raised in the Netherlands. During his time persecutions compelled many to seek refuge in other lands for a season. Yet these were only harbingers of a policy that was to bring these lands to the brink of ruin.

When Philip II took upon himself the government of these territories that had yielded such rich profits, he displayed a much greater reluctance to temporize.[6] Under him foreign troops together with the Spanish Inquisition were introduced, in order to achieve a religious unity that all the placards of his father had failed to secure. Now the majority of the people—irrespective of either social position or ecclesiastical affiliation—rose in rebellion. Thus within ten years after his accession to power the war of independence broke out in eighty years of fury.[7] During the early decades of that struggle the Reformed church was to be organized and recognized as the religion of the land and the Dutch people were to become a free nation among the other nations of the world.

The Early Years of the Reformation

The rise of Protestantism in the Netherlands distinguishes itself in several respects from that in neighboring lands. Here was no outstanding leader to rally the people around his standard. Much less do we find the Reformation inaugurated or encouraged by political authorities. Instead it developed gradually among the masses who listened to the teaching and preaching of individuals dissatisfied with conditions in the church.

This pattern compelled those inclined to the new way to be content with a day of small beginnings. Rather than accepting Protestantism in one form and by a common act, the Netherlanders had to make it a matter of personal decision. Thus the movement spread from individual to individual, from one family and community to another, often leaving large areas undisturbed for a long time in their allegiance to Roman Catholic doctrine and practice. Only in this restricted sense can it be called a popular movement. This accounts also for its comparatively slow and at times unsteady progress, as well as for the wide variety of opinions propagated especially in the early years. This does not mean that the Netherlands proved to be hard and unfruitful soil for ecclesiastical reformation. On the contrary, the ground had been prepared by individuals and movements and circumstances for more than a century and a half before Luther nailed his 95 theses to the church door in Wittenberg.

Especially in this country a growing and sustained interest developed in what took place in other parts of the world. Here men enjoyed more than average proficiency in learning and letters. The people boasted that even fishermen who dwelt in the huts of Friesland could read and write and discuss how the Bible should be understood. Waldensians had found shelter in these lands during the thirteenth and fourteenth centuries.[8] The Brethren of the Common Life, a lay organization committed to educating the people and increasing their piety, led many to a deeper spirituality.[9] Famous preachers like Ruysbroec stressed simple truths of the gospel that had been so long neglected by ecclesiastical leaders.[10] By 1445 the literary organizations, known as "Rederijkerskamers," had passed from clerical to lay control and thus could engage much more freely in criticizing abuses within the church.[11] Before the Reformation many books were being published in the land, partly in consequence of the work of Laurens Jansz. Koster who vies with Gutenberg as the inventor of moveable type.

It comes as no surprise, therefore, that even without strong indigenous leadership Protestantism quickly took root.

Two matters of significance with respect to ecclesiastical organization in that day deserve mention. These affected the turn of events for both church and state in the years that followed and indicate why the concerns of both were so interrelated until and even after the days of Dort.

The first was the lack of unified organization for the church throughout the Netherlands. For a land with a burgeoning population in the opening years of the fifteenth century the number of bishoprics was unusually small. No reform on this score was suggested by Rome. Meanwhile the bishop of Liege ruled over Dutch territory that sustained no political ties with the rest of the country. All the other provinces, duchies, and cities were integrated for control into episcopal provinces with sees in either France or Germany, thus further dividing the allegiance of the people. When reform on this score finally came in 1559, it was too late. Large numbers had broken with finality with the Roman Catholic Church. And all the inhabitants, Catholic as well as Protestant, were by that time rightly suspicious that both religious and secular authorities were conspiring to destroy the last vestiges of liberty.[12]

The second was the strange admixture of ecclesiastical and civil control. In several areas the church had preceded the establishment of any political administration. Often a rich landowner had erected and endowed a chapel. In time a village sprang up around the church. The right of appointing the officiating priest remained with the descendants of the original donor. Not infrequently under such circumstances the church through its clergy acted in civil capacities. All this explains, at least in some measure, why the authority of church and state were so peculiarly bound together in the minds of many people. This helped to perpetuate the medieval notion of one church in one state for one and the same people—a pattern that the followers of Arminius and the political leaders who supported them defended with vigor in the days immediately prior to the Synod of Dort. At issue between Calvinists and Remonstrants (as the Arminians were called) was not only the matter of sound doctrine but also that of the degree of authority of the state over the church.

Protestantism, as Noted Before, Sprang Up in the Netherlands Early

By 1518 monks of the Augustinian order, to which Luther himself had belonged, went through the country preaching evangelical doctrines. Soon after his New Testament appeared in the German language in 1522, it was translated into Dutch and published at Antwerp. Numerous other editions of the Scriptures also began to flood the market.[13] At no time could the presses keep pace with the popular demand for this and other religious materials. Yet those with "Lutheran inclinations" did not produce an ecclesiastical organization.

Another group, influential especially in the early days of the Reformation, were the "Sacramentarians." These people, found especially among the more educated, were thoroughly dissatisfied with conditions in the church. Among their number was Cornelis Hoen, attached to the government of Holland, whose reading of the writings of Wessel Gansfort stimulated him to put his views concerning the Lord's Supper in print.[14] These were circulated among such leading reformers as Luther, Zwingli, Bucer, and Oecolampadius by Hinne Rode, rector of a school at Utrecht. In many places such people met in conventicles to read and interpret the Scriptures and engage in preaching. From among them were drawn the first evangelical martyrs in the land. At no time, however, did they organize themselves, with the result that when first Anabaptism and then a decade or two later Calvinism arose, the influence of these men was submerged and for a season quite forgotten.

Much more significant on the score of winning the Netherlands for the Protestant faith was the Anabaptist movement.[15] By 1529 or 1530 Melchior Hoffman sent his emissary into the land to preach an apocalyptic message. The people were urged to look forward to a complete redemption from all their miseries, since Christ would soon return to make an end of the evils that they had so long endured. But when Hoffman was imprisoned in Strasburg and Trijpmaker was executed in the Hague, this movement fell into the hands of leaders of a more aggressive kind. Large groups now led insurrections against the civil magistrates in several cities. For a time the town of Bloemkamp (Oudeklooster) in Friesland was in their possession. People ran naked through the streets of Amsterdam. When the leaders gained control in Munster, a large fleet filled with sympathizers intent on joining their co-religionists was intercepted at Genemuiden and the pilgrims dispersed. Because of these and similar activities the entire Anabaptist movement was discredited in the eyes of the Lutherans and Calvinists as well as of the Roman Catholics. Nor was this suspicion mitigated when the antinomianism of David Joris and the antitrinitarianism of Adam Pastor as recognized Anabaptists became known.

Meanwhile the movement had made itself strong by providing the people with a simple ecclesiastical organization that appealed directly to Scripture for support. It sought to establish a "pure" church with room only for the regenerate. Discipline was strictly and even rigorously enforced. But when early disciples disagreed with each other on the true meaning of Scripture, the movement suffered from innumerable quarrels and dissensions and schisms. Soon large numbers were thoroughly disenchanted, so that when Calvinism appeared on the scene after 1540 even the new approach of Menno Simons could not prevent many from embracing the Reformed faith. As a result the organized Anabaptists remained a relatively small group in the land. Their indirect influence through numerous accessions to the Reformed church, however, should not be discounted.

Calvinism was the last of the reformatory movements to gain a foothold in the Netherlands. Its appearance in organized form can hardly be said to antedate the year 1544.

Usually its introduction has been traced to influences that spread from Geneva through France to the southern provinces where the French language was widely spoken. Indeed, here the churches were first organized. Yet its coming was a far more complex phenomenon.[16] By at least three avenues it found its way into the lives of the Netherlanders. At an early date the writings of Calvin as well as those of Zwingli, Oecolampadius, and Bullinger were read by Dutchmen interested in reforming the church. Many of the leaders also found themselves in exile from time to time. Some went to Geneva. Others, and this group was far more numerous, fled as merchants with their families or as students to places where Reformed churches in exile were being organized. This accounts for the powerful influence exerted by such congregations as Emden, Wesel, London, Frankfort-on-the-Main, and especially Heidelberg on the development of the ecclesiastical life in the Netherlands after 1550.[17] The third method by which Calvinism infiltrated the land is to be sought in the vigorous labors of those who returned to the southern provinces to organize and lead Reformed congregations. Thus what today is Belgium became the cradle of Dutch Calvinism. Here its confession was composed, officially adopted, and widely disseminated. Here its first congregations were duly organized, and its first synods convened in great secrecy. Here it suffered its severest persecutions, but here it also registered for a small season some of its greatest triumphs. Only the changing political scene that within two decades rent the southern provinces from the north compelled Calvinism to seek support and strength almost exclusively in the north.

What was there about the Calvinistic faith that appealed to such large numbers in that land? Several answers can be given. None, however, can be correctly assessed apart from the political and ecclesiastical oppressions of Spain and the disillusionment of the people with the Anabaptist movement.

The Reformed faith appealed to the intelligent and thoughtful layman who knew the need of thoroughgoing reform of the church. Here was a biblical system of doctrine that set forth in all its glory the evangelical faith. Its stress on divine sovereignty provided strength in the struggles of life and encouragement in the face of death. It was deeply concerned with the issue of true liberty. Its emphasis on a well-ordered discipline for the church and its membership appealed to many who, while convinced that sound doctrine must result in a godly life, had been disappointed with the irregularities and rigors of Anabaptism. And while under Menno Simons this movement had become orderly, its quietistic acceptance of tyranny could not win the hearts of the liberty-loving Netherlanders. When, then, Calvin in his writings defended the rights of the people under their magistrates to oppose the tyranny of kings and emperors, his views were embraced eagerly by those Dutchmen who saw in their struggle for freedom not only political but also religious dimensions.[18] For them the war against Spain became increasingly a profoundly spiritual issue. On the basis of Scripture they believed they could defend themselves before God as well as man. This assurance that God approved of their resistance to a tyranny not only cruelly but especially illegally inflicted upon them strengthened their hearts. From the beginning humanists and Roman Catholics joined in the war of independence. However, it was brought to a successful conclusion only through the dogged persistence of the Calvinists. The humanists wrote much but fought little. And when the nobility of the southern provinces drew away from the leadership of William of Orange, the Calvinists found themselves within less than ten years standing quite alone. In the years that followed, the union between the Dutch church and state was fused, without which the Arminian controversy could never have assumed the proportions that it did.

The Organizational Development of the Reformed Churches

Philip II upon his accession to sovereignty pursued the same policy that had guided his father, but with unparalleled rigor. Fisher writes of him, "Political and religious absolutism was the main article of Philip's creed. His ideas were few in number, but he clung to them with the more unyielding tenacity. The liberties of Spain had been destroyed at the beginning of Charles' reign; and the absolute system that was established there Philip considered to be the only true or tolerable form of government."[19]

He repelled the people by his aloofness and arrogance. When he spoke, it was always in a foreign tongue. Instead of appointing a regent from among the nobles, he preferred his sister, Margaret of Parma. At her side he placed Granvelle, the bishop of Arras, thus betraying suspicion of his own appointees, which marred all his dealings with others. Both were accomplished in the art of dissimulation and succeeded in arousing the king's jealousy of the nobles, especially of William of Orange. Soon all control devolved on Granvelle. This set the stage for striking fear and terror into the hearts of the people.

In violation of the rights of the provinces several regiments of Spanish soldiers were retained in the land. Philip's pledge to withdraw them within a few months was broken. When the church was reorganized in 1559 with the creation of many new bishoprics, each bishop clothed with inquisitorial powers to enforce discipline and exterminate heresy, the plans of Philip became transparent. All the edicts of Charles V were renewed. Men were forbidden to own a heretical book, to read the Scriptures, or to attend any conventicle where points of doctrine were discussed. Failure to inform against persons suspected of heresy made one guilty of treason. The goods of those convicted of heresy were confiscated, a share assigned to the accusers. Severe penalties were prescribed for all who in any way pleaded their cause.

To carry out such a program Charles V had already established an Inquisition independent of the clergy. To it all inhabitants were answerable. Although it lacked some of the more barbarous features of the Holy Office in Spain, it aroused the hostility of the people and the princes even when loyal to the Roman Catholic Church. Especially Granvelle, who in all things was unswervingly loyal to his sovereign, was blamed when persecution increased in thoroughness and intensity. But when the king removed him from office, this did not ameliorate the sufferings. The Inquisition proceeded with even greater vigor in burning and burying its victims alive. Even those suspected of heresy were put to death. At last the Prince of Orange broke his reserve and in a bold, powerful speech warned the council of the consequences of Philip's determination to carry out the decrees of the Council of Trent. Count Egmont was sent to Madrid to plead with the king. But with duplicity the old policy was not merely continued but strengthened. Merchants in large numbers fled the land. Others deprived of their livelihood soon followed. Agriculture as well as commerce ground to a halt. The cost of living soared. The population of cities and villages dropped dangerously. The once prosperous lands were on the verge of total economic collapse.[20]

In the summer of 1565 events moved swiftly. More than three hundred of the gentry supported by the burghers signed the "Compromise," in which they pledged to assist each other, restore wherever possible the rights of the people, and resist the Inquisition. The nobles, led by William of Orange, stood aloof. They realized that little could be done with a government that ruled with duplicity. Soon severer oppressions were inflicted. Large numbers of the people assembled outside of the city walls to listen to evangelical preaching, a practice to which the Regent acquiesced. Philip, however, refused all requests for moderating his policies. The next summer the storm of iconoclasm broke over the land. In many church buildings statues, paintings, and even windows were destroyed.[21] Now the regent was compelled to make a truce with the nobles who promised to quell the disturbances in exchange for toleration of the Protestant faith. However, when German troops were engaged to punish several of the cities and the Catholic nobility rallied around the government, William of Orange regretfully withdrew to his ancestral possessions in Nassau to prepare for the conflict that he realized was inevitable.

Enraged at what had happened, Philip sent the Duke of Alva with a large, well-trained Spanish army into the land. Now the Regent was divested of her powers. A fearful tribunal, called the "Council of Blood" by the people, was organized. In less than three months some two thousand, including many from among the wealthy and the nobility, were tortured and put to death.[22] Crowds of refugees fled the land. By February of 1568 all the inhabitants of the Netherlands with the exception of those specifically named were condemned to death for heresy.

During this year the Prince of Orange began to strike back. His brother defeated a large Spanish army at Heiligerlee only to suffer defeat a few months later. To strike terror into all hearts Alva retaliated by having the Catholic nobles Egmont and Hoorn with twenty others executed without due process of law. Exorbitant taxes were imposed, which led to the closing of all shops for a season. The Inquisition accelerated its murderous work, so that within three years more than eighteen thousand were put to death. War raged throughout the land. The zenith of revolt was reached when all parts of the country joined in the "Pacification of Ghent" in 1576, shortly after Antwerp was sacked with barbarous ferocity. But less than two years later, when the Catholic nobility repudiated William of Orange as leader and entered into secret negotiations with archduke Matthias, the unity was broken. The result was the League of Arras, in which the south promised to defend the Catholic religion and support the king subject to his observance of certain political stipulations. The north replied with its Union of Utrecht in January, 1579, in which Holland, Zeeland, and five other provinces entered a confederacy for common defense.[23] Two years later they declared their complete independence from Spain.

In these turbulent years the Reformed church of the Netherlands grew up. Its first general assemblies had already been held in great secrecy in the south. With the spread of the new faith, leaders felt the need for greater consolidation and organization. A number of ministers, elders and other members met in the German town of Wesel to draw up a series of proposed regulations for ecclesiastical life and order. Three years later, while persecution and war and economic distress ravaged the land, elected representatives of the churches adopted the first official Church Order.[24]

From its inception the church was constituted on the basis of the Belgic Confession. This had already been proposed by the "Convent of Wesel," which demonstrated its conviction that without sound preaching on the basis of a common confession the churches could not live together in unity. All ministers and teachers were to subscribe to the articles of the Belgic

Confession, promising to teach nothing contrary to what was therein set forth. The churches regarded themselves as completely sovereign to manage all their ecclesiastical affairs, electing their own officiary and exercising discipline in matters of doctrine and conduct over the members as well as the ministers. But when succeeding synods met on Dutch soil at Dordrecht (1574), Dordrecht (1578), Middelburg (1581) and the Hague (1586) concessions were made to the magistrates. This allowed the state a large measure of control over the churches, so that, greatly to the advantage of the Arminian party, no national synod could be held for thirty years.

When the Netherlands attained independence, the Reformed religion was officially recognized as the religion of the land.[25] The force of this must not be misunderstood. Here was no attempt to suppress the conscience of those who refused to express agreement with Calvinistic teaching. Lutherans, Anabaptists, and even Roman Catholics were tolerated in the land. However, these groups were at a decided disadvantage. They could worship together only in private dwellings. All church edifices were allotted to the Reformed. Funds necessary for the maintenance of ecclesiastical life were provided by the government out of vast holdings confiscated from the Roman Catholic Church at the time of independence. Meanwhile the churches agreed to allow civil representatives to attend their assemblies, lest the latter meddle in matters that were political. Not only the church orders, modified from time to time, but also the persons of those elected to office in the churches were subject to the approval of the authorities. The church's struggle to maintain its right to internal managing of its affairs reached a climax at the time of the Synod of the Hague (1586).[26] Fearing the growing power of the Reformed church throughout the land, the States-General thereafter refused permission for a national synod until 1618. Thus the church, while officially recognized, was fettered by the opposition of the very government that recognized and owed so much to it.

This opposition centered especially in the political authorities led by Johan van Oldenbarnevelt.[27]

The ideal had been a free church in a free land. What made the ideal unattainable were these complex relationships of church and state. At no time had the Reformed faith won over the majority of the inhabitants. Yet leadership in the struggle for independence had been increasingly assumed by avowed Calvinists. For them religious and political liberties were bound up together. Even the political authorities recognized that the will to resist came largely from this group. During the opening years of the struggle the Inquisition, which intended to maintain Spanish rule, was greatly aided by bishops and priests. Large numbers of Jesuits managed to enter the northern provinces, attempting to keep the people loyal to both the king and the Roman Catholic Church. Thus although the Reformed never totaled more than ten percent of the population, the Netherlands could never have waged the war successfully without them. In consequence, those who aspired to political office or desired to teach in the schools had to be members of this church. But this policy, which aimed at unifying the nation, weakened the church from within.

Large numbers with Sacramentarian or Anabaptist roots and those with pronouncedly humanistic leanings joined. Criticism may easily be leveled against the States-General for promoting the policy of recognizing the Reformed religion, thus curtailing some of the ideals of William of Orange concerning liberty, as well as against the church for accepting this privileged position. But in the face of the withdrawal of the southern nobility from the war, the activities of the Jesuits and others, and the fearful reverses sustained from time to time in the war, nothing but the closest relations between church and state seemed to offer any hope. In such a confusing situation for the Reformed churches the Arminian controversy arose.

As Far as the Church Was Concerned Two Issues Were at Stake

The first concerned itself with matters of doctrine. Were Arminius and those who embraced his teachings in accord with the Belgic Confession and the Heidelberg Catechism? To these they as well as all other officiaries in the church had solemnly pledged their agreement.

The second concerned itself with matters of church polity and government. Did this confessional Reformed church have the right to depose from office, especially the ministry of the Word and sacraments, those whose teachings were in conflict with the creeds?

Although the government in theory had acknowledged this right by approving the church orders, it could nullify it in two ways.

The local magistrates, to whom belonged a measure of supervision over the churches in their respective areas, maintained in office several men whom the churches in their classes and provincial synods had judged worthy of deposition. Thus in the period between Middelburg (1586) and Dort (1618–19) a growing number of ministers was upheld contrary to the desires of the congregations and the decisions of ecclesiastical assemblies. Especially after 1610 this produced friction and even schism. Many congregations refused to listen to the preaching of those who inclined to Arminianism. Often such people assembled for worship in warehouses, private dwellings and fields. And when the civil magistrates attempted to halt such activities by force, the nation was faced with the specter of civil war. Those who had fought for their liberties refused to submit callowly to the erosion of their rights and the confessional emasculation of their churches.

The only hope for a fruitful resolving of the doctrinal conflict lay in convening a national synod. Here representatives from the churches of all the provinces could act in concert. But permission for such an assembly had to be granted by the States-General.

Time and again this was urged, only to meet the resistance of the province of Holland under the strong leadership of van Oldenbarnevelt. At long last Prince Maurice, counseled by his cousin the stadtholder of Friesland, cast in his lot with the churches. Only in this way could he save the unity of a threatened nation. Under pressure from him the States-General decided to convene a synod. To this the States of Holland refused to agree. They passed a resolution that asserted the principle of provincial independence, which threatened the unity of the nation, allowed levies of local militia (*"waardgelders"*) to enforce their will, and instructed the army that it owed no allegiance to the "generality." The Prince together with the States-General took swift reprisals to preserve national unity. Leaders of the opposition were removed from their positions, the army rallied to the support of the States-General, and van Oldenbarnevelt was imprisoned, tried, and later executed.

Arminius, who had been professor at Leiden, died before the controversy within the churches reached its climax. At the beginning he had been willing to have the matter that concerned him discussed at a national synod. He and especially in later times his followers, however, increasingly embraced a view of the government of the church that favored a large measure of control by the state. Even more devastating for the welfare of the church according to the Calvinists was their repeated insistence on greater toleration in matters of doctrine. Many of their opinions were ambiguously presented and championed, so that the Calvinists rightly feared that any yielding on their part would open the way to even more radical departures from the creeds. No attempt on the part of the state to mediate proved fruitful in the controversy, which was far more extensive than a dispute between a few professors of theology. When by 1610 the Arminians clearly saw that the majority within the church adamantly opposed any weakening of the Calvinistic position, they began to fear nothing so much as a national synod.

When the Synod was finally convened, the Arminians refused to acknowledge its synodical character in accordance with the specific declarations on this point of the church order. At best they were willing to discuss as equal partners. Already at the opening sessions it became clear that a frank and full declaration of their views would not be forthcoming. By several means they tried to pursue the dialogue in their own fashion in the hope of preventing a clear-cut decision that they realized would go against them. Thereupon they were publicly rebuked by the representatives of the States-General for obstructing the course of business for which the Synod had been convened. No other alternative seemed open than that of dismissing them and deciding their case from their own writings but in their absence. For this procedure neither the ecclesiastical delegates nor the representatives of the government were to blame but the Arminians themselves.

Dort marks the close of the first period in the history of the Reformed churches in the Netherlands.

Its significance in this respect can hardly be overrated. Even the well-known historian Philip Schaff, who does not disguise the fact that he was out of sympathy with its doctrinal decisions and does not hesitate to aver that the Remonstrants "had no fair hearing," affirmed,

> It was undoubtedly an imposing assembly; and, for learning and piety, as respectable as any ever held since the days of the Apostles. Breitinger, a great light of the Swiss Churches, was astonished at the amount of knowledge and talent displayed by the Dutch delegates, and says that if ever the Holy Spirit were present in a Council, he was present at Dort. Scultetus, of the Palatinate, thanked God that he was a member of that Synod, and placed it high above similar assemblies. Meyer, a delegate of Basel, whenever afterwards he spoke of this Synod, uncovered his head and exclaimed 'Sacrosancta Synodus!' Even Paolo Sarpi, the liberal Catholic historian, in a letter to Heinsius, spoke very highly of it. A century later, the celebrated Dutch divine, Campegius Vitringa, said: 'So much

learning was never before assembled in one place, not even at Trent.'[28]

At this assembly the pattern early adopted by the churches was firmly fixed. Matters pertaining to the confessions and the church order, to preaching and catechesis for the children of the church, to the training of ministers and Bible translation and missions were thoroughly discussed and decided. And although the churches would still remain bound to the state in several respects so that for another two centuries no national Reformed synod would be convened, their passionate concern to remain confessionally Reformed triumphed. The church could be in practice what it claimed to be. For that faith tens of thousands had been put to death, and more than ten times that number had suffered the ravages of persecution, torture, and war together with the hardships of exile. But their blood and tears had not been spilled in vain. Dort secured that for which they had suffered. For on the soil of the Netherlands there now flourished for a season a strong confessing church, one whose influence increased among all ranks of society, to whose schools students came from all corners of Europe, and through whose missionary efforts the gospel of Jesus Christ was propagated for a time in all parts of the world.

2 THE BACKGROUND OF THE ARMINIAN CONTROVERSY (1586–1618)

Louis Praamsma

Arminianism was not a meteoric phenomenon, nor was Arminius a "homo novus" in the story of the Reformed churches in the Netherlands. Fragments of new opinion had raised their heads, now here and then there. Splinters had fallen from the wall of the Reformed structure before the crisis came. All these were signs of a coming conflict.

Historians differ in their diagnosis of the situation which culminated in the great Synod of Dort. Actually a long historiographical controversy characterizes the history of the origin and essence of Dutch Arminianism.

During the post-Dort period this controversy was set in bold relief by the appearance of two great works: the first, De Kerckelycke Historie by the Arminian Uytenbogaert in 1646 and the other, *Kerckelycke Geschiedenissen* by the Calvinist Triglandius in 1650. Thereupon in the nineteenth century such men as Ypey and Dermout, Hofstede de Groot, Glasius, Gooszen, Reitsma, and Lindeboom defended Arminianism against such proponents of Calvinism as Vander Kemp, Groen van Prinsterer, Abraham and H. H. Kuyper, Geesink, Hania, Wijminga, Wagenaar and Kaajan.

What was the Arminian Thesis in this Historiographical Controversy?

Simply stated, it was the theory of a third kind of reformation, a *tertium genus Reformationis* which differed from the movements inspired by Luther and Calvin. According to this position it was represented on the European scene by such reformers as Bullinger, à Lasco and Melanchthon. In the Netherlands it appeared as a special Dutch kind of religion marked by moderation, by the absence of speculation and dogmatism, by a preference for the plain words of the Bible (especially of the New Testament), and by a strong interest in a broad-minded education. This special Dutch form of religion has been frequently characterized as a kind of biblical humanism.

Able and enthusuastic men of learning have written on the origin and development of this biblical humanism. It is highly questionable, however, whether its proponents have the right to include in the movement such men as Bullinger and à Lasco, both of whom plainly confessed the great Reformation doctrine of justification by faith only. To call this movement a third type of Reformation both confuses and blurs the meaning attached to the term Reformation. Furthermore, to speak of a special Dutch form of religion smacks of the spirit of nineteenth century Romanticism which was tempted to interpret religion and religious differences in the light of nationalism and national characteristics. It is also a bold assumption to call Erasmus "a typical Dutchman," and even more so to speak of Calvin in this way despite the fact that once he said that he might perhaps be considered a Netherlander.[1] Both assumptions are clearly unwarranted speculations.

Mention has now been made of Erasmus, that prince of humanists who died in Basle in 1536. Although a church historian of the first half of the nineteenth century called him a Dutch reformer, he was no more a reformer than his English friend, Thomas More, or his Italian admirer, Jacopo Sadoleto to whom Calvin wrote his famous letter. Nevertheless Erasmus should be mentioned in this connection for two reasons. His Semi-Pelagianism accorded with that of the later Arminians, and he also greatly influenced the famous Dutch humanist, Coornhert, who has often been called one of the precursors of Arminianism.

Precursors of Arminianism

This term should be used with the same discretion as the phrase "precursors of the Reformation." Were there really Arminians before Arminius?

When we consider those who are usually called by this title, we discover several who were in no way associated with each other or presented a united front in opposition to others. These men were generally isolated individuals. As individualists, each had his own peculiar objections to the church of Rome without wholeheartedly embracing the tenets of the Reformation. Each lived as it were on the border between two worlds, in both of which he felt ill at ease. Each experienced his peculiar difficulties after the establishment of the Dutch Reformed Church. Among such "precursors" the following are most frequently mentioned: Dirk Volkertszoon Coornhert (1552–1509), Hubertus Duifhuis (1531–1581), Caspar Coolhaes (1536–1615), Herman Herberts (1540–1607), Cornelis Wiggerts (d.1624), Adolphus Venator (d.1619), Taco Sybrants (d.1613), and perhaps also Jelle Hotzes Snecanus (1540–1600).

The most isolated of these figures was Coornhert. This self-made man was not a minister but rather a talented man of letters and an able politician. In his religious feelings he was more Stoic than Christian, even though he remained a member of the Roman Catholic Church until his death. He took the position that outward ceremonies did not require the involvement of the heart.[2] The early Arminians customarily denied their affinity with Coornhert. Yet in common with them he had a deep-felt aversion to predestination. Also his more-than-Arminian Pelagianism, his pleading for an unrestricted toleration, and his recognition of the civil magistrate as the final judge in matters of religion were views which the Arminians in one form or another also championed. When Arminius was minister in Amsterdam, his consistory asked him to refute Coornhert's ideas on predestination. But upon studying the matter, Arminius discovered his own doubts increasing to such an extent that he never finished this task.[3]

All the other "precursors" were ministers. With the exception of Snecanus they were all involved in ecclesiastical difficulties and procedures too numerous to mention here. However, what they had in common deserves mention at this point.

First of all—and this is perhaps the most important—all of them came into conflict with a confessional church which wanted to maintain its doctrinal standards as Forms of Unity without any compromise. The real issue between these precursors and the confessional church they held to be that of freedom of conscience. This tenet of theirs they viewed as a fundamental principle of the Reformation. All historians who have defended the Arminians have maintained that the Reformed churches should have been "liberal" from the beginning, liberal in the sense of accepting a complete freedom of individual opinions around an open Bible. However, the story of the precursors plainly demonstrates that the churches wanted allegiance to the doctrinal standards.

That these men were judged in the light of these standards is evident from the following instances. When the unreformed opinions of Duifhuis (founder of an independent church in Utrecht) became known, the consistory of Delft admonished him in a letter to subscribe to the Belgic Confession. It also warned that should he refuse to do this, he would openly be declared to be outside of the Reformed Church.[4] Sybrants, his successor, resigned from the office of minister because he could not honestly subscribe to that creed. Coolhaes was required by the Synod of Middelburg (1581) to sign the confession.[5] Herberts, of whom the same was asked by the Synod of the Hague (1586), complied but with reservations. Wiggerts was reminded by the Synod of North Holland that he had signed the Belgic Confession.[6] Venator's doctrine was declared inconsonant with the Word of God and the doctrines of the Reformed Church as contained in the Belgic Confession and the Heidelberg Catechism.[7] Throughout this entire period the regulation of the first Synod of Emden (1571) was in force; namely, that unity of doctrine on the part of all the Dutch congregations was to be demonstrated by having all ministers subscribe to the creeds.[8]

In the second place, all the precursors had in common their objections of several sorts to the doctrine of predestination. At times these objections seemed minor. Duifhuis, for example, declared himself an adherent of the Reformed doctrine but without wanting to go as "deep and high" as the Calvinists did. Herberts also claimed his readiness to agree with the confession, provided he might interpret article 16 as not intending to mean that God was the author of sin (as if any sound exegesis of said article ever allowed God as the author of sin!). However superficial these objections of Duifhuis and Wiggerts may seem, the old Semi-Pelagianism of the Roman Catholic Church was actually deeply rooted in their hearts. After Duifhuis had read in the Dutch language the anti-Calvinistic works of Castellio, he opposed the doctrine of predestination much more openly than before.[9] This was also true of Herberts who with the other precursors championed a universalism in his concept of the doctrine of grace.[10]

In the third place, their erroneous constructions of the doctrine of predestination led all of them into other errors. Predestination as the free act of God in bestowing grace according to his will immediately evolves the central teaching of justification by faith apart from any meritorious works. On this score Herberts opposed the doctrine of the imputation of Christ's righteousness.[11] Wiggerts taught that all men were justified by Christ.[12] In the later Arminian conflict this doctrine of justification by faith always turned up for discussion. However, also other doctrines were involved. Geesink rightly claims that Wiggerts was in agreement with the later Arminians in his errors with respect to the image of God in man, providence, original sin, the recovery of fallen man, predestination, free will, good works, and the perseverance of the saints.[13]

In the fourth place, all these men were Erastian rather than Reformed with respect to church polity and government. They recognized the civil government as the highest authority in ecclesiastical matters and sought to maintain their position in the churches by means of the strong support of local and provincial authorities. Often these magistrates, usually drawn from the merchant class, manifested a measure of doctrinal indifference.

The influential secretary of state, Oldenbarnevelt, adopted as his motto, "Tutissima fides nil scire."[14] He also wanted a national church which would make room for all shades of religious opinion. And in that church the civil authorities would have power to appoint office-bearers as well as to convene and supervise ecclesiastical assemblies. Coolhaes, Duifhuis, Venator, Herberts and Wiggerts all gained the support of and at the same time supported the claims of their respective local magistrates, those of Leiden, Utrecht, Alkmaar, Gouda and Hoorn.

A few evidences of the coalition between the Arminians and the magistrates should be cited here.

The Coolhaes-conflict began in 1579, when by an official decision the magistrates of Leiden demanded the right to appoint the members of the consistory. When twenty two of the twenty four members of the consistory refused to comply with this new order, they were summarily dismissed from office. Thereupon the magistrates appointed twenty two others who had been proposed by Coolhaes. Meanwhile his colleague, the Calvinist Cornelisz, was also removed from office. Coolhaes defended this usurpation of power in his *Justification of the Magistrates of Leiden*. In characteristic Erastian fashion he argues that discipline should be exercised by the magistrates in cooperation with the office-bearers of the church, that these office-bearers are not qualified to excommunicate anyone from the church, and that there is no need for a consistory in those places where the government is Christian.[15]

Venator, although suspended from office in 1608, was upheld by the political authorities. Thus he could continue in the ministry of the Word and the sacraments. When during the next year the States of Holland dismissed the consistory of Alkmaar and appointed new office-bearers, many members of the congregation began to worship in neighboring churches. This was the beginning of schism in the Reformed churches.

The Views of Arminius

All these conflict-situations were more or less incidental. Although in the seven provinces of the Netherlands there was a Reformed church with a Presbyterian-synodical form of church government and Calvinistic creeds, there was as yet no organized Arminian party. All the above incidents, however, constituted a prelude to the Arminian concerto soon to reverberate throughout the land. The first blast of the Arminians trumpet was heard, when Jacobus Arminius (1560–1609) preached a series of sermons on Paul's epistle to the Romans.

What did this brilliant pupil of Beza, who had just completed his studies in Geneva, have to say about this letter of Paul? When preaching on the first chapters, he, according to Triglandius, upon more than one occasion ironically remarked that his hearers would have done better to remain in the Roman Catholic Church, because then at least they would be doing good works in the hope of eternal reward while now they did none at all. In his exposition of Romans 5 and 6 he taught that death would have been inevitable even if man had never sinned, since God alone is immortal. He declared Romans 7 to be reminiscent of Paul in his unregenerate state. Therefore its description of man's experience should not be ascribed to the regenerate. In preaching on Romans 8 through 11 he stressed man's free will, and in explaining Romans 13 he ascribed to the civil government the highest authority in ecclesiastical and religious matters.[16] Small wonder, then, that Triglandius after reviewing these sermons remarks on their effect,

> And when he brought these thoughts forward with great zeal and seriousness on different Sundays and in different churches, the whole congregation was greatly disturbed by it.

His colleague Plancius also accused him of holding Socinian opinions.[17] In the ensuing discussions Arminius revealed his doubts concerning article 16 of the Belgic Confession but promised to adhere to what it taught.

This was the beginning of endless controversy in the life of this conscientious objector to Calvinism, a conflict which continued until his early death in 1609.[18] We should pay him tribute as a faithful pastor, a man of rare scholarly abilities, a man of peace and sensitivity who against his will was always at war, a man eager to serve God. On the other hand, we must also agree with the charge often leveled against him that he was not free from a certain kind of duplicity. No matter how clearly his views represented a marked departure from the Reformed faith, he always hid himself under the cloak of orthodoxy. The verdict of Roger Nicole on Arminius cannot be contravened:

> His attitude toward confessional standards was open to question, for a theologian of his caliber must have realized that there was a substantial rift between his views and the system of teaching as well as the express utterances of the Heidelberg Catechism and the Belgic Confession. Nevertheless, he paraded under the flag of allegiance and under the vows of conformity from the time of his ordination to his death. He repeatedly promised not to teach anything from the pulpit or the university chair which might be out of keeping with the standards. Obviously, if he had done just that, it is unlikely that he would have been the center of such storms and the rallying point of a whole group of uneasy spirits, whose heterodoxy was often more pronounced that his own.[19]

The Major Issues in Dispute

Within the space allotted it is not possible to relate in detail the successive stages in which the Arminian controversy developed before the Synod of Dort. However, attention should at least be drawn to the main points in dispute, points which run parallel to those already noted in the preceeding period.

First of all, the permanence of the character and authority of the confessional standards was at stake. Arminius and his followers (who upon his death organized themselves in 1610 at Gouda under the leadership of Uytenbogaert and were called Remonstrants)[20] never wearied of expressing themselves in favor of a revision of those standards. What kind of revision did they have in mind? Was it to be a revision of grammar and style? Was it a revision of details in those articles to which they had specific objections? Indeed not. They had in mind a permanent attitude of openness and freedom. These men argued that a binding confession ultimately conflicted both with the authority of Scripture and with the freedom of the individual conscience.

In their Counter Remonstrance, authored by Festus Hommius as pastor of the Leiden congregation, the Calvinists agreed that the confessional standards were not to be placed on a par with God's Word, yet they regarded them as necessary both to preserve the unity of the churches and to avoid the multiplication of sects. They also declared it hazardous to call the creeds into question lightly. Their position was that anyone, convinced that something in these standards was contrary to the Word of God, should reveal such convictions so that both the official doctrine of the church and the objections to it could be tested in the light of Scripture. This method of procedure, so the Calvinists urged, was open to anyone who had subscribed to the Forms of Unity without being accused of perjury, provided he express a willingness to submit to the consensus of the church.[21]

All this shows that an important principle was at stake. Was the Reformed church to be confessional or liberal?[22] Was it to be a church with unity in doctrine or one which allowed large freedom for differing views? Was it to be a church "contending for the faith once for all delivered to the saints" (Jude, verse 3) or a church "tossed to and fro and carried about with every kind of doctrine" (Eph. 4:14)? That this principle was clearly at stake becomes even more apparent, when we remember that the Arminians of that period were both unwilling and seemingly unable to raise specific objections to both Confession and Catechism. When finally compelled to state their objections openly at the Synod of Dort, the English reporter Hales called them "a poor impertinent stuff."[23] Increasingly it became clear that what the Arminians wanted was full doctrinal freedom, while the Calvinists insisted on doctrinal unity and stability.

Secondly, the doubts and objections of both Arminius and his followers centered in the doctrine of predestination. Already at an early date Arminius had revealed some of his doubts on this subject, but he suppressed them in later discussions. Then he concentrated his chief attacks on the supralapsarian positions of Beza and his own colleague at Leiden, Gomarus, while claiming in this the help of many Dutch infralapsarians.[24] However, it soon became plain that Arminius went far beyond the infralapsarian view both in denying that faith is the fruit of election and in asserting that predestination unto salvation is based on divine foreknowledge. As a result the Dutch infralapsarian, Donteclock, declared already in 1609 that Arminius deviated from the doctrine of the Reformation, that both infra- and supralapsarians were in essential agreement on the doctrine of predestination since both confessed the absolute sovereignty of God, and that by positing a human decision prior to the divine decision a new doctrine was being introduced in the churches.25 The issues were confused, however, because Arminius tried to make use of orthodox terms as much as possible. In this also his followers patterned after him. Concerning them Bavinck's judgment rings true,

> Gradually they laid the decision in the hands of man as appears clearly in the later Arminian writings, in the letter of Episcopius to the Reformed abroad, in the second Remonstrance of the year 1617, in the Confession and Apology of the Confession of Episcopius, in the dogmatic works of Uytenbogaert, Episcopius, and Limborch. Arminianism prepared the way for rationalism.26

In the third place, the Arminian heresy proved far from being an isolated doctrinal opinion of little relevance. It affected and infected the whole system of Reformed doctrine. This helps to explain why Gomarus as the champion of Calvinism from Leiden attacked Arminius' view in the High Council. Arminius interpreted the doctrine as teaching that man is justified before God not on the basis of the imputed righteousness of Christ but by the human act of believing which constituted his righteousness before God. Manifestly this conflicted with the teachings of question and answer 61 of the Heidelberg Catechism Roger Nicole has called attention to two other opinions of Arminius which conflicted with Reformation teaching. The first was his restriction of the term *autotheos*[27] to God the Father in such a way that according to him the Son is subordinate to the Father. This subordinationism (not without kinship to Socinianism) was later developed by the Arminians. The second opinion was that of perfectionism, a notion which Arminius himself never strongly affirmed.[28]

That careful nineteenth century historian, William Cunningham, in attempting to be as fair to Arminianism as possible, has summarized the development of its ideas in these words:

> Arminius himself does not seem—as far as his views were ever fully developed—to have gone further from scriptural truth than to deny the Calvinist doctrine of election, particular redemption, efficacious and irresistable grace in conversion, and to doubt, if not to deny, the perseverance of the saints. But his followers, and particularly Episcopius and Curcellaeus, very soon introduced further corruption of scriptural truth; and made near approaches, upon these and kindred topics, to Pelagian and Socinian views.[29]

Here it is again apparent that there never seems to be a half-way house on the road to heresy. It is amazing how soon minor doubts and difficulties blossomed into major errors and deviations. In the fourth place, the Arminian movement prior to Dort was marked by increasing attacks on the autonomy or, if one prefers to speak of it in another way, the Christonomy of the churches. Together with this there developed among them a perplexing display of "liberal intolerance."

On this score three famous exponents of Arminian theory and practice must be mentioned. The first is Uytenbogaert who, upon the death of Arminius, became the leader of the Arminian minority within the Reformed church. The second is the influential Erasmian humanist, Grotius, known as the oracle of Delft. The third is the able statesman, Oldenbarnevelt, who served for many years as advocate of Holland.

In 1610 Uytenbogaert published his *Tract on the Office and Authority of a Higher Christian Government in Ecclesiastical Affairs*. In this book he defended the thesis that the highest authority in the affairs of the church belonged under God and his Word to the States of every province in the Netherlands. In accordance with this view the States had authority to call and install ministers, elders and deacons, to supervise the preaching, to frame an order for the churches, to convene ecclesiastical assemblies as well as to preside over them.[30]

In 1614 Grotius drafted his "Resolution for Peace in the Churches," according to which the States of Holland had the right of prohibit preaching on controversial points. His ideal was the English archbishop Laud, well-known as one who persecuted the Puritans in his own country. This controversial figure stated his views clearly in 1638, when he wrote,

> In England you can see how well the extermination of harmful doctrines has advanced, above all by reason of the fact that the persons who have there taken this holy work upon themselves have not intermingled anything new, anything of themselves, but have focussed their gaze on better ages.[31]

These better ages, according to Laud, were to be found in the period of the Constantinian state-church, of which he believed he saw a new embodiment in the Anglican Church before his aristocratic mind finally found its rest in the bosom of the Roman Catholic hierarchy.

Oldenbarnevelt is best remembered as the father of the "Sharp Resolution" of 1617 in which the States of Holland decided that no national synod was to be convened, that the States would retain their authority in ecclesiastical matters, and that the cities were authorized to levy soldiers in defense of the Remonstrants. In his classic description of this conflict Groen van Prinsterer rightly said,

> Oldenbarnevelt and his followers permitted the Arminians to propagate their doctrine in the name of tolerance. They imposed silence on others to suppress discord. But those whom they wanted to silence refused to abandon their duty to the Judge Supreme. For this refusal they were banished from the church as if they were rebelling against legitimate superiors. Excluded from places of worship they, with their faithful followers, took refuge in private buildings in order to worship. That refuge, however, was also forbidden. The civil authorities, fearing schism, intervened in the name of public order. To maintain this imposed silence the authorities used violence. Faithful pastors were forbidden to preach; separatist meetings were not tolerated; houses, barns and ships used for assembling were confiscated; various methods of intimidation were applied to laymen who joined the meetings of the faithful. Such were bereft of the right of citizenship. In other

words, their means of existence, including their daily bread, was taken away. In this manner, under the pretext of public order and tolerance, a systematic oppression of the Reformed Church and its faith was organized.[32]

These words of Groen can be amply substantiated. The historian Triglandius relates how in Rotterdam the Calvinistic minister Geselius was deposed from office by the magistrates; how in the Hague the Rev. Rosaeus was suspended; how in Schoonhoven, Gouda, Brielle, Hoorn, Alkmaar, and other towns separate meetings were held by groups of Reformed people who called themselves the *Doleerende* church (the church in "mourning").[33]

After much hesitation Prince Maurice of Orange took action. Early in 1617 he declared at a session of the magistrates of Holland that he would keep his oath to defend the Reformed faith. In July of the same year he openly attended the services of the *Doleerenden* in the Hague. After the "Sharp Resolution" was passed in that year he at the urging of his cousin, William Louis of Friesland, went through the provinces of Holland and Utrecht at the head of soldiers faithful to him and succeeded in discharging the regiments which had been hired by the municipal authorities. When the States of Holland still persisted in their opposition to the convening of a national synod, he took Oldenbarnevelt, Grotius and four other leaders of the opposition into custody. In the meanwhile the States-General by majority vote decided to call a national synod so that the controversy which had agitated both state and church for at least two decades could finally be settled.

Not since 1586 had such a national synod been held. Now after some thirty two years the church would finally be allowed to make its own decisions on matters of common concern. This was an answer to countless prayers. Yet the victory was hardly complete. Synod could convene only under the tutelage of the Illustrious and Most Mighty States-General of the land. This definite drawback was the product of the prevalent view of those days concerning the relationship of church and state and in turn resulted in another recess of some two hundred years. Yet for a brief season the door was open. The churches were permitted at the Synod of Dort to express themselves and make decisions which insured the maintenance of the pure doctrine of the Gospel.

Appendix on the Collatio Hagiensis of 1611

In 1611 the States of Holland summoned a meeting of six representatives of the Remonstrant party and six of the Contra-Remonstrants. The aim was to reach some settlement in the controversy or, at least, to arrive at a definition of the "status questionis." Because of the city in which it was held, this gathering received the name of "Collatio Hagiensis" or Conference of the Hague. In a sense it constitutes a landmark in the history of the controversy, since here was presented the famous Counter Remonstrance which likely was authored by Festus Hommius. A report of this meeting was published in 1612. According to Professor Dr. A.D.R. Polman in an article entitled "The Doctrine of Eternal Reprobation in the Hague Conference of 1611"[34] special attention should be paid to this report in our day.

The Polman-study is highlighted in a number of theses, to the third and sixth of which we would now refer.

The third thesis asserts that it is impossible to make clear in the doctrine of *predestinatio gemina* (double predestination) the essential assymetry (inequality) of election and reprobation. This doctrine, according to the professor, is not a religious confession but rather a disastrous penetration of a philosophical determinism by which the structural difference between divine election and reprobation is eliminated by the thesis of a causal determinism.

In his sixth thesis he maintains that the Bible does not know of a pre-temporal decree which determines all things and causally settles them. Rather, it speaks of a gracious election of God in Christ before the foundation of the world and a reprobation in the midst of history wherein God's reaction is seen against man's rebellion and revolution. In reading this kind of differentiation into Scripture, so the professor insists, we are not arguing in favor of autonomizing sinful activity over against God's command but simply recognizing in clear fashion the limits of our reflection.

The Background of the Arminian Controversy

After positing these theses Polman summarizes in six other theses his opinion of the Conference at the Hague. Of these especially the following deserve our attention.

The Remonstrant protest against positing an absolute sovereignty and an absolute decree wherein always and again the false parallelism of election and reprobation appears was perfectly well grounded. Equally well grounded was their protest against reducing the confession of the God and Father of our Lord Jesus Christ to an abstract recognition of God's absolutely free sovereignty. Although Polman would not urge that Calvin's doctrine of predestination was completely expressed at the Conference, he reminds his readers that during the controversy between Remonstrants and Contra-Remonstrants many individuals wholeheartedly defended the well-known definition of Calvin:

> For they are not all created[35] in an equal condition, but eternal life is foreordained for some, and eternal damnation for others. Every man, therefore, being created for one or the other of these ends, we speak of him as predestinated either to life or to death (*Institutes*, III, xxi, 5).

In the debate the Remonstrants did not ask merely "hair-splitting and subtle questions." While it is understandable that the Contra-Remonstrants halted further questioning about predestination and did not want to decide on the issues involved in supra- and infralapsarianism, they thereby admittedly blocked one road to discovering whether the manner in which the Conference posited the problem was unbiblically abstract. The Contra-Remonstrants should have responded to at least two of the seven questions which were asked. One question concerned the meaning of divine pleasure, a biblical aspect of the doctrine of salvation which the Contra-Remonstrants reconstructed into a sovereign decretive power isolated from the Gospel. The other focussed on whether in divine election Christ appears only as the executor of the sovereign decree of God's will. That these questions should have been honored was the more imperative, according to Polman, because during the Conference many expressions were used by the Contra-Remonstrants which seemed to indicate that they believed that the decision of God concerning elect and reprobate was taken without any manifest involvement of Christ.

Polman informs us that during the Conference the Contra-Remonstrants wanted to discuss only the central issues at stake, whereas the Remonstrants desired clarification of seven subsidiary but relevant theological matters prior to any consideration of the central issues. This the Contra-Remonstrants refused to grant for several motivated reasons.

Within the scope of this Appendix there is no need to pass judgment on Polman's position regarding election and reprobation. He has expressed this clearly enough by speaking of "a gracious election of God in Christ before the foundation of the world, and a reprobation in the midst of history in which the reaction of God is seen against our rebellion and revolution." Evidently he accepts reprobation as an open possibility (and reality) in time; not as a decree of God preceeding human actions. The point which should engage our attention, however, is whether Polman's criticism of the Contra-Remonstrants at the "Collatio Hagiensis of 1611" is well founded.

Although in subsequent writings he abundantly praises the Contra-Remonstrants for their emphasis on election and for their denial of a logical symmetry of election and reprobation, he accuses them of essentially two weaknesses. The first is their abstract idea of an absolute decree of the all-determining God. The second is their neglect in answering the question whether Christ is the foundation of election or only its executor.

The first accusation can hardly be substantiated by the facts.

At the Conference the Contra-Remonstrants were very careful not to express themselves in those terms which Polman imputes to them. They therefore complained with justification of the strategy employed by the Remonstrants who, in order to justify their opposition to Calvinism, capitalized on some immoderate expressions which their opponents had used in the heat of the debate a year earlier. Now, however, the Contra-Remonstrants showed how "piously and religiously" they sought to handle this doctrine, declaring that

> ... as far as the high doctrine of predestination is concerned, we in our churches used to speak of it moderately and carefully

according to the rule of the Word of God, only upholding the undeserved grace of God, taking away all human merit and worthiness, and strengthening the steady comfort of the believers in such a manner that no one needs to be offended by it.36

To this they added,

It should satisfy our brethren that we again declare as our belief that God condemns no one unrighteously neither has determined so to condemn anyone. He only condemns righteously because of one's own sins.37

In repeating the reasons why the Contra-Remonstrants did not answer the Remonstrants in the way they wanted at this Conference, Triglandius in 1650 concludes with these words:

This is certainly the difference between believers and unbelievers, that the former are justified from their sins while the latter are still in their sins. This difference must be made between corrupted and corrupted men: that the one, enlightened, gifted with faith, regenerated by the Spirit of God, becomes a new man and a new creature; and the other, being in corruption and blindness, remains an unregenerated old man. Whence does this difference come? No one who knows what it is to believe and to be born again will be able to deny that this difference comes from God. God makes this difference according to his merciful and absolutely free purpose, having mercy on whom he will and hardening whom he will. This is the defect of the Remonstrants that they refuse to attribute this difference to God. If they would do so, there would be no question at all, and they neither could nor would have written their articles. But because they do not attribute this difference to God, they transfer it to the indifferent will of man, and from there they bring it back to God in the sense of chance or fortune.38

The second objection of Polman concerns the function of Christ in election. It is again understandable that the Contra-Remonstrants refused to respond to the question raised in this connection. This did not spring from an inability on their part to meet the question, but rather because they insisted that this concerned only a *theologoumenon*39 and not an officially endorsed doctrine of the church. At the outset they made clear that they were not conferring as a group of theological experts to discuss dogmatic intricacies but rather as delegates of the churches called together to speak on confessional matters.[40] They were entirely correct, therefore, in maintaining that the seven questions posed by the Remonstrants did not belong to the framework of Confession and Catechism and thus should be disputed in the universities instead of in the pulpits.

The question raised by Polman may, perhaps, be stated in this way: Did Christ come only to save the elect of the Father, or did he come to offer salvation to all men? Actually this is not an either/or question. It is quite easy to quote biblical texts to demonstrate the paradoxical character of this positing of the problem. The best response to it is given by the Canons of Dort in these words:

> Election is the unchangeable purpose of God whereby, before the foundation of the world, he has out of mere grace, according to the sovereign good pleasure of his will, chosen from the whole human race, which had fallen through their own fault from their primitive state of rectitude, a certain number of persons to redemption in Christ, whom he from eternity appointed the Mediator and Head of the elect and the foundation of salvation.

3 LEADING FIGURES AT THE SYNOD OF DORT

Simon
Kistemaker

BOGERMAN, Johannes (1576–1637)

"He was a very remarkable man physically and mentally. He had a fine presence—was tall, straight, and well proportioned. His forehead was high. His features were expressive and his eyes sparkling and piercing. A magnificent beard, of a light color like his hair, descended to his waist. He had a full voice, and his gestures, when he was excited (which was not seldom, for he was a man of strong passions), were very impressive. With intense convictions, he was impulsive and imperious in his manner of uttering them."[2]

Bogerman was born at Uplewert, East Friesland, in 1576 into a family that had several vocations to the ministry: father Johannes Bogerman became pastor of the Reformed Church at Bolsward in 1580; the junior Johannes wished to follow his father's calling, and, blessed with a clear mind and phenomenal memory, he enrolled at the Academy of Franeker on May 23, 1591. Besides studying Latin, he became an ardent student of Hebrew under the tutelage of Drusius. He stayed at Franeker for five years, studied successively at the universities and academies of Heidelberg, Geneva (where he listened to Theodore Beza, then

80 years old), Zürich, Lausanne, Oxford, and Cambridge. During the late summer of 1599 he returned to the Netherlands as a candidate to the ministry; soon afterwards he accepted a call to the Reformed Church of Sneek, where he was ordained to the Gospel ministry on September 23, 1599.

This gifted man, who served three congregations and who was delegated to provincial and national synods, received an appointment as professor of theology at the Academy of Franeker in 1617. However, at that time the States-General as well as the consistory of the congregation he served did not want to let him go. In 1633 he received another appointment to the Academy of Franeker; but because of his task of translating the Scriptures, he could not begin his professorate until December 7, 1636. Nine months later on September 11, 1637, he died.

Johannes Bogerman is chiefly known for his role at the Synod of Dort, where he was elected president; less well-known, yet of equal importance, is his work of translating the Scriptures. At the sessions of Synod his qualities of leadership were displayed, but in translating the Old Testament—which was primarily his work—Bogerman demonstrated his biblical scholarship.

Delegated by the provincial Synod of Friesland to the National Synod of Dort (1618–1619), Bogerman was elected president during the second session together with Jacob Rolandus (first assessor), Herman Faukelius (second assessor), Sebastian Dammannus (first clerk), and Festus Hommius (second clerk).[3] As president he revealed his personality dramatically: during the sixth session and the one hundred fifty-third, Bogerman led in prayers that expressed his deepest convictions; during the lengthy sessions Bogerman conducted the proceedings with firm hand, especially at the time when he denied the Remonstrants the right to be present at Synod as delegates. The passionate Bogerman lost his temper during the fifty-seventh session on Monday morning the fourteenth of January 1619. With thundering voice the president expostulated,

You boast that many foreign divines did not refuse to grant your request. Their moderation arose from a misunderstanding. They now declare that they were deceived by you. They say that you are no longer worthy of being heard by the Synod. You may pretend what you please, but the great point of your obstinacy is that you regard the Synod as a party in the case. Thus you have long delayed us. You have been treated with all gentleness, friendliness, toleration, patience, and simplicity. Go as you came. You began with lies and you end with them. You are full of fraud and double-dealing. You are not worthy that the Synod should treat with you further. Depart! Leave! You began with a lie, with a lie you ended! Go![4]

The effect was startling, for the Remonstrants stood up and left—not only the floor of Synod—against the ordinances of Synod they left the city of Dordrecht.

Yet Bogerman was a peace-loving president, who through patience and kindness was able to control the emotional and even quarrelsome natures of the delegates. A controversy between Sibrandus Lubbertus and Johannes Maccovius, for example, was brought to a peaceful conclusion towards the end of the Synod.[5]

EPISCOPIUS, Simon (1583–1643)

As chief spokesman for the Remonstrants, Simon Episcopius was told by the States of Holland and West Friesland to be in Dordrecht by November 1, 1618. However, he learned that the Synod would not convene on the first day of the month but on the thirteenth; therefore, he met with a number of Remonstrants in Leiden on the eleventh of November to decide how they should conduct themselves at Synod.[6] They decided to send a large number of Remonstrants to Dordrecht, who would have the freedom to give an account of their teachings. When Episcopius, with some other Remonstrants, arrived on the eighteenth of November, he learned that Synod had decided on the fifteenth of that month to request the presence of thirteen Remonstrants: three from Gelderland, five (among whom was

Episcopius) from South Holland, two from North Holland, two from Overijsel, and one from Walloon churches.[7] Episcopius received a written summons from Synod's moderamen in which he was requested to be present "within fourteen days after receipt of this letter, without tardiness or excuse."[8] More than two weeks later (to be precise the seventh of December during the twenty-third session) Episcopius with the other twelve Remonstrants appeared and took a place opposite the president, Johannes Bogerman. In fact, Episcopius acted as if he were the elected president of a Remonstrant synod. Episcopius pleaded innocence, calling upon the name of the Savior: "Dear Jesus, from thy throne how much hast thou heard or seen against us, simple and innocent people."[9] Later in his speech he asked for freedom, "We have not kept before us, have not wished, have not sought anything else than that golden liberty which keeps the middle road between servitude and licentiousness."[10] He concluded his oration by saying,

> Therefore whoever does not come here in such a frame of mind that he is ready to permit anyone to speak freely because he does not favor him, and judges or puts wrong to him whom he loves, truly he is not worthy that he has a voice in this gathering. Our friend must be Plato, our friend Socrates, our friend the synod. Above all our rock must be the Truth.

After the delivery, President Bogerman asked Episcopius for a copy of the oration. His reply, however, was that the copy that he had was not neat enough to be handed to the clerks; yet upon further deliberation, he submitted a rewritten copy to the President (which document, reportedly, was not the original). Bogerman received the copy almost a week later (December 12); however, he took the opportunity to admonish Episcopius for speaking out of turn—as he had not yet received permission from Synod to deliver his oration—and for hurling accusations against fellow-ministers so as to seek a following and to embitter his opponents.[11]

During the one hundred thirty-eighth session (April 24, 1619), Synod expressed its feelings toward the Remonstrants; but Episcopius had to wait for the final text in the Hague where he was asked to sign a document to lay the doctrinal controversy to rest. Episcopius refused to sign, was declared an insurgent, and was banished from the Netherlands. For at least six years he lived abroad in Antwerp and Cologne, to return to the Netherlands in 1625.

Although Episcopius was a witty debater, a congenial controversialist, and a knowledgeable student of the Scriptures, his theology was unscriptural and uncertain. His conception of the plan of salvation was this: all people may avail themselves of election if they believe in Christ, the Redeemer. He argues that the ethical aspect of Christianity is more important than the doctrinal, that Christianity is not so much a doctrine as a life.

Already in 1609, Episcopius had been so fervent in theological debate that he seriously offended his professor Sibrandus Lubbertus on the interpretation of Romans 7 and was forced to leave the Academy of Franeker in February of the following year.[12] Also, because of his Arminian beliefs he was at one time driven from Amsterdam by a blacksmith, attempting to brand him with a hot iron and shouting: "Stop the Arminian disturber of the Church." Yet amidst all the opposition, his supporters were strong enough to gain him an appointment to the University of Leiden, where he occupied the position of Professor of Theology vacated by Franciscus Gomarus. In 1612, Simon Episcopius began his lectures at the University of Leiden, where he stayed until his exile seven years later. After his banishment, he provided leadership in the Remonstrant Church. He consecrated the church of Amsterdam and became the head of the growing Remonstrant Seminary in that city in 1634. Episcopius died there on April 4, 1643.

GOMARUS, Franciscus (1563–1641)

Years of theological training at many universities prepared Franciscus Gomarus professionally and spiritually for such tasks in the church as pastor, teacher, leader, and defender of the truth.

In Strasburg he took a course in humanistic studies under Johann Sturm; at Neustadt he sat at the feet of Zacharias Ursinus; he also studied at Oxford, Cambridge, and Heidelberg. After serving the Dutch refugee church in Frankfurt from 1586 to 1594, he accepted the appointment to become the third professor of theology at the University of Leiden. A few weeks after receiving the appointment, he was promoted to the doctorate in theology at the University of Heidelberg.

When the pestilence of 1602 took the lives of the other two theological professors at Leiden, the Board of Curators appointed Jacobus Arminius to fill the vacancy of at least one of them. Gomarus had misgivings about the unscriptural doctrines of Arminius because of the latter's exegesis of Romans 7. Friction between Gomarus and Arminius soon became apparent as it centered on the doctrine of predestination. For a time peace prevailed between the two professors when they declared before the Board of Curators that in the fundamental doctrines they did not differ. However, peace was of short duration; the doctrine of predestination was again discussed, first by Arminius and later by Gomarus.[13] The breach that once was healed seemed to be permanent—according to Gomarus, Arminius did not teach in harmony with Scripture and the Confessions.

In disputes, Arminius displayed equanimity; he assured the audience that he did not seek quarrels and disharmony, and he asserted that he would not be the cause of a schism in the church. Gomarus, however, though his arguments against Arminius were Scripturally sound, expressed himself passionately and vindictively.

Yet in all fairness, at the Synod of Dort Gomarus did not take a front line position, shunned publicity, and avoided militancy.[14] As in his conflicts with Arminius, at the Synod he preferred to remain aloof from controversy, hesitated to enter the arena of debate; only when he felt that continued silence would be detrimental to the cause of truth did he speak, but then strongly and forthrightly. When the Remonstrants appeared before

Synod, however, and the delegates heard the oration of Episcopius and his associates, Gomarus remained remarkably quiet. Only once did he ask for the floor, and that was in reaction to the assertion of Episcopius that the Calvinists taught absolute reprobation. No one, according to Gomarus, taught that God rejected man absolutely without regard to man's sin. Before and after the appearance of the Remonstrants, Gomarus spoke on various issues on the floor of Synod. Prior to the arrival of the Remonstrants, for example, while Synod debated the feasibility of a new Bible translation, Gomarus declared that he opposed the inclusion of the apocryphal books in the new translation, and that the name "Jehovah" should be maintained and not be translated by "Lord." He was appointed revisor of the Old Testament, which assignment suggests his scholarliness and erudition. After the departure of the Remonstrants, Gomarus entered into a spirited debate with foreign delegate Matthias Martinius, professor of theology at Bremen, concerning the execution of election. At first the debates were rather militant, for in the opinion of Gomarus and others, Martinius leaned toward the Remonstrant doctrines. When the English delegates reasoned with Martinius privately, the latter promised meekness at Synod so that no disunity would result.[15] Gomarus, though generally reserved, continued to be a zealous defender of the Reformed faith.

Life in academic surroundings was not easy for Gomarus. After a six-year period of strife between Gomarus and Arminius, Arminius died on October 19, 1609. In his place, the Board of Curators wished to appoint Conrad Vorstius, professor of theology at Steinfurt. Because Vorstius also followed Arminius in his teachings, the Board of Curators, wishing to avoid further debate, precluded the advice and opinion of Gomarus. Hence, when the appointment was conferred and subsequently accepted, Gomarus resigned his post as professor of theology to become pastor of the Reformed Church at Middelburg. Both the schools of Saumur and Groningen had been observing Gomarus and desired to have him as professor of theology. In 1615, he received an appointment from the Seminary at Saumur; and no sooner had he accepted the appointment than Groningen offered him a similar post. He stayed at Saumur for three years and then in 1618 went to the University of Groningen, where he taught until his death on January 11, 1641.

Gomarus was known for his vigorous and able defense of the Reformed faith—he remained a supralapsarian until his death—and for his great erudition church and university relied on him for counsel and instruction.

LUBBERTUS, Sibrandus (1555–1625)

In the year 1555 at Langwarden, East Friesland, Sibrandus Lubbertus was born into a soundly Reformed family. His parents soon discovered that young Sibrandus was endowed with keen intellect, which, as they rightly observed, had to be developed in the famous school of Molanus in the city of Bremen. At this school Lubbertus learned Ciceronian Latin and Greek; he mastered these languages so that his Latin was comparable to that of Cicero and he was able to correspond in Greek. From Bremen he went to Wittenberg, and shortly afterwards to Geneva, where he studied under Theodore Beza. For reasons unknown, he stayed in Geneva for only one year, traveled by way of Basel to Marburg, where he learned about the doctrinal conflicts between the Lutherans and the Calvinists. Two years later he enrolled at the Calvinistic Seminary of Neustadt, to study under Zacharias Ursinus. Here he perfected his knowledge of Hebrew, so that on occasion he excelled his master Ursinus. At Neustadt, Lubbertus completed his theological studies and was ready for service in the church; also, in those years his character was formed through academic interests and by his acquaintance with eminent contemporary theologians.

During the spring of 1582, Lubbertus, having declined a call to Brussels, accepted the invitation to become pastor of the church at Emden with the special mandate to minister to the spiritual needs of the sick. But the States of Friesland also desired to have this promising theologian; they called him indirectly to establish a Reformed seminary in Friesland and directly to be minister-at-large in that state. In November 1583 he received the call and in May of the following year he accepted. The acceptance of this call marks the beginning of a lifelong career in church and academy of Friesland. On the twenty-ninth of July 1585, he began his work at the newly founded Academy of Franeker with two other professors. His task was to teach Old Testament and New Testament because of his peerless knowledge of Hebrew and Greek. Lubbertus, however, began his work at the seminary without the title of doctor of theology, though all along he hoped for promotion at the University of Heidelberg, which once more had become a bulwark of Calvinism. During the month of June 1587, Sibrandus Lubbertus earned his doctorate, so that upon returning to Franeker he continued his teaching with the dignity and enhanced qualification of a degree.

Besides his controversy with Rome (which involved the works of Bellarmine), Lubbertus is known for his stand against Socinianism. In 1611 he published a book entitled *Jesus Christ, the Redeemer,* which, dedicated to the Reformed church at London, became a useful weapon against Socinianism in Poland and Prussia. However, Lubbertus did not attack Socinianism merely by writing a book; Socinianism came within the very gates of the Reformed Church of the Netherlands in the person of Conrad Vorstius, who was to succeed Arminius at the University of Leiden. When Franciscus Gomarus indicated his strong opposition by withdrawing from the lectern at Leiden in exchange for the pulpit of the Middelburg congregation, Lubbertus took up the fight against Conrad Vorstius. Then, when followers of Vorstius published a booklet of Socinian teachings and had it circulated in the churches, the battle against Socinianism in general and specifically against Vorstius broke loose. From that moment the terms Remonstrant and Socinian became synonymous among Calvinists in the

Netherlands. Furthermore, Vorstius became a pawn in an international theological chess game in which James I of England played his part as king.[16]

Although delegated to the Synod of Dort, Lubbertus was absent during the early sessions because of a controversy at the Academy in Franeker. During the sixty-second session on January 17, 1619, he delivered a discourse in which he asked the Remonstrants the question whether from John 3:36; 6:40; Hebrews 11:6; and 1 Corinthians 1:12 they could prove that the decree to save believers is the entire decree of predestination.[17] Lubbertus supported the other professors at Synod, yet he was not afraid to give his own opinion whenever necessary. Thus he distinguished himself from Gomarus by stating his infralapsarian sentiment.

Nevertheless, during his professorate at the Academy of Franeker, he was willing to go the second mile to maintain peace. Socinianism excepted. The lines were sharply drawn for him when Socinian doctrine confronted the church.[18] In that respect he was a true defender of the orthodox faith and a genuine disciple of John Calvin.

UYTENBOGAERT, Johannes (1557–1644)

A famous and influential leader of the Dutch Remonstrants was Hans Uytenbogaert, born in the city of Utrecht on February 11, 1557, of Roman Catholic parents. After attending the school of St. Jerome in that city and taking up the study of law, he became a notary public when he was twenty-one years old. He broke with the Roman Catholic church when he was told not to listen to the sermons of an evangelical preacher, Huibert Duifhuis. Within two years, civic leaders of Utrecht sent Uytenbogaert, at the expense of the city, to Geneva, where he studied theology under Theodore Beza. While studying in the Academy of Geneva, Uytenbogaert learned to know his countryman and fellow student, Jacobus Arminius, who had come to study under Beza one year later (1581). Soon a close friendship developed between the two students, which lasted until the death of Arminius in 1609. Already in Geneva Uytenbogaert was influenced by his friend; he refused to listen to his teacher Beza, and after staying in Geneva four years, he returned to Utrecht, where he became a pastor until 1590. In that year, because of an ecclesiastical conflict, he was honorably discharged.

Although his doctrinal moorings were tenuous, his personal charm and rhetorical fervor on such subjects as piety and the renewal of life secured him an invitation from Prince Maurice to come to the Hague in 1591. He was installed as preacher of the Walloon congregation where the Prince and his nobles worshiped. Uytenbogaert soon gained the favor of the Prince, who appointed him as private instructor to his son Prince Frederik Hendrik. Also in ecclesiastical matters, the counsel of this eloquent preacher and charming instructor was constantly sought.

Championing the cause of freedom of speech, Uytenbogaert applied his influence to appoint his friend Arminius as professor of theology at the University of Leiden. When Arminius received and accepted the appointment, it was Uytenbogaert who tried to make peace between the followers and opponents of his friend. Then, upon the death of Arminius, Uytenbogaert showed his real allegiance by accepting the position of leader of the Arminians. He called together forty Arminian pastors and drew up the Five Articles of the Remonstrance on January 14, 1610.

But this position of leadership did not gain him approbation when he persuaded the Board of Curators to appoint Conrad Vorstius to take the place of Franciscus Gomarus at the University of Leiden. He suffered for his diplomacy when Prince Maurice ceased to favor him and later renounced Uytenbogaert's preaching. Having fallen into disrepute and knowing that he could not avoid a conflict at the National Synod—which against his wishes was to convene in November of 1618—Uytenbogaert lost courage in the spring of that year.[19] Episcopius was required to take his place as spokesman for the Arminians at the Synod: Uytenbogaert fled to Rotterdam and from there to Antwerp.

When the Synod of Dort concluded its work (after the foreign delegates had left), it stipulated on May 24, 1619, that Johannes Uytenbogaert be expelled from the Dutch Republic, and that his goods be confiscated because of teachings that were contrary to the Reformed truth. Uytenbogaert spent his time in exile giving leadership to the Remonstrant church in Antwerp until October 1621, and thereafter residing in Rouen, France. When he learned that Prince Maurice had died on April 23, 1625, and that his son Frederik Hendrik had taken his place, Uytenbogaert took the chance of returning secretly to the Netherlands, hoping that his former pupil would be gracious to him. He returned to Rotterdam on September 26, 1626, and Prince Frederik Hendrik, having learned of his old mentor's return, granted him permission to stay. Once again at home in the Hague, Uytenbogaert spent the rest of his life preaching and writing, quietly supporting and stimulating the cause of the Remonstrants.

VOETIUS, Gijsbertus (1589–1676)

The fiery and disputatious Gijsbert Voetius was born of aristocratic parents at Heusden in 1589. He studied theology at the University of Leiden under Franciscus Gomarus, who made a profound and lasting impression on him. After seven years of study at Leiden, he accepted a call to become the pastor of the Reformed church of Vlijmen and Engelen in 1611. Six years later he became the pastor in his native town, despite the well-known text that a prophet is not honored in his own country. He served that congregation until 1629; and he gained further respect by being appointed to the National Synod of Dort as a delegate of the provincial Synod of South Holland. From 1629 to 1634 he served the church at 's-Hertogenbosch, diligently building up a congregation, stressing the supreme necessity of living a life consecrated to God and based on fidelity to the Scriptures.

As a student, Voetius had impressed his professors with his industry and extraordinary memory. The virtue of conscientious stewardship of time he cultivated throughout his life.

Besides studying theology, he steeped himself in the study of Hebrew, Arabic, Syriac, logic, and physics. This interest in theology and Oriental languages brought about an appointment to a professorate at the University of Utrecht in 1634. For forty-two years he was professor of theology and Oriental languages there until his death in 1676.

Although Voetius was not one of the great leaders at the Synod of Dort, his influence became apparent when he began a teaching career at the University of Utrecht. Like his former instructor Franciscus Gomarus, Voetius defended and promoted strict Calvinism. In 1636, for example, he issued a work of practical theology that attests to his dedicated life and orthodox faith; the work is entitled *Proof of the Power of Godliness* and is indicative of Puritan influence. Voetius taught that scholarliness and piety must be life partners of the Christian student.

In addition to his work at the University, Voetius served the church with advice in theological matters, filled the pulpit many Sundays, and gave leadership in ecclesiastical gatherings. Courageously, he wrote against prominent false doctrines and philosophies of his day: he opposed Remonstrants, Roman Catholics, and teachers of the philosophy of Descartes. Voetius is known as the leader of the Reformed Church during the middle of the seventeenth century.[20]

VORSTIUS, Conrad (1569–1622)

Although Conrad Vorstius did not appear on the floor of the Synod of Dort, his influence in the decade preceding that gathering was particularly great. When Arminius died on October 19, 1609, the Board of Curators of the University of Leiden were advised by Johannes Uytenbogaert and others to appoint Vorstius, at that time professor of theology in Steinfurt. Because of his Arminian doctrines—which came close to Socinian teachings—Reformed theologians in continental Europe attacked him, and even King James I of England vehemently opposed this enemy of the faith. James I informed the States-General of the Netherlands that he would consider them his enemies if they tolerated the presence of Conrad Vorstius at the University of Leiden. Vorstius was dismissed by the States-General—who were under obligation to continue his salary—and settled in nearby Gouda in May of 1612.

From Gouda, Vorstius continued his polemical writings against the orthodox theologians of the Netherlands. His persistent and energetic polemical writing became too much even for his closest friends, who tried to persuade him not to publish anymore lest their position also be further imperiled. Uytenbogaert knew that all these publications caused increased antagonism to the cause of the Remonstrants; and when he learned that Sibrandus Lubbertus and Conrad Vorstius were attacking each other's publications before they were properly off the press, he cried out, "O wretched theology and wretched theologians! What, I ask, will ever set this man [Vorstius] free from this labyrinth!"[21] In the fall of 1613, the flood of pamphlets that Vorstius was directing against his enemies became so distasteful to Uytenbogaert that he wrote this in a letter to his friend:

> That you keep yourself busy with short studies against Sibrandus, I do not condemn. But when will there be an end to all this writing? Believe me, with all those pamphlets you achieve nothing. You will never extricate yourself. You will have to choose one of the two: either by recanting some things shake hands or depart, that is, give up your public office.[22]

Vorstius refused to recant.

When the Synod of Dort convened, the delegates ruled that Vorstius' goods be confiscated and that he be exiled from the Netherlands. For three years he lived in hiding near Utrecht, until in 1622, he openly professed Socinianism.

Vorstius was born in Cologne in 1569 of Roman Catholic parents, and studied theology (from 1583 to 1587) at the College of St. Lawrence in his native city. Unable to obtain a degree because of his refusal to subscribe to certain theological doctrines, he pursued a mercantile career for two years. In 1589 he enrolled at the Calvinistic University of Herborn to continue his theological studies. From Herborn he went to Heidelberg, where he received a doctorate in theology in 1594. Universities and academies throughout Western Europe coveted this brilliant theologian, who in 1596 accepted the position of professor of theology at the Seminary of Steinfurt. Soon the academic centers of Saumur (France) and Marburg and Hanau (Germany) offered him similar appointments. He declined them, but accepted the appointment to the University of Leiden in 1611.

4 THE DOCTRINAL DELIVERANCES OF DORT

Fred H.
Klooster

The chief significance of the Synod of Dort is due to its doctrinal deliverances—the Canons of Dort. The doctrinal dispute between the Calvinists and the Arminians was the occasion for calling the Synod, the major item on the agenda, and the reason for the presence of delegates from other Reformed churches of Europe.

In the Canons of Dort the Synod sought to maintain and defend the biblical doctrine of the free and sovereign grace of God in man's salvation. The Arminian teachings were viewed as a revival of the Semi-Pelagian heresy, and their presence in the Reformed churches was judged intolerable. The Arminian doctrines were found to conflict with scriptural teaching and to threaten the confessional character of the Reformed churches whose faith was expressed in the Belgic Confession and the Heidelberg Catechism.

The Canons of Dort emphasize both divine sovereignty and human responsibility. It is misleading—indeed, wholly false and untenable—to contend that Dort defended divine sovereignty while the Arminians defended human responsibility. Both Dort and the Arminians held to divine sovereignty and human responsibility. But two different and contradictory theologies were involved. The Synod of Dort reaffirmed the Calvinistic doctrine of divine sovereignty and human responsibility expressed in terms of unconditional election, limited or definite atonement, man's total depravity, God's irresistible grace, and the perseverance of the saints through God's preserving grace. The Arminians, on the other hand, revived a modified Semi-Pelagian doctrine of divine sovereignty and human responsibility expressed in terms of election conditioned by foreseen faith, universal atonement, man's partial depravity and the cooperative ability of his fallen will, resistible grace, and the possibility of a complete fall from grace on the part of the regenerate.

In this Arminian teaching Synod saw an infringement of God's sovereignty as it is revealed in Scripture. To that extent it emphasized the sovereignty of God in man's salvation over against the Arminians. But Dort clearly maintained and emphasized human responsibility as well.

Historical Background

The Reformed Churches of the Netherlands confessed their faith according to the Belgic Confession of 1561 and the Heidelberg Catechism of 1563. All ministers subscribed to these confessions, and they were expected to abide by these confessions in their preaching and teaching. If difficulties arose from their further study of Scripture, they were expected to pursue a recognized ecclesiastical procedure before making such difficulties public. Jacobus Arminius and the other Arminians or Remonstrants were initially members of the Reformed churches, and they had freely indicated their agreement with these creeds.

As is described elsewhere in this volume in greater detail, the controversy originated when Arminius,[1] an able student and strict Calvinist, was called upon to defend the views of Beza, his former teacher, from the attacks made upon them by Coornhert. The attack centered upon Beza's view of predestination. Coornhert (1522–1590), who remained a member of the Roman Catholic Church until his death, had been influenced by Erasmus and his Semi-Pelagianism. When the Amsterdam consistory requested Arminius to refute Coornhert's attack, he discovered that his own convictions with respect to predestination began to waver and his doubts increased. Eventually he found himself unable to carry out the assignment. Later when Arminius delivered a series of sermons on Paul's *Epistle to the Romans*, serious suspicions were aroused as to whether Arminius was still faithful to the Reformed confessions. One of his fellow ministers in Amsterdam, Plancius, accused him of Socinism. When Arminius became professor of theology at the University of Leiden, the staunch supralapsarian Gomarus attacked his views and questioned his orthodoxy.

During the lifetime of Arminius, the controversy centered upon him and his personal views. However, after his death in 1609, party formation in defense of Arminian views developed, and the unity of the Reformed churches was threatened. In spite of his variant views,[2] Arminius continued to claim adherence to the Belgic Confession and the Heidelberg Catechism. He engaged in criticism of the accepted doctrines, but he did not work out or develop the system of doctrine that has come to be called by his name. This was done mainly by his successors, the learned Simon Episcopius (1583–1644), who succeeded Arminius as professor of theology at Leiden, and by Johannes Uytenbogaert (1557–1644), an eloquent preacher at the Hague who for a time was chaplain of Prince Maurice. Episcopius and Uytenbogaert, the theological leaders of the Arminian party, were supported by the statesman Johan van Oldenbarnevelt (1547–1619) and the many-sided scholar, Hugo Grotius (1583–1645).

The positive expression of the Arminian creed was drawn up by Uytenbogaert in Five Articles called a Remonstrance and presented to the representatives of Holland and West Friesland in 1610. This document was signed by forty-six ministers. A Counter Remonstrance, written mainly by Festus Hommius, was then issued, and the two parties held a conference at the Hague in 1611, the Collatio Hagiensis. No agreement was reached there. Another discussion was held at Delft in 1613. In 1614 the States of Holland offered an edict prepared by Grotius recommending peace, but this was unsuccessful also.

Thus a considerable period of unrest preceded the convening of the Synod of Dort in 1618. Writings of Arminius had long circulated. The Arminian credo had been expressed in the Five Articles. And other more extensive writings had appeared from

Arminian authors. However, the Five Articles of the Arminians, as understood and explained in other writings and public discussions, were the major concern of the Synod of Dort. In addition the Arminian party led by Episcopius was urgently requested by the Synod to set forth its opinions more fully. This was done in the so-called *Sententia Remonstrantium*, the Opinions of the Remonstrants. The Canons of Dort are formulated with these two Arminian statements clearly in mind—the Five Articles and the *Sententia Remonstrantium*. One will best understand the Canons if he studies these documents carefully and observes the specific response of the Canons to these Arminian views. (The reader will find these statements in the appendix to this volume.)

As has already been stated, the views of the Arminians were not really new. What was new, however, was that these views were promulgated within a Reformed church by men who still claimed fidelity to the Reformed confessions. Nevertheless, as Arminianism developed, the criticism of the Reformed confessions increased, and calls for revision were increasingly voiced.

The forerunners of Arminianism are traced in these words by William Cunningham:

> The doctrines of Arminius can be traced back as far as the time of Clemens Alexandrinus, and seem to have been held by many of the fathers of the third and fourth centuries, having been diffused in the church through the corrupting influence of pagan philosophy. Pelagius and his followers, in the fifth century, were as decidedly opposed to Calvinism as Arminius was, though they deviated much further from sound doctrine than he did. The system of theology which has generally prevailed in the Church of Rome was substantially very much of the same as that taught by Arminius, with this difference in favor of the Church of Rome, that the Council of Trent at least left Romanists at liberty to profess, if they chose, a larger amount of scriptural truth, upon some important points, than the Arminian creed, even in its most evangelical form, admits of—a truth strikingly confirmed by the fact, that every Arminian would have rejected the five propositions of Jansenius, which formed the ground of the Jansenistic controversy, and would have concurred in the condemnation

which the Pope, through the influence of the Jesuits, pronounced upon them.³

More immediate influences were made upon Arminian leaders by Erasmus. An advocate of the freedom of the will in contrast to Luther's bondage of the will, Erasmus was held in esteem by many of his Dutch countrymen. Already before the turn of the century, his influence was directly mediated through Coornhert who attacked Calvin and Beza on predestination and also harshly criticized the Heidelberg Catechism. Another forerunner of Arminianism was Caspar Coolhaes. This Leiden minister had been protected by the civil magistrates but was excommunicated in 1582 by the provincial Synod at Haarlem. Arminians were also influenced in varying degrees by Castellio, Bolsec, and Huber.

The five doctrines that were in dispute at the Synod of Dort have come to be called the five points of Calvinism. Reference will be made to this in what follows. Here attention is called to the fact that these five points reflect the major differences between Arminianism and Calvinism. However, the fact that a different theology is involved shows itself as much in the later development as in the specific differences evident at Dort. Note has already been taken that Arminius did not formulate his views to the extent that his successors, especially Episcopius, did. But the later development of the Arminian views also helps to show the seriousness of the issues at stake. Cunningham contrasts Arminius with his successors as follows:

> Arminius himself does not seem—so far as his views were ever fully developed—to have gone further in deviating from scriptural truth than to deny the Calvinistic doctrines of election, particular redemption, efficacious and irresistible grace in conversion, and to doubt, if not to deny, the perseverance of the saints. But his followers, and particularly Episcopius and Curcellaeus, very soon introduced further corruptions of scriptural truth, especially in regard to original sin, the work of the Spirit, and justification; and made near approaches, upon these and kindred topics, to Pelagian or Socinian views.⁴

What was then the central issue in the Arminian controversy? The five points on each side do have a central focus. Philip Schaff designates it "the problem of the ages," a problem "which again and again has baffled the ken of theologians and philosophers, and will do so to the end of time: the relation of divine sovereignty and human responsibility."[5] Approaching the question from a different angle, William Cunningham regards the fundamental characteristic of Arminianism to be ". . . a scheme for dividing or partitioning the salvation of sinners between God and sinners themselves, instead of ascribing it wholly, as the Bible does, to the sovereign grace of God—the perfect and all-sufficient work of Christ,—and the efficacious and omnipotent operation of the Spirit."[6] "Arminianism, in any form," he continues, "can be shown to involve the ascription to men themselves—more directly or more remotely—of a place and influence in effecting their own salvation, which the Bible denies to them and ascribes to God."[7] G. C. Berkouwer puts it this way: "No one will object when we assert that the central intention of the Canons is the unmerited election, the sovereignty of grace in the way of salvation, election as the fountain of all redemptive good."[8] While the Canons maintain human responsibility within the context of the sovereignty of God, Arminianism is characterized by conditionalism. "Theologically, Arminianism is a mediating system throughout. Its most characteristic feature is conditionalism. Absolutism is its persistent opposite; moderation, the mark of its method . . . The supreme principle of Arminianism is conditionalism."[9]

The central issue involves divine sovereignty and human responsibility; another way of putting that is that it involves differing views of God and man. "But whilst the peculiarity of Calvinism is found in holding fast to the absolute idea of God in opposition to all 'idolatry of the creature,' the center of gravity of the Arminian system is found in the sphere of anthropology. Its doctrine of man probably differentiates it more definitely from Calvinism than its doctrine of God."[10]

How were these differences to be resolved? Although the binding character of the creeds was involved, and the Arminians were first opposed in Holland because of their alleged infidelity to the Reformed creeds to which they had voluntarily subscribed, it was decided that the Synod of Dort would judge the issues solely from Scripture. By the time Synod was convened, the Arminian party had increasingly called into question the legitimacy of binding creeds and had openly challenged the biblicalness of various confessional teachings. Furthermore, the political authorities, who were also involved at that age in ecclesiastical controversy, stipulated that the Arminians were not to be judged by any human writings. They were to be judged solely by the criterion of the Word of God.

This was all for the good. However convinced one may be that his confession is faithful to Scripture, careful reexamination in the light of the Word can only lead to needed improvement or deepened conviction. The Arminian controversy had reached such an impasse that only a renewed examination of the disputed doctrines by the norm of Holy Scripture could hopefully lead to resolution of the controversy. Appropriately then, each member of Synod took the following solemn oath before the Synod proceeded to its business:

> I promise before God, in whom I believe, and whom I worship, as being present in this place, and as being the Searcher of all hearts, that during the course of the proceedings of this Synod, which will examine and decide, not only the five points, and all the differences resulting from them, but also any other doctrine, I will use no human writing, but only the Word of God, which is an infallible rule of faith. And during all these discussions, I will only aim at the glory of God, the peace of the Church, and especially the preservation of the purity of doctrine. So help me, my Savior, Jesus Christ! I beseech him to assist me by his Holy Spirit![11]

Thus one finds in the Canons quotations only from Scripture. These references are simply quoted and explanation or exegetical considerations are not provided, though this can hardly be expected within the brevity of a confession. In the Conclusion of the Canons we hear this testimony:

> And this is the perspicuous, simple, and ingenuous declaration of the orthodox doctrine respecting the five articles which have been controverted in the Belgic Churches; and the rejection of the errors, with which they have for some time been troubled. This doctrine the Synod judges to be drawn from the Word of

God, and to be agreeable to the confession of the Reformed Churches.[12]

While Synod appealed to Scripture, it here expressed the judgment that what was found or rediscovered was also "agreeable to the confession of the Reformed Churches." The same thought is expressed in the Formula of Subscription drawn up by the Synod of Dort and still in use in Reformed churches, which include the Canons of Dort in their doctrinal standards. Dort was an elaboration of these doctrines already found in the Reformed confessions; it was not new dogmatic pronouncement.[13]

However, the assertion and belief that the Canons were drawn from and in harmony with Scripture does not exempt us from making our own review and hopefully expressing that same conviction for ourselves. The fact that the Arminians made essentially the same claim for their position indicates the continuing complexity of one's Scriptural appeal. Not only did Arminius and his followers claim the support of Scripture for their views, but the Five Articles of their Remonstrance (1610) also make this claim:

> These Articles, thus set forth and taught, the Remonstrants deem agreeable to the Word of God, tending to edification, and, as regards this argument, sufficient for salvation, so that it is not necessary or edifying to rise higher or to descend deeper. [14]

However, as Frederic Platt, himself a Wesleyan Methodist, states: "Arminianism was always most successful when its argument proceeded upon principles supplied by the moral consciousness of man."[15] On the other hand, history has often heard opponents charge that the Canons of Dort reflect Aristotelian logic and scholasticism.[16] We shall return to this question of the biblical basis for the Canons after we have reviewed their main emphases.

The Interrelatedness of the Five Heads of Doctrine

We have observed that the central issue at the Synod of Dort concerned the doctrine of the sovereignty of God and the responsibility of man. The Arminians called into question certain doctrines that had been regarded as biblical and Reformed by the

Reformed churches of the Netherlands and elsewhere. The initial and focal point of the Arminian attack was the doctrine of predestination. But it soon became evident that other doctrines such as the nature and the extent of the atonement, the nature and extent of man's corruption and depravity, as well as the nature of God's grace and the possibility of a total fall from grace were also intimately involved.

These five heads of doctrine are intimately related. One will discover that while each head of doctrine of the Canons of Dort is devoted to one of these five points, the other four also come into each section explicitly or implicitly as the context and presupposition of the specific doctrine that is being explained. The same is true of the Five Articles of the Arminians. Furthermore, the five doctrines are themselves part of a larger theological perspective. These articles represent a Semi-Pelagian or Arminian theology, while the Canons represent an Augustinian-Calvinistic theology. The differences between Dort and the Arminians on the five disputed doctrines are reflective of differing views of God and man, of sin and grace. Hence differing views of the gospel were at stake.

In this chapter a survey of the doctrinal deliverances of Dort has been requested. An attempt will be made to highlight the major differences between Dort and the Arminians as well as to pinpoint some of the major issues in dispute to this day. But it will be impossible to present a commentary on the Canons of Dort within the space limitations prescribed for this chapter. It will also be impossible to develop in detail any of the disputed issues. The reader is urged to consult and study both the Canons of Dort themselves as well as the Arminian Five Articles and the Opinions of the Remonstrants delivered at the Synod of Dort (*Sententia Remonstrantium*). One will discover that the Canons are drawn up with these two Arminian documents clearly in view.

The Arminian attack upon the Reformed doctrines began with the doctrine of predestination and continued to center upon this doctrine. Thus the Arminian Articles begin with the doctrine of predestination, and this has also determined the order of the Canons of Dort. This is unfortunate and has too often led superficial readers or commentators to suggest that election or predestination is the central principle of Calvinism from which everything else is deduced. Nothing is further from the truth, and a responsible reading of the Canons will readily show the falsity of this interpretation. Election is no more the central or primary doctrine of the Canons than it is of Calvin himself.[17] Since the doctrine of election received the brunt of Arminian opposition, not to mention calumny and caricature, the Canons of Dort first deal with this subject. However, the First Head of Doctrine begins with reference to man as fallen into sin and then goes on to speak of the preaching of the gospel by which faith is awakened. Only then, in the sixth article of the First Head does election receive its explanation. It would probably have been better if the Canons had begun with what are now the Third and Fourth Heads of Doctrine. There the historical order of creation, fall, and redemption—which is basic to the entire doctrine of the Canons—is explicated in further detail. Yet that is also touched upon briefly at the outset of the First Head of Doctrine. In this summary of the doctrine of the Canons of Dort I have chosen to begin with Head of Doctrine III–IV. This reversal of the order will involve no injustice to the Canons, nor is it meant to be an attempted improvement upon them. The chief benefit of this rearrangement is brevity in restatement. Hopefully, in addition to brevity, the rearrangement may enable some to see the positive teaching of the Canon in a truer perspective.

The Creation, Corruption, and Conversion of Man (Third and Fourth Heads of Doctrine)

The Canons of Dort begin with reference to the fact that "all men have sinned in Adam, lie under the curse, and are deserving of eternal death" (I, 1).[18] Since this subject is more fully explained in the Third and Fourth Heads of Doctrine, it will better serve our purpose to follow that fuller explanation first. While the Arminians had set forth their view of man's fall and corruption in one article and their view of grace and man's conversion in another article, the Synod of Dort considered it necessary to unite these two subjects, and thus we have the combined Third and Fourth Heads of Doctrine.

The Arminians did not call into question the doctrines of man's creation by God and his rebellious fall into sin. The chief point of difference concerned the effect of the fall upon man and the extent of his corruption. And this affected their view of how grace operates in man's conversion. Over against the Arminian view of man's partial depravity and retention of the will's cooperative ability, the Synod of Dort affirmed what it believed to be the biblical doctrine of man's total depravity and his loss of a free will. And over against the Arminian view of a grace common to all men with which they were free to cooperate or not cooperate in conversion, Dort affirmed the irresistible grace of God that works true conversion in the sinner's heart. The Canons set forth this doctrine, however, by following the biblical sequence of man's originally perfect creation, his rebellious fall into sin and the corruption of his whole nature as well as all of his posterity, and the renewal of fallen man by the Holy Spirit through the holy Gospel.

Thus the Canons begin this section by recalling that man was "originally formed after the image of God." In this perfect state of creation "his understanding was adorned with a true and saving knowledge of his Creator, and of spiritual things; his heart and will were upright, all his affections pure, and the whole man was holy" (III/IV, 1). But the fall or revolt of Adam changed all this: "revolting from God by the instigation of the devil and by his own free will, he forfeited these excellent gifts; and in the place thereof became involved in blindness of mind, horrible darkness, vanity, and perverseness of judgment; became wicked, rebellious, and obdurate in heart and will, and impure in his affections" (III/IV, 1). This total corruption or depravity due to Adam's fall is passed on to his descendants, not by imitation, "but by the propagation of a vicious nature, in consequence of the just judgment of God" (III/IV, 2). With the sole exception of Jesus Christ who is sinless, "all men are conceived in sin, and are by nature children of wrath, incapable of saving good, prone to evil, dead in sin, and in bondage thereto; and without the regenerating grace of the Holy Spirit, they are neither able nor willing to return to God, to reform the depravity of their nature, or to dispose themselves to reformation" (III/IV, 3, cf. III/IV, par. 1–5).

While the Canons insist upon the radical corruption of man's nature as a result of Adam's fall, man is not regarded as ceasing to be man and becoming "senseless stocks and blocks" (III/IV, 16). Rather, it is asserted that "man by the fall did not cease to be a creature endowed with understanding and will, nor did sin which pervaded the whole race of mankind deprive him of the human nature." However, the fall has "brought upon him depravity and spiritual death." As a result, unless God intervene with the regenerating grace of the Holy Spirit, man "can have no hope of being able to rise from his fall by his own free will, by which, in a state of innocence, he plunged himself into ruin" (III/IV, 16).

Thus the Canons also state that "there remain, however, in man since the fall, the glimmerings of natural light, whereby he retains some knowledge of God, of natural things, and of the difference between good and evil, and shows some regard for virtue and for good outward behavior" (III/IV, 4). These "glimmerings" have sometimes been referred to as general revelation or fruits of common grace.[19] But the Canons do not allow these remaining "glimmerings" to become the basis for a natural theology or a common grace that provides a neutral area for believer and non-believer. The Canons not only state that "this light of nature" is far "from being sufficient to bring him to a saving knowledge of God and to true conversion," but they emphatically add that he is also "incapable of using it aright even in things natural and civil. Nay further, this light, such as it is, man in various ways renders wholly polluted, and hinders in unrighteousness, by doing which he becomes inexcusable before God" (III/IV, 4). They specifically reject the error of those who teach "that the corrupt and natural man can so well use the common grace (by which they understand the light of nature), or the gifts still left him after the fall, that he can gradually gain by their good use a greater, that is, the evangelical or saving grace, and salvation itself" (III/IV, par. 5).

In addition to "the light of nature," the Canons refer to the law of the Decalogue. While the law "reveals the greatness of sin, and more and more convinces man" of his sin, yet it cannot obtain saving grace for him. "It neither points out a remedy nor imparts strength to extricate him from this misery," and therefore "leaves the transgressor under the curse" so that "man cannot by this law obtain saving grace" (III/IV, 5).

This view of man's fall and resultant corruption (total depravity) underlies the exposition that the Canons give in the other articles as well. Having thus emphasized the biblical view of man's creation and fall with the resultant total depravity of the entire race, the Canons turn attention to the gospel by which God provides for man's salvation. Corrupt man's conversion to God occurs by means of God's irresistible grace. "What, therefore, neither the light of nature nor the law could do, that God performs by the operation of the Holy Spirit through the word or ministry of reconciliation; which is the glad tidings concerning the Messiah, by means whereof it has pleased God to save such as believe, as well under the Old as under the New Testament" (III/IV, 6; cf. also I, 2, 3).

The differences between the Old and the New Testaments are fully acknowledged. During the Old Testament period God revealed the mystery of his will "to but a small number" while under the New Testament "he reveals it to many." The cause of this difference "results wholly from the sovereign good pleasure and unmerited love of God"; it is not due to "the superior worth of one nation above another, nor to their better use of the light of nature." How men are to respond to this "sovereign good pleasure" of God is also described: those who receive this gracious, undeserved blessing in spite of their demerits "are bound to acknowledge it with humble and grateful hearts, and with the apostle to adore, but in no wise curiously to pry into, the severity and justice of God's judgments displayed in others to whom this grace is not given" (III/IV, 7).

However, here as elsewhere the Canons of Dort emphasize the meaningfulness of history and the seriousness of human responsibility both for belief and unbelief. Hence the urgency of preaching is stressed. "As many as are called by the gospel are unfeignedly called (*serio vocantur*)" (III/IV, 8). In his Word God has earnestly and truly declared what is acceptable to him, namely "that those who are called should come unto him. He also seriously promises rest of soul and eternal life to all who come to him and believe" (III/IV, 8). When men refuse to come and be converted, "the fault lies in themselves" (III/IV, 9). Thus the reason for unbelief is ascribed to human responsibility: "it is not the fault of the gospel, nor of Christ offered therein, nor of God, who calls men by the gospel and confers upon them various gifts" (III/IV, 9). The various responses that the gospel preaching evokes is recognized in terms of the parable of the sower in Matthew 13 (III/IV, 9) (cf. similarly I, 3–5; II, 5–7; III/IV, 6–10, 17; V, 14).

On the other hand, when the preaching of the gospel leads to conversion and faith, this "must be wholly ascribed to God." This difference is important: while all are "seriously called," unbelief is wholly due to the unbeliever himself, but faith is wholly due to God's sovereign grace. The Arminian idea that those converted have properly exercised their wills in cooperation with a common grace equally furnished to all is rejected. Conversion and faith "must be wholly ascribed to God, who, as he has chosen his own from eternity in Christ, so he calls them effectually in time, confers upon them faith and repentance, rescues them from the power of darkness, and translates them into the kingdom of his own Son" unto his own glory and praise (III/IV, 10).

Though conversion and faith are wholly due to the grace of God, God works this conversion and faith through means which also employ responsible human activity. When God works true conversion in the elect, "He not only causes the gospel to be externally preached to them, and powerfully illuminates their minds by his Holy Spirit, that they may rightly understand and discern the things of the Spirit of God; but by the efficacy of the same regenerating Spirit he pervades the inmost recesses of man; he opens the closed and softens the hardened heart, and circumcises that which was uncircumcised; infuses new qualities into the will, which, though heretofore dead, he quickens; from being evil, disobedient, and refractory, he renders it good, obedient, and pliable; actuates and strengthens it, that like a good tree, it may bring forth the fruits of good actions" (III/IV, 11). This regeneration of the totally depraved sinner by the Spirit is extolled in Scripture as "renewal, new creation, resurrection from the dead, making alive." God works it in us "without our aid." While it takes place through the use of means, it is not worked simply by the external preaching of the gospel, nor by moral suasion, nor by man's cooperation. Rather it is "a supernatural work, most powerful, and at the same time most delightful, astonishing, mysterious, and ineffable." It is "not inferior in efficacy to creation or the resurrection from the dead . . . so that all in whose heart God works in this marvelous manner are certainly, infallibly, and effectually regenerated, and do actually believe." While the will of fallen man is dead and in bondage, no longer free, and unable to cooperate in regeneration, yet in the renewed man the will is "not only actuated and influenced by God, but in consequence of this influence becomes itself active." Thus the Synod of Dort did not hesitate to say that therefore "also man himself is rightly said to believe and repent by virtue of that grace received" (III/IV, 12).

Article 16 of the same head of doctrine further elaborates this frequently misunderstood and caricatured doctrine. Denial of the Arminian contention that man's will after the fall is still able to cooperate in the use of common grace did not lead the Synod to deny that fallen man was still man or to deny the use of the will by renewed man. The Canons specifically state that "this grace of regeneration does not treat men as senseless stocks and blocks, nor take away their will and its properties, or do violence thereto." Rather the regenerating grace "spiritually quickens, heals, corrects, and at the same time sweetly and powerfully bends it (the will), that where carnal rebellion and resistance formerly prevailed, a ready and sincere spiritual obedience begins to reign." In this, the Canons declare, "the true and spiritual restoration and freedom of our will consist" (III/IV, 16).

Thus the Canons stress the sovereign, efficacious, irresistible grace of God in regeneration and conversion. Unless "the admirable Author of every good work so deal with us, man can have no hope of being able to rise from his fall by his own free will" (III/IV, 16). The Synod asserted that man was not able to free himself. In faith it also asserted that it is the supernatural work of the Holy Spirit that frees the will from its bondage and regenerates and quickens it. But at the same time, Synod confessed that this supernatural activity was incomprehensible: it is "at the same time most delightful, astonishing, mysterious, and ineffable" (III/IV, 12). "The manner of this operation cannot be fully comprehended by believers in this life" (III/IV, 13). But believers are "satisfied to know and experience that by this grace of God they are enabled to believe with the heart and to love their Savior" (III/IV, 13).

The Canons continue by making doubly clear that faith is "to be considered as the gift of God . . . because it is in reality conferred upon him, breathed and infused into him." It is not, as the Arminians contended, "offered by God to man, to be accepted or rejected at his pleasure." Nor does God "bestow the power or ability to believe, and then expect that man should by the exercise of his own free will consent to the terms of salvation and actually believe in Christ." It is a gift of God "because he who works in man both to will and to work, and indeed all things in all, produces both the will to believe and the act of believing also" (III/IV, 14).

Since those who do believe are no more deserving than others, and since "God is under no obligation to confer this grace upon any," he who becomes "the subject of this grace owes eternal gratitude to God, and gives him thanks forever." Haughtiness is out of place in the recipient of free, sovereign grace. Furthermore, "it is our duty to pray to God" for those who have not yet been called, while we must speak in the most favorable manner of those who have professed their faith and amended their lives" (III/IV, 15).

This head of doctrine on total depravity and irresistible grace concludes with another facet of human responsibility. Just as God "brings forth and supports this our natural life" through the use of means, so this "supernatural operation of God by which we are regenerated" requires the use of means, namely the gospel which he has "ordained to be the seed of regeneration and food of the soul." We must follow the example of the apostles and teachers in using the means of the Word, the sacraments, and ecclesiastical discipline. The church today may not tempt God "by separating what he of his good pleasure has most intimately joined together." For grace is conferred by means of admonitions; and the more readily we perform our duty, the more clearly this favor of God, working in us, usually manifests itself, and the more directly his work is advanced; to whom all the glory, both for the means and for their saving fruit and efficacy, is forever due. Amen" (III/IV, 17). Thus this important section of the Canons concludes by joining together both divine sovereignty and human responsibility. Sovereign, irresistible grace works in the conversion of corrupt sinners through the means God has commanded men to employ in faith.

Divine Predestination (First Head of Doctrine)

The above summary of the Third and Fourth Heads of Doctrine was presented first because it provided the fuller exposition of that with which the First Head actually begins. Before describing predestination, the Canons here speak of the fact that "all men have sinned in Adam, lie under the curse, and are deserving of eternal death" (I, 1). Hence God would have done no injustice if he had left all to perish and had delivered them over to condemnation because of their sin as Romans 3:19, 23 and 6:23 teach (I, 1). "But in this the love of God was manifested, that he sent his only begotten Son into the world, that whosoever believeth on him should not perish, but have eternal life" (1 John 4:9; John 3:16) (I, 2). In order that "men may be brought to believe, God mercifully sends the messengers of these most joyful tidings to whom he will and at what time he pleases." By this "ministry men are called to repentance and faith in Christ crucified," (I, 3). Those who believe in Jesus Christ are delivered from "the wrath of God and from destruction, and have the gift of eternal life conferred upon them," but "the wrath of God abides upon those who believe not this gospel" (I, 4). Again, before speaking of predestination, the Canons assert man's responsibility: "the cause or guilt of this unbelief as of all other sins is no wise in God, but in man himself" (I, 5). However, faith in Jesus Christ and salvation through him "is the free gift of God" as Ephesians 2:8 and Philippians 1:29 teach. It is certainly clear that these teachings here so briefly set forth are more fully explained in III/IV. What the First Head of Doctrine works out more fully now is the relation of God's predestination to the administration of his grace.

The Canons come to the doctrine of predestination in I, 6 in a way that reminds one of Romans 9. Calvin, who also discusses predestination within the context of soteriology, does so with the opening observation that the preaching of the gospel leads to two types of response and sees behind this the counsel or decree of God.[20] Similarly the Canons: "That some receive the gift of faith from God, and others do not receive it, proceeds from God's eternal decree" (I, 6. Acts 15:18 & Eph. 1:11 are quoted). God's eternal decree is referred to in the singular, and subsequently in the same article reference is made to "that decree of election and reprobation, revealed in the Word of God." According to this decree, God "graciously softens the hearts of the elect, however obstinate, and inclines them to believe; while he leaves the non-elect in his just judgment to their own wickedness and obduracy." In his eternal decree God discriminates between men, but these men are regarded as "equally involved in ruin." Thus the Canons regard God in his decree as presupposing man as fallen. Yet the decree is eternal and as such the decree precedes man's actual existence and fall into sin. Although the doctrine here set forth does not include speculation concerning a logical order of the divine decrees, the manner of presentation is more congenial to the infralapsarian view than to the supralapsarian view.[21] It hardly seems correct, however, to say that the Canons of Dort are specifically infralapsarian. Fortunately, they have bypassed the subtle speculation that led many theologians of that period to set forth what they believed to be the logical order of the decree concerning creation, fall, and predestination.

In the "decree of election and reprobation" Synod saw displayed "the profound, the merciful, and at the same time the righteous discrimination between men equally involved in ruin." Confessing this doctrine because revealed in the Word of God, they add that while "men of perverse, impure, and unstable minds wrest it to their own destruction" yet "to holy and pious souls (it) affords unspeakable consolation" (I, 6). The Canons then go on to speak of election in ten articles (I, 7–14, 17–18) and reprobation in two articles (I, 15–16).

Unconditional, Gracious Election

Election is defined as unconditional, particular, and gracious. In contrast to this view is that of the Arminians who saw election conditioned by foreseen faith. While the Arminians also believed in election and reprobation, they did not believe that God elected specific men, but held that God elects to save those who believe and rejects those who do not believe. While they expressed it in subtle ways, the Arminians believed that men believe by an act of the will cooperating with God's common, enabling grace. Dort's contrast is unmistakable:

> Election is the unchangeable purpose of God, whereby, before the foundation of the world, he has out of mere grace, according to the sovereign good pleasure of his own will, chosen from the whole human race, which had fallen through their own fault from their primitive state of rectitude into sin and destruction, a certain number of persons to redemption in Christ, whom he from eternity appointed the Mediator and Head of the elect and the foundation of salvation. This elect number, though by nature neither better nor more deserving than others, but with them involved in one common misery, God has decreed to give to Christ to be saved by him, and effectually to call and draw them to his communion by his Word and Spirit; to bestow upon them true faith, justification, and sanctification; and having powerfully preserved them in the fellowship of his Son, finally to glorify them for the demonstration of his mercy, and for the praise of the riches of his glorious grace (I, 7. Eph. 1:4–6 & Rom. 8:30 are quoted).

In this comprehensive exposition of the doctrine of election a number of emphases deserve our special attention. First, we see that election unto salvation is an election *in Christ*. In the Arminian Articles of 1610, election was described as God's determination "to save in Christ, for Christ's sake, and through Christ, those who through the grace of the Holy Ghost shall believe on this his Son Jesus, and shall persevere in this faith and obedience of faith" (Art. I). This Arminian emphasis upon Christ, however appealing, was vitiated by the conditionality involved in referring to foreseen faith. While compelled by Scripture to reject this Arminian exposition, the Synod of Dort did not turn away from the emphasis upon election in Christ. The decree of election is the choosing of "a certain number of persons *in Christ* unto salvation" as the Latin should be more accurately rendered.[22] Christ is "from eternity appointed the Mediator and Head of the elect and the foundation of salvation." Furthermore, the Canons state that God decreed to give this elect number "to Christ to be saved by him and effectually call and draw them to his communion by the Word and Spirit." This beautiful, biblical emphasis upon election in Christ is not always adequately noted by commentators.

Secondly, election is not merely the divine decision concerning an end or goal, namely, the eternal salvation of the elect. Election also includes the means to this end. Here, too, election in Christ is central. To effectuate the salvation of the elect, God decreed the means for the achievement of this goal. This elect number "God has decreed to give to Christ to be saved by him, and effectually to call and draw them to his communion by his Word and Spirit." And he has also decreed "to bestow upon them true faith, justification, and sanctification; and having powerfully preserved them in the fellowship of his Son, finally to glorify them for the demonstration of his mercy, and for the praise of the riches of his glorious grace" (I, 7). This exposition follows the biblical teaching of Ephesians 1:4–6 and Romans 8:30. Election includes the means as well as the goal.

Thirdly the Canons stress "one and the same decree" rather than various decrees of election. The Arminians taught that there were various kinds of election: "one general and indefinite, the other particular and definite." The latter was again considered to be either "incomplete, revocable, non-decisive, and conditional, or complete, irrevocable, decisive, and absolute" (I, par. 2). The Arminians also distinguished election unto faith and election unto salvation, so that the former might lead to justifying faith but not to eternal salvation. All this Synod rejected as contrary to Scripture and the result of the fancy of man's inventive mind (I, par. 2). Thus Dort affirms "not various decrees of election, but one and the same decree respecting all those who shall be saved, both under the Old and the New Testament" (I, 8). In the light of Ephesians 1:4–5, and 2:10, Dort states that there is but one decree whereby God has "chosen us from eternity, both to grace and to glory, to salvation and to the way of salvation, which he has ordained that we should walk therein" (I, 8).

Fourth, while the Arminians taught that God elects on the basis of foreseen faith, Dort maintains that faith is itself the fruit of God's election. In the light of Ephesians 1:4 Dort states that "men are chosen to faith and to the obedience of faith, holiness, etc." (I, 9). Election itself is confessed to be "the fountain of every saving good, from which proceed faith, holiness, and the other gifts of salvation, and finally eternal life itself, as the fruits and effects . . ." (I, 9). As is abundantly clear from Romans 9:11–13 and Acts 13:48, election does not rest upon men's works or foreseen faith: "the good pleasure of God is the sole cause of this gracious election" (I, 10). Hence the certainty and unchangeableness of election roots in the very nature of God himself who is "most wise, unchangeable, omniscient, and omnipotent" (I, 11). Thus "the election made by him can neither be interrupted nor changed, recalled, or annulled; neither can the elect be cast away, nor their number diminished" (I, 11). The assurance of election and the means of attaining it are also considered in I, 12 and 13. We shall consider this matter later when we survey the doctrine of the perseverance of the saints in the Fifth Head of Doctrine.

Finally, under the discussion of election the Canons speak of the manner in which this doctrine is to be published. Since God himself has revealed the doctrine of election in Scripture, and the prophets, the apostles, and indeed Christ himself have declared it, we are certainly to do the same. Thus the doctrine of election is "still to be published in due time and place in the Church of God, for which it was peculiarly designed, provided it be done with reverence, in the spirit of discretion and piety, for the glory of God's most holy Name, and for enlivening and comforting his people, without vainly attempting to investigate the secret ways of the Most High" (I, 14).

Sovereign and Just Reprobation

After this rather extensive consideration of election, the Canons turn to a brief discussion of reprobation. As we have observed above, they view God's eternal decree as conceiving the race as fallen and corrupt. The decree of election and reprobation displays "the profound, the merciful, and at the same time the righteous discrimination between men equally involved in ruin" (I, 6). With respect to *"men equally involved in ruin"* it is said "that some receive the gift of faith from God, and others do not receive it, proceeds from God's eternal decree" (I, 6). The Canons are explicit in stating that the "wrath of God abides upon those who believe not this gospel" (I, 4). They are equally explicit in stating that "the cause or guilt of this unbelief as well as of all other sins is no wise in God, but in man himself" (I, 5). Now, while election is the basis for the elect's receiving the gift of faith, it is also stated that the fact that others do not receive the gift of faith proceeds from God's eternal decree (I, 6). That is, "He leaves the non-elect in his just judgment to their own wickedness and obduracy" (I, 6). This is "the righteous discrimination between men equally involved in ruin" (I, 6).

Now in I, 15 reprobation is explained more fully:

> What peculiarly tends to illustrate and recommend to us the eternal and unmerited grace of election is the express testimony of sacred Scripture that not all, but some only, are elected, while others are passed by in the eternal decree; whom God, out of his sovereign, most just, irreprehensible, and unchangeable good pleasure, has decreed to leave in the common misery into which they have willfully plunged themselves, and not to bestow upon them saving faith and the grace of conversion; but, permitting them in his just judgment to follow their own ways, at last; for the declaration of his justice, to condemn and punish them forever, not only on account of their unbelief, but also for all their other sins. And this is the decree of reprobation, which by no means makes God the Author of sin (the very thought of which is blasphemy), but declares him to be an awful, irreprehensible, and righteous Judge and Avenger thereof (I, 15).

As one examines this article, he discovers some of the same considerations involved in I, 6. The decree of reprobation conceives of men as willfully fallen into a common misery. Reprobation is not the cause nor the explanation of man's sin and unbelief. The article concludes again with the emphasis that this decree of reprobation "by no means makes God the Author of sin (the very thought of which is blasphemy)." The major emphasis in the Canons falls upon the preterition aspect of reprobation, the passing by: God has "decreed to leave in the common misery into which they have willfully plunged themselves, and not to bestow upon them saving faith and the grace of conversion." Thus God permits "them in his just judgment to follow their own ways." While reprobation includes condemnation, this had direct reference to their sins. Thus "at last, for the declaration of his justice," "God decreed to condemn and punish them forever, not only on account of their unbelief, but also for all their other sins."

Thus according to the Canons, while reprobation as election is sovereign as God's decree, election displays grace and mercy that reprobation does not. Reprobation displays God's "sovereign, most just, irreprehensible and unchangeable good pleasure." But reprobation is not the cause nor the explanation of man's sin. "The common misery into which (men) have willfully plunged themselves" is "no wise in God, but in man himself." Reprobation is God's decree to pass by some men thus fallen, to leave them in this common misery into which they have willfully plunged themselves, not to bestow upon them saving faith and the grace of conversion, permitting them to follow their own ways, and finally to condemn and punish them for all their sins.

In Article 16 Synod expresses a pastoral concern with respect to the doctrine of reprobation and the response of three types of people to this doctrine. Those who are weak in faith and lack the assurance of faith are urged not to be alarmed at the mention of reprobation so long as they make use of the means of grace that God has appointed. Much less should those be "terrified by the doctrine of reprobation" who are serious in the use of the means of grace but who have not yet reached the measure of holiness to which they aspire. But the Canons realistically add that "this doctrine is justly terrible to those who, regardless of God and of the Savior Jesus Christ, have wholly given themselves up to the cares of the world and the pleasures of flesh, so long as they are not seriously converted to God" (I, 16). Notice that even in this last category, the Canons do not regard any men in history however careless as certainly reprobate and beyond hope. It speaks this warning with the addition—"so long as they are not seriously converted to God."

The First Head of Doctrine on divine predestination concludes with two articles that reflect a warm pastoral note and an urgent exhortation. The pastoral note in the very context of predestination expresses a moving, personal concern. A comforting word is addressed to believers who have lost infant children. "Since we are to judge the will of God from his Word, which testifies that the children of believers are holy, not by nature, but in virtue of the covenant of grace, in which they together with the parents are comprehended, godly parents ought not to doubt the election and salvation of their children whom it pleases God to call out of this life in their infancy" (I, 17). Genesis 17:7, Acts 2:39, and 1 Corinthians 7:14 are listed in support of this pastoral consolation.

The final words of this section echo the response of Paul to objectors: "To those who murmur at the free grace of election and the just severity of reprobation we answer with the apostle: Nay but, O man, who are thou that repliest against God" (Rom. 9:20). The words of our Savior are also added: "Is it not lawful for me to do what I will with mine own?" (Matt. 20:15). What other answer can one utter in faith? And thus the Synod concludes "with holy adoration of these mysteries" in citing the doxology with which Paul concluded Romans 11 (I, 18).

The Death of Christ and Man's Redemption (Second Head of Doctrine)

The dispute between the Arminians and the Reformed churches also concerned the nature and the extent of the atonement provided by Jesus Christ. The Arminians taught that the atonement was universal in its extent, while the Synod of Dort maintained a limited or definite atonement; that is, those for whom Christ died are also effectually saved.

Let us begin by considering the Arminian doctrine as it was set forth in the second of their Five Articles. They confessed that

> ... Jesus Christ, the Savior of the world, died for all men and for every man, so that he has obtained for them all, by his death on the cross, redemption and the forgiveness of sins, yet that no one actually enjoys this forgiveness of sins, except the believer, according to the Word of the Gospel of John 3:16 and 1 John 2:2 . . . (Art. II).

This view of the Arminians can accurately be called "universal atonement" because they contended that Christ "died for all and every man" in the sense "that he has obtained for them all, by his death on the cross, redemption and the forgiveness of sins." According to the Arminian system of doctrine, the appropriation of this salvation depends upon man's use of his free will cooperating with the common grace bestowed by God upon all men.

This emphasis of the Arminian teaching comes out even more clearly in the "Opinions" submitted to the Synod on December 17, 1618. They express their views as follows:

> 1. The price of the redemption which Christ offered to God the Father is not only in itself and by itself sufficient for the redemption of the whole human race but has also been paid for all men and for every man, according to the decree, will, and grace of God the Father; therefore no one is absolutely excluded from participation in the fruits of Christ's death by an absolute and antecedent decree of God.
>
> 2. Christ has, by the merit of his death, so reconciled God the Father to the whole human race that the Father, on account of that merit, without giving up his righteousness and truth, has been able and has willed to make and confirm a new covenant of grace with sinners and men liable to damnation (*Acta*, pp. 130–132).
>
> 3. Only those are obliged to believe that Christ has died for them for whom Christ had died . . . (p. 132).

In contrast to this Arminian doctrine of universal atonement and particular redemption, the Synod of Dort reaffirmed the doctrine of particular atonement and particular redemption. The atonement through Jesus Christ is a perfect atonement that effectually redeems those for whom Christ died.

In the Second Head of Doctrine the Canons begin with the recognition that "God is not only supremely merciful, but also supremely just" (II, 1). According to God's Word, his "justice requires that our sins committed against his infinite majesty should be punished, not only with temporal but with eternal punishment, both in body and soul; which we cannot escape, unless satisfaction be made to the justice of God" (II, 1).[23] Since man is unable to make that satisfaction himself or to deliver himself from God's wrath, God "has been pleased of his infinite mercy to give his only begotten Son for our Surety, who was made sin, and became a curse for us and in our stead, that he might make satisfaction to divine justice on our behalf" (II, 2).

Then in II, 3 & 4 the Canons speak of the sufficiency of Christ's death as the death of the person of the infinite Son of God. Synod did not affirm limited atonement because there were inherent limits in Christ's sacrifice. The definite or particular focus of the atonement stems from the sovereign will and design of God himself, not from inherent limitations in Christ's work. On the other hand, while the Canons speak of the sufficiency of Christ's death, they do not teach that Christ has "paid for all men and for every man" as did the Arminians. Let us examine the precise teaching of the Canons since this too has often been misconstrued.[24]

With respect to the sufficiency of Christ's death, they say: "The death of the Son of God is the only and most perfect sacrifice and satisfaction for sin, and is of infinite worth and value, abundantly sufficient to expiate the sins of the whole world" (II, 3). Furthermore, Christ's death is "of such infinite value and dignity because the person who submitted to it was not only really man and perfectly holy, but also the only begotten Son of God . . . and, moreover, because it was attended with a sense of the wrath and curse of God due to us for sin" (II, 4). The distinction between the Canons and the Arminian position is clear and important; it is unfortunate that confusion arises when these distinctions are not fully observed. While the Canons speak of "the death of the Son of God" as "abundantly sufficient to expiate the sins of the whole world," the Arminians speak of a sufficiency because of a universal expiation. According to the Arminians, Christ's death is "sufficient for the redemption of the whole human race" because he has "paid for all men and for every man, according to the decree, will, and grace of God the Father" (Opinion 2). They maintained that "Christ has merited reconciliation with God and remission of sins for all men and for every man" because "he has obtained for them all, by his death on the cross, redemption and forgiveness of sins" (Art. II). According to the Arminian doctrine, men are called upon to believe that Christ died for them, because he has actually died for all in the sense of expiating sin and propitiating God. That doctrine is radically different from the Synod's recognition that Christ's death was "abundantly sufficient to expiate the sins of the whole world" (II, 3). It is wholly misleading and in conflict with the teaching of the Canons to claim that they teach "universal atonement" in II, 3, 4 and particular redemption in II, 8. They speak of the sufficiency of Christ's death, but not of the sufficiency of the atonement or of the satisfaction made. They speak of Christ's death as "abundantly sufficient to expiate the sins of the whole world," but they do not teach that Christ's death did actually expiate the sins of the whole world. The Arminians taught that, but the Canons reject it. This comes out more clearly if we also examine the Rejection of Errors on this subject.

The Arminians taught that as a result of Christ's universal atonement, "all men have been accepted unto the state of reconciliation and unto the grace of the covenant, so that no one is worthy of condemnation on account of original sin, and that no one shall be condemned because of it, but that all are free from the guilt of original sin." This teaching is specifically rejected by the Synod in II, par. 5. Dort held that by the death of Christ, God has *confirmed* the new covenant of grace through Christ's blood, but rejects the teaching that as a result of Christ's death God has established an entirely new covenant including all men in which are prescribed new conditions dependent upon the free will of man (II, par. 2, 3). The Arminians held that Christ had paid for the sins of all men by his death, so that the guilt of original sin is now removed for all, and all come into a new state of reconciliation and into a new covenant of grace. Thus they contended that the one sin for which man could be condemned was the sin of unbelief—rejecting the message that Christ died for them.[25]

The basic thrust of II, 3–4, in contrast to the Arminian doctrine of universal atonement, is the recognition that limited atonement is not due to inherent limitations in Christ's sacrificial death. In spite of Synod's disagreement with the Arminians, they did not hesitate to acknowledge that the death of Christ was indeed "of infinite worth and value, abundantly sufficient to expiate the sins of the whole world." The Canons continue by frankly acknowledging that the doctrine of limited or definite atonement does not in any way curtail the universal preaching of the gospel. "The promise of the gospel is that whosoever believes in Christ crucified shall not perish, but have eternal life" (II, 5). And they do not hesitate to add that "this promise, together with the command to repent and believe, ought to be declared and published to all nations and to all persons promiscuously and without distinction, to whom God out of his good pleasure sends the gospel" (II, 5). Thus the meaningfulness of history, the responsibility of men in preaching, and the urgency of this preaching is clearly maintained. Whatever paradox there may be between limited atonement and the universal call of the gospel, the Synod of Dort affirmed both and curtailed neither—convinced that this was scriptural.

In this context, as elsewhere throughout the Canons, unbelief in the face of the preaching of the gospel is always ascribed to man's sin while faith is the work of God's grace (cf. I, 4 & 5 with II, 6 & 7). Unbelief is wholly imputed to man's sin: "and, whereas many who are called by the gospel do not repent nor believe in Christ, but perish in unbelief, this is not owing to any defect or insufficiency in the sacrifice offered by Christ upon the cross, but is wholly to be imputed to themselves (II, 6).[26] On the other hand, faith and deliverance from sin is solely due to the grace of God: "But as many as truly believe, and are delivered and saved from sin and destruction through the death of Christ, are indebted for this benefit solely to the grace of God given them in Christ from everlasting, and not to any merit of their own" (II, 7).

Definite Atonement Explained

Only after all these important explanations and clarifications in II, 1–7, do the Canons specifically set forth their view of definite atonement in contrast to the Arminian view of universal atonement. Although the term "atonement" is not employed by the Canons, this term is, strictly speaking, applicable only to II, 8 and 9. Here the Reformed doctrine of "limited atonement" is explained:

> For this was the sovereign counsel and most gracious will and purpose of God the Father that the quickening and saving efficacy of the most precious death of his Son should extend to all the elect, for bestowing upon them alone the gift of justifying faith, thereby to bring them infallibly to salvation; that is, it was the will of God that Christ by the blood of the cross, whereby he confirmed the new covenant, should effectually redeem out of every people, tribe, nation, and language, all those, and those only, who were from eternity chosen to salvation and given to him by the Father; that he should confer upon them faith, which, together with all the other saving gifts of the Holy Spirit, he purchased for them by his death; should purge them from sin, both original and actual, whether committed before or after believing; and having faithfully preserved them even to the end, should at last bring them, free from every spot and blemish, to the enjoyment of glory in his own presence forever (II, 8).

It is clear that in this article the Canons are not simply speaking of particular redemption or the saving efficacy of the death of Christ in distinction from a more universal atonement described earlier. That interpretation frequently heard of late does injury to the specific teaching of the Canons. In fact it is specifically rejected in II, par. 3. The difference between the Synod of Dort and the Arminians was not confined to the question of the extent of the atonement. The question of the extent of the atonement also involves the question as to the nature of the atonement. Both the nature and extent of the atonement is the subject of II, 8. Let us look at this article more closely.

Dort links redemption or the application of salvation directly to the death of Christ and the sovereign counsel of God. As we have already seen in the articles on election, the means to the attainment of God's decreed goal are included in his decree. Means are not separate from end or goal. The same teaching is evident here. This is stated a second time in II, 8 when in an explanatory way it is added: "that is, it was the will of God that Christ by the blood of the cross, whereby he confirmed the new covenant, should effectually redeem . . . all those, and those only, who were from eternity chosen to salvation and given to him by the Father" and that "he should confer upon them faith, which, together with all the other saving gifts of the Holy Spirit, he purchased for them by his death . . ." (II, 8). The Canons do not view the application of redemption as something divorced from or distinct from the atonement. The atonement describes what God intended (willed) and what Christ actually achieved by his death. While the Arminians viewed the atonement as obtaining redemption and the forgiveness of sins for all men so that all are now brought into a state of reconciliation, and salvation is available for all, they did not regard the application of redemption as included in the atonement. The atonement does not insure saving efficacy. Hence they taught universal atonement but particular redemption. The Canons specifically reject this view. Dort views the atonement as including effective application; saving efficacy is included in God's will and Christ's atonement. Hence Dort here teaches a definite or particular atonement that includes definite or particular redemption.

Canons II, 8 is also a striking illustration of the interrelatedness of the five points of doctrine on which the Arminians and Calvinists disagreed. In this article one sees definite atonement, unconditional election, irresistible grace, and the perseverance of the saints all interrelated in God's gracious redemption of men who are totally depraved. Efficacy, application, salvation, perseverance, and glorification are unitedly willed by God in his good pleasure and achieved, obtained, purchased by Christ in his atoning death. All the saving gifts that the Holy Spirit applies to the elect were purchased by the Son and decreed by God. There is no disunity, only harmony and unity, in the work of the Father, the Son, and the Holy Spirit in man's salvation. All this is involved in Dort's doctrine of limited atonement. The Arminians taught universal atonement and particular redemption; efficacy and application are divorced from Christ's atoning death. The Synod of Dort taught particular atonement and particular redemption; efficacy and application are included in Christ's atoning death. To confuse these matters is to do violence to the Canons of Dort.

The Second Head of Doctrine concludes its positive presentation with a believing application of this comforting doctrine:

> This purpose (*Consilium*), proceeding from everlasting love towards the elect, has from the beginning of the world to this day been powerfully accomplished, and will henceforward still continue to be accomplished, notwithstanding all the ineffectual opposition of the gates of hell; so that the elect in due time may be gathered together into one, and that there never may be wanting a Church composed of believers, the foundation of which is laid in the blood of Christ; which may steadfastly love and faithfully serve him as its Savior (who, as a bridegroom for his bride, laid down his life for them upon the cross); and which may celebrate his praises here and through all eternity (II, 9).

The reader will do well to study carefully the seven paragraphs in the Rejection of Errors in order to understand better the implications of the Arminian position and that of Dort as well. It is also important to observe that here as well as in all of the Canons except the First Head of Doctrine, most of the Scripture passages upon which the position of the Synod of Dort is based are found in the sections on the rejection of errors.

The Perseverance of the Saints (Fifth Head of Doctrine)

Since this survey of the doctrinal deliverances of the Synod of Dort began with the Third and Fourth Heads of Doctrine, we now move from the Second Head to the Fifth, from limited atonement to the perseverance of the saints. This is also useful because it brings out the clear link between God's sovereign, efficacious and irresistible grace. Although the Canons realistically and biblically recognized the constant presence of sin in the believer, they also affirm the perseverance of the saints by means of God's preservation. Here divine sovereignty and human responsibility again go hand in hand.

The Canons affirm that with respect to God "it is utterly impossible" that the true believer should "totally fall from faith and grace" or "continue and perish finally in (his) backslidings" (V, 8). This is not due to the believer's inner personal strength;

the reason is that God's "counsel cannot be changed nor his promise fail; neither can the call according to his purpose be revoked, nor the merit, intercession, and preservation of Christ be rendered ineffectual, nor the sealing of the Holy Spirit be frustrated or obliterated" (V, 8). Thus the perseverance of the saints is linked to God's counsel of election, Christ's efficacious work, and the Holy Spirit's sovereign application. That emphasis is found in the opening words of this section also: "Those whom God, according to his purpose, calls to the communion of his Son, our Lord Jesus Christ, and regenerates by the Holy Spirit, he also delivers from the dominion and slavery of sin, though in this life he does not deliver them altogether from the body of sin and from the infirmities of the flesh" (V, 1).

Perfection is not possible in this life, even though the saints persevere and their sanctification progresses. Daily sins and blemishes "cleave even to the best works of the saints" (V, 2). Such daily sins are "to them a perpetual reason to humiliate themselves before God and to flee for refuge to Christ crucified; to mortify the flesh more and more by the spirit of prayer and by holy exercises of piety; and to press forward to the goal of perfection, until at length, delivered from this body of death, they shall reign with the Lamb of God in heaven" (V, 2). Thus we see a beautiful exhortation to responsible human activity also on the part of believers in the use of God-ordained means with an eschatological perspective.

The Canons contain a measure of repetition at this point in order to bring out various nuances of the biblical doctrine. Because of indwelling sin and the temptations of the world and Satan, those who are converted cannot persevere in their own strength. "But God is faithful, who, having conferred grace, mercifully confirms and powerfully preserves them therein, even to the end" (V, 3). "Although the weakness of the flesh cannot prevail against the power of God, who confirms and preserves true believers in a state of grace," yet true believers are not always "so influenced and actuated by the Spirit of God" that they do not fall into serious sin. "Great and heinous sins by the flesh, the world, and Satan" may result such as the Bible itself describes in "the lamentable fall of David, Peter, and other saints" (V, 4). There is no minimizing of the sins of believers that arise when they neglect to be "constant in watching and prayer"; for then, "sometimes by the righteous permission of God (they) actually are drawn into these evils" (V, 4). The seriousness of such sins by careless believers is fully acknowledged: "By such enormous sins, however, they very highly offend God, incur a deadly guilt, grieve the Holy Spirit, interrupt the exercise of faith, very grievously wound their consciences, and sometimes for a while lose the sense of God's favor, until, when they change their course by serious repentance, the light of God's fatherly countenance again shines upon them" (V, 5).

Thus the Canons do not mean by the doctrine of the perseverance of the saints, that the once-converted are kept from all sin and never resist the grace of God, or neglect the means of grace, or succumb to temptation. Rather, they mean that God's preserving grace guarantees their persevering. Furthermore the perseverance of the saints is not seen apart from their personal perseverance in faith. Basically the ground for perseverance is the sovereignty of God's grace: "But God, who is rich in mercy, according to his unchangeable purpose of election, does not wholly withdraw the Holy Spirit from his own people even in their grievous falls; nor suffers them to proceed so far as to lose the grace of adoption and forfeit the state of justification, or to commit the sin unto death or against the Holy Spirit; nor does he permit them to be totally deserted, and to plunge themselves into everlasting destruction" (V, 6).

The Canons stress the perseverance of the saints by means of God's continuous work of grace in them as they also make use of the means of grace in terms of human responsibility: "For in the first place, in these falls he preserves in them the incorruptible seed of regeneration from perishing or being totally lost; and again, by his Word and Spirit he certainly and effectually renews them to repentance, to a sincere and godly sorrow for their sins, that they may seek and obtain remission in the blood of the Mediator, may again experience the favor of a reconciled God, through faith adore his mercies, and henceforward more diligently work out their own salvation with fear and trembling" (V, 7). Thus their perseverance is "not in consequence of their own merits or strength, but of God's free mercy." A total fall from grace "with respect to themselves is not only possible, but would undoubtedly happen"; but such a total falling away "with respect to God, . . . is utterly impossible" because God's counsel and promises cannot fail, because Christ's work cannot be rendered ineffectual, and because the sealing of the Holy Spirit cannot be frustrated or obliterated (V, 8). But according to the Canons "this preservation of the elect to salvation and their perseverance in the faith" (V, 9) are always correlative.

The Canons state that true believers "may and do obtain assurance" of God's preservation and their perseverance. But this assurance will vary "according to the measure of their faith" (V, 9). They gain this assurance as they believe "that they are and ever will continue true and living members of the Church, and they have the forgiveness of sins and life eternal" (V, 9). However, this assurance is "not produced by any peculiar revelation contrary to or independent of the Word of God." It comes via human responsibility; it "springs from faith in God's promises, which he has most abundantly revealed in his Word for our comfort, from the testimony of the Holy Spirit, witnessing with our spirit that we are children and heirs of God (Rom. 8:16); and lastly, from a serious and holy desire to preserve a good conscience and to perform good works (V, 10). So important is this assurance that if the elect were deprived of it "they would be of all men the most miserable" (V, 10). Carnal doubts and grievous temptations often keep believers in this life from "this full assurance of faith and certainty of persevering" (V, 11). But God, "the father of all consolation," does not allow believers to be tempted without giving the way of escape and endurance (1 Cor. 10:13), and the "Holy Spirit again inspires them with the comfortable assurance of persevering" (V, 11).

The common charge against this doctrine is that it leads to a spirit of pride and carnal security. Not so, say the Canons; "this certainty of perseverance . . . is the real source of humility, filial reverence, true piety, patience in every tribulation, fervent prayers, constancy in suffering and in confessing the truth, and of solid rejoicing in God" (V, 12). Rather than leading to laxity and carelessness, "consideration of this benefit should serve as an incentive to the serious and constant practice of gratitude and good works, as appears from the testimonies of Scripture and the examples of the saints" (V, 12).

What about those who are "recovered from backsliding"? Would they not tend from this experience to disregard piety and tend toward licentiousness? Not at all, say the Canons; "it renders them much more careful and solicitous to continue in the ways of the Lord, which he has ordained, that they who walk therein may keep the assurance of persevering." Here too a false security in the face of faithlessness is not encouraged by this doctrine. The warning is expressed that the believer must continue in the way of faith to persevere and to be assured of persevering, "lest, on account of their abuse of his fatherly kindness, God should turn away his gracious countenance from them . . . and they in consequence thereof should fall into more grievous torments of conscience" (V, 13).

Perseverance of the saints works through means, just as the beginning of faith is worked through means. "As it has pleased God, by the preaching of the gospel, to begin this work of grace in us, so he preserves, continues, and perfects it by the hearing and reading of the Word, by meditation thereon, and by the exhortations, threatenings, and promises thereof, and by the use of the sacraments" (V, 14).

Finally Synod stated that while this doctrine of the perseverance of the saints is clearly revealed in Scripture, yet "the carnal mind is unable to comprehend" it (V, 15). God has revealed this doctrine "for the glory of his Name and the consolation of pious souls," but "Satan abhors it, the world ridicules it, the ignorant and hypocritical abuse it, and the heretics oppose it." "But the bride of Christ has always most tenderly loved and constantly defended it as an inestimable treasure." And the confidence is expressed that "God, against whom neither counsel nor strength can prevail, will dispose her so to continue to the end." Thus this positive section of the Canons concludes with the doxology: "Now to this one God, Father, Son, and Holy Spirit, be honor and glory forever. Amen" (V, 15).

Divine Sovereignty and Human Responsibility

Now that we have completed our survey of the various sections of the Canons, attention will be directed to a few final considerations.

It was stated above that it is too simplistic to maintain that the Arminians defended human responsibility while the Synod of Dort defended divine sovereignty. Both parties held to both divine sovereignty and human responsibility. The conflict concerned the nature of divine sovereignty and the nature of human responsibility. Dort contended that the Arminian views were in conflict with Scripture both with respect to divine sovereignty and human responsibility. While Dort has come to be known for its emphasis upon the sovereign grace of God in man's salvation, it also defended what it believed to be the scriptural teaching of man's responsibility. In fact, human responsibility pervades the Canons. Without wishing to minimize Dort's emphasis upon divine sovereignty, one will nevertheless discover that in terms of space the Canons devote more attention to human responsibility than they do to divine sovereignty.

A brief survey of these themes in the Canons may be helpful. The comprehensive survey of the main sections of the Canons has, of course, included this concern. Here a cross section of the teaching of the Canons will be made in order to highlight the present subject. In general it may be said that Dort maintains a divine sovereignty that operates through human responsibility or a human responsibility that is enveloped by and subordinate to the divine sovereignty. The Arminians, on the other hand, conceived of God in his sovereignty placing man in such a situation that human responsibility is thereby given a more autonomous character.

The Canons begin with reference to man's responsibility for his sin, and this emphasis pervades the entire confession. "As all men have sinned in Adam, lie under the curse, and are deserving of eternal death, God would have done no injustice by leaving them all to perish and delivering them over to condemnation on account of sin . . ." (I, 1). Thus the whole human race has "fallen through their own fault from their primitive state of rectitude into sin and destruction" (I, 7). While God created him in his image, perfect, righteous, and holy, man is responsible for his fall and depravity. "Revolting from God by the instigation of the devil and by his own free will, he forfeited these excellent gifts" (III/IV, 1). The presence of sin in the regenerate also is traced to human responsibility, and its seriousness is not minimized (V, 1ff.). In a word, sin is throughout traced to human responsibility.

Especially since the time of Calvin, most Reformed theologians speak of Adam's fall as somehow included in God's decree. They also stressed man's responsibility in sin and denied that God was in any sense the author of sin. For this reason they usually spoke of God's decree with respect to sin as a "permissive decree."[27] But the Canons refrain from making any link between man's sin and God's decree. Dort was satisfied simply to stress the fact of sin and the corruption of the entire race as a result of Adam's fall. Human responsibility is wholly adequate to explain the origin of sin. Thus reference is throughout made to "men equally involved in ruin" (I, 6 etc.). Reprobation, which is indeed confessed as rooted in God's decree, is not the reason for man's sin and unbelief. To speak otherwise is to do injustice to the Canons. Furthermore, the Canons specifically state that the decree of reprobation does not make God the author of sin and emphatically adds that this "very thought . . . is blasphemy" (I, 15).

Human responsibility is stressed throughout the Canons also with respect to the serious, well-meant, universal call of the gospel (I, 4; II, 5; III/IV, 7, 8). The "promise of the gospel is that whosoever believes in Christ crucified shall not perish, but have eternal life" and "this promise, together with the command to repent and believe, ought to be declared and published to all nations, and to all persons promiscuously and without distinction, to whom God out of his good pleasure sends the gospel" (II, 5). God's sovereignty is indeed recognized in the last part of that statement as it is elsewhere: "God mercifully sends the messengers of these most joyful tidings to whom he will and at what time he pleases" (I, 3). Nevertheless, human responsibility in preaching, in evangelizing, in missions is clearly emphasized in these references and throughout the Canons.

Again, as the Canons reflect upon the response to that preaching of the gospel, human responsibility is recognized in the response that the gospel awakens—but human responsibility with a difference. Without exception, the response of unbelief is always man's responsibility: "the cause or guilt of this unbelief as of all other sins is no wise in God, but in man himself" (I, 5; cf. 1, 4; II, 6; III/IV, 9). This unbelief is "wholly to be imputed to themselves . . . whereas many who are called by the gospel do not repent nor believe in Christ, but perish in unbelief, this is not owing to any defect or insufficiency in the sacrifice offered by Christ upon the cross, but is wholly to be imputed to themselves" (II, 6). Yet this emphasis on human responsibility is different from that of the Arminians, who taught a universal atonement and a common grace given to all. The Arminians held that unbelief was wholly due to man because God had placed him in a situation in which the mere use of his will in cooperating with the grace of God would have enabled him to appropriate the salvation universally available. That was a different view of human responsibility from that of Dort. And yet Dort does not hesitate meaningfully to relate all sin to man's fall and man's responsibility. "It is not the fault of the gospel, nor of Christ offered therein, nor of God, who calls men by the gospel and confers upon them various gifts, that those who are called by the ministry of the Word refuse to come and be converted. The fault lies in themselves" (III/IV, 9). Also the sin still present in regenerated believers is laid at the door of human responsibility. This emphasis runs through the Fifth Head of Doctrine. It cannot be gainsaid that the Canons stress human responsibility throughout when referring to sin and unbelief in all its forms and manifestations.

However, when the Canons reflect upon the response of faith that arises when the gospel is preached, emphasis falls on the sovereignty of God's grace. Sin and unbelief must wholly be imputed to man; faith and obedience, however, must be wholly ascribed to God. "But that others who are called by the gospel obey the call and are converted is not to be ascribed to the proper exercise of free will . . . but it must be wholly ascribed to God" (III/IV, 10). Again, "as many as truly believe, and are delivered and saved from sin and destruction through the death of Christ, are indebted for this benefit solely to the grace of God given them in Christ from everlasting, and not to any merit of their own" (II, 7). This response of faith, which is "wholly ascribed to God" and "not to any merit of their own" does, of course, involve human activity and thus human responsibility. But this human activity is linked to God's gracious election, Christ's efficacious death, and the irresistible grace of the Holy Spirit. Thus human responsibility in faith and obedience is embraced within the sovereignty of God. Strikingly different is the human responsibility in sin and unbelief, which is "wholly to be imputed" to man.

Thus as the Canons ascribe the faith-response to the grace of God, they focus attention upon God's sovereignty in predestination and atonement. As was noted above, Paul in Romans 8 to 11 turns to consider predestination against the background of faith and unbelief. Calvin presents his teaching on predestination also within the context of soteriology in Book III of the *Institutes*. So too, the Canons: "that some receive the gift of faith from God, and others do not receive it, proceeds from God's eternal decree" (I, 6). One must not fail to recall that this statement is made of "men equally involved in ruin" (I, 6). Again it cannot be overemphasized, the statement "that some receive the gift of faith from God and others do not receive it" is *not* made with respect to sin and unbelief. Failure to observe this distinction has frequently led to caricature and misrepresentation of the Canons. Dort considered the matter so important that it reappears in the Conclusion. There the teaching "that in the same manner in which the election is the fountain and cause of faith and good works, reprobation is the cause of unbelief and impiety" is declared to be one that the Reformed Churches "not only do not acknowledge, but even detest with their whole soul."

The grace of God manifested to men in history by which some receive the gift of faith flows from God's eternal election (I, 7ff.). This same "sovereign counsel and most gracious will and purpose of God the Father" is seen in the atoning death of Jesus Christ: "it was the will of God that Christ by the blood of the cross, whereby he confirmed the new covenant, should effectually redeem out of every people, tribe, nation, and language, all those, and those only, who were from eternity chosen to salvation and given to him by the Father," (II, 8). Faith and all the other saving gifts of the Holy Spirit, Christ has "purchased for them by his death" (II, 8). Faith and conversion are therefore "wholly ascribed to God" because as "he has chosen his own from eternity in Christ, so he calls them effectually in time, confers upon them faith and repentance, rescues them from the power of darkness, and translates them into the kingdom of his own Son" (III/IV, 10).

Throughout the Canons this sovereign grace of God is understood to work through means so that men are brought to believe actively and dynamically. Although the grace of regeneration is a supernatural work of God, it "does not treat men as senseless stocks and blocks, nor take away their wills and its properties, or do violence thereto" (III/IV, 16). Rather, this sovereign grace of God, "spiritually quickens, heals, corrects, and at the same time sweetly and powerfully bends" man's will so that "a ready and sincere spiritual obedience begins to reign" (III/IV, 16). As God's sovereignty over our ordinary life "does not exclude but requires the use of means" so too the "supernatural operation of God by which we are regenerated in no wise excludes or subverts the use of the gospel" (III/IV, 17). After regeneration takes place, God still works through the means of the Word, the sacraments, and ecclesiastical discipline. Therefore we are not "to presume to tempt God by separating what he of his good pleasure has most intimately joined together. For grace is conferred by means of admonitions"—that might be regarded as a summary of the way in which the Canons mainly view the interrelation between divine sovereignty and human responsibility.

It is not unimportant to observe how the Canons relate divine sovereignty and human responsibility in connection with the doctrine of reprobation. To repeat, perhaps not unnecessarily, according to the Canons God's eternal, sovereign decree views men as fallen in Adam and "equally involved in ruin." Thus the decree of reprobation is first of all referred to as a passing by (preterition). The decree of reprobation is not the cause of man's sin; this is wholly to be imputed to man himself. In the decree of reprobation God "leaves the non-elect in his judgment to their own wickedness and obduracy" (I, 6). These non-elect are "passed by in the eternal decree." In his "sovereign, most just, irreprehensible, and unchangeable good pleasure," God "has decreed to leave them in the common misery into which they have willfully plunged themselves, and not to bestow upon them saving faith and the grace of conversion." Rather he permits them "in his just judgment to follow their own ways" and "at last, for the declaration of his justice, to condemn and punish them forever, not only on account of their unbelief, but also for all their other sins" (I, 15). The Canons are serious in stating that this decree of reprobation "by no means makes God the Author of sin, the very thought of which is blasphemy." But this decree of reprobation "declares him to be an awful, irreprehensible, and righteous Judge and Avenger" of sin (I, 15). There is no conflict on this matter between the Canons and the Conclusion as is sometimes superficially claimed. There too the claim that this doctrine makes God the Author of sin is vigorously rejected. To hold such a doctrine would be "nothing more than an interpolated Stoicism, Manicheeism, Libertinism, Turcism." The Conclusion rejects the idea that sovereignty in reprobation means that "God, by a mere arbitrary act of his will, without the least respect or view to any sin, has predestinated the greatest part of the world to eternal damnation, and has created them for this purpose." No one could legitimately draw this conclusion from the Canons. It is one of the calumnies heaped upon the doctrine of the Reformed churches.

Thus we have seen how Dort defended both divine sovereignty and human responsibility. It did not play off the one over against the other. Believing both to be clearly revealed by the Word of God and seeing divine sovereignty especially but also the right understanding of human responsibility endangered by the Arminian teachings, Dort set forth and defended both. This doctrine, derived from Scripture, Dort desired to direct "to the glory of the Divine name, to holiness of life, and to the consolation of afflicted souls" (Conclusion).

The Biblical Basis of the Canons

The Canons claim to be rooted in Scripture. It is admitted that the doctrine set forth is beyond human comprehension. What Dort specifically says of the doctrine of the perseverance of the saints might be said of all its teachings: "Satan abhors it, the world ridicules it, the ignorant and hypocritical abuse it, and the heretics oppose it" (V, 15). But Dort confessed because it believed these to be the doctrines "which God has most abundantly revealed in his Word" (V, 15). Thus the opening words of the Conclusion affirm: "This doctrine the Synod judges to be drawn from the Word of God, and to be agreeable to the confession of the Reformed Churches."

In the early part of this chapter we noted that Dort decided to examine the Arminian position simply by the norm of Scripture and not by any human or churchly authority. Hence there is almost no reference to existing creeds or theologians.[28] The appeal of the Canons is to Scripture, and this appeal is pervasive throughout. Ultimately every judgment with respect to the Canons must be made by the same criterion. No other standard can withstand the judgment of God!

It is a curious fact that most of the biblical passages are cited in the paragraphs that reject the positions of the Arminians. The positive articles in which the doctrine of Dort is set forth contain few of the biblical citations. The most striking exception is the First Head of doctrine in which biblical passages are found profusely in both the positive and the negative sections. Although it might have been preferable to include the biblical passages in both sections throughout, one will not do justice to the biblical appeal of the Canons without taking both sections of each head of doctrine into account. Those churches that have accepted only the positive sections of the Canons, such as the Reformed Church in America, have greatly impoverished the confession by eliminating the section containing the majority of the Scripture quotations.

An examination of the Canons indicates that a vast number of biblical passages are directly cited. Others are referred to without quotation. At least 136 verses of the Bible are referenced, and the vast majority of these are quoted. While such confessions as the Heidelberg Catechism and the Westminster Confession have a much larger number of Scripture references, these are simply appended to the confession by means of the chapter and verse reference. But in the Canons of Dort these biblical references are an integral part of the text of the confession, being woven into the doctrinal statements in a variety of ways. One will be hard pressed to produce another confession in the entire history of the church that includes greater scriptural material into the document itself. Anyone who objects to the fact that the passages are simply cited and not exegeted hardly raises a legitimate objection. No other creed includes exegesis of the passages appealed to. A confession can hardly do anything else than cite its scriptural support. Exegesis will have to precede its inclusion into the confession, and the *Acta* provide ample evidence that the Synod of Dort engaged in study and debate as to the meaning of the passages to which appeal was made. Furthermore, any objection made to the appeal of the Canons to the passages cited will have to support that objection by sound exegetical considerations. Generalizations, more important, personal dislike, will carry no weight with those who seek to conform their thinking to the authoritative Word of God written.

In view of the issues in dispute between the Arminians and Dort, it is not surprising that Paul is the biblical author to whom the greatest appeal is made. The number of references from Paul is 75. From John's writings there are 20 quotations; from Luke and Acts 12; from Matthew 8; and from Hebrews 5. In the Pauline writings Romans predominates with 38 references; Ephesians is second with 28 quotations. Nine references come from other writings of Paul: Philippians (2), 1 Corinthians (4), Galatians (1), 1 Timothy (1), and 2 Thessalonians (1). In addition to those mentioned there are two other New Testament references, one each from 1 and 2 Peter. The Old Testament quotations are less frequent: Genesis (3), Deuteronomy (2), Psalms (3), Isaiah (2), Jeremiah (3), and Ezekiel (1). That the majority of these passages are key passages of crucial doctrinal significance is understandable.

Within the confines of this chapter it is obviously not possible to assess the exegetical validity of the use made of passages cited. A separate study of extensive proportions would be required for that purpose. But perhaps it is in order to call attention to one major issue. Until recently the Reformed churches that accept the Canons of Dort have generally defended their confession as required by the obedience of Scripture in the face of continued opposition, caricature, and even calumny from opponents on many fronts. Recently, however, increasing difficulties and objections have been heard from within the Reformed churches especially with respect to the doctrine of reprobation as found in the Canons. The issue is too complex to survey here, but one central feature may be mentioned.

While the Arminians opposed predestination and limited atonement in the context of a theology that rejected total depravity, irresistible grace, and the perseverance of the saints, objections within the Reformed churches today have a different context. These objections to predestination (especially reprobation) and limited atonement are made by those who claim to accept the doctrines of sovereign grace, total depravity, irresistible grace, and the perseverance of the saints. Whether they can continue to maintain these doctrines while rejecting other sections of the Canons is not our major concern. History might provide a warning in this connection because of the biblical inter-relatedness of these doctrines. However, our major interest in this brief reference concerns the objection that is raised to the biblical support primarily of the doctrine of reprobation. Is the doctrine of reprobation that is set forth in the Canons largely a logical deduction made from other doctrines that are clearly taught in Scripture? This not entirely new objection is increasingly heard within the Reformed churches today.

The major biblical appeal made in the Canons for the doctrine of reprobation is Pauline. Romans 8 to 11 is the major passage to which appeal is made. Paul's reference to the fact that God "worketh all things after the counsel of his will" (Eph. 1:11) is also involved. But Romans 9 is certainly of central significance, as Berkouwer indicates in his article, which gives a survey of the objections that have been expressed with respect to this doctrine of the Canons.[29] In this connection Berkouwer refers to an undeniable shift in the exegesis of Romans 9–11 that does not warrant the appeal made by the Canons in connection with reprobation. While the Canons follow a tradition of exegesis that sees two themes involved in Romans, namely the undeserved election and the absolute sovereignty of God in general (cf. I, 18), the shift in the exegesis of Romans 9 touches precisely this matter: there are not two themes but the one theme, namely, merciful election which issues in the doxology.[30] Now that a certain shift in the exegesis of Romans 9–11 is noticeable among Reformed theologians can not be denied. But the question remains whether that new exegesis does full justice to the teaching of Romans. Is Romans only concerned with the problem of the election of Israel as a nation in connection with the Gentiles? Or is Romans also concerned with an election that took place within Israel itself? The exegesis focuses upon such questions. Is there a sovereign discrimination within Israel, between Isaac and Ishmael, between Jacob and Esau? And what is the bearing of that teaching in Romans, especially Romans 9:6ff.?

Since Berkouwer's article was published, the second volume of John Murray's commentary on Romans has appeared. In a painstakingly detailed exegesis of Romans 9, Murray observes that more than national election is involved. Observing the distinctions Paul makes between Israel and *true* Israel, children and *true* children, seed and *true* seed, elect Israel and elect *of* Israel, he weighs the various alternatives and reaches this conclusion. "The conclusion, therefore, is that when Paul says 'the purpose of God according to election' he is speaking of the electing purpose of God in a discriminating, differentiating sense that cannot apply to all who were embraced in the theocratic election."[31] After a careful and detailed analysis of Romans 9:6–13 he says: "We are compelled, therefore, to find in this word a declaration of the sovereign counsel of God as it is concerned with the ultimate destinies of men."[32] I must frankly confess that there are emphases in Paul's teaching in Romans that the newer exegesis to which Berkouwer refers seems largely to bypass. And it is precisely these emphases, so carefully examined in Murray's commentary, that favor Dort's appeal to Romans for its teaching on predestination. The Reformed community will have to test its difficulties by the authoritative Scripture. Likes and dislikes, logical deductions and scholastic speculations, of course, have no place in the church's confession. But there are no easy *a prioris* by which to determine which is which. Only the most open, honest, and careful listening to Scripture in faith will suffice.

Conclusion

The crisis that the Reformed churches face in connection with the anniversary of the Synod of Dort is basically the same crisis that the Reformed churches faced three-and-one-half centuries ago—namely, obedience to God as he has revealed himself in his Word. This writer openly and gratefully acknowledges that his listening to the Word of God leads him to whole-hearted agreement with the Canons of Dort. Speaking of eternal predestination, I can only say what Calvin said in this connection: "I can, with all truth, confess that I never should have spoken or written on this subject unless the Word of God in my own soul had not led the way."[33]

Again, in the words of Calvin, is not the following true and entirely in harmony with Scripture?

> The covenant of life is not preached equally to all, and among those to whom it is preached, does not always meet with the same reception. This diversity displays the unsearchable depth of the divine judgment, and is without doubt subordinate to God's purpose of eternal election.[34]

Awesome as is the contemplation of God's sovereignty, the believer's response can only lead to magnify the boundless mercy of God. As Calvin so well expresses it:

> We shall never feel persuaded as we ought that our salvation flows from the free mercy of God as its fountain, until we are made acquainted with his eternal election, the grace of God being illustrated by the contrast—viz. that he does not adopt promiscuously to the hope of salvation, but gives to some what he denies to others.[35]

Appropriate and challenging as we conclude this survey is the prayer with which the Synod of Dort concluded its doctrinal deliverances:

May Jesus Christ, the Son of God, who seated at the Father's right hand, gives gifts to men, sanctify us in the truth; bring to the truth those who err; shut the mouths of the calumniators of sound doctrine, and endue the faithful ministers of his Word with the spirit of wisdom and discretion, that all their discourses may tend to the glory of God, and the edification of those who hear. Amen.[36]

5 THE SYNOD AND BIBLE TRANSLATION

Marten H. Woudstra

The question of a new translation of the Bible in the Dutch language was the first regular item of business on the agenda of the famous Synod of Dort. After the necessary organizational details had been addressed, the Synod devoted itself to this important question during the sixth and subsequent sessions. The entire discussion regarding this matter extended from November 19 to 27, 1618.

Earlier Protestant Translations of the Bible in Dutch[1]

The Liesveldt Bible

One of the most widely used versions of the Bible used by Protestants in the Netherlands prior to the Synod of Dort had been the so-called Liesveldt Bible, so named after its publisher, Jacob Van Liesveldt Antwerp. It had first been published in 1526 and was a literal translation into Dutch of the German Luther Bible. It went through many editions. In 1542 it was provided with a set of marginal notes. These notes expressed the principles of the Reformation doctrines so unambiguously that Liesveldt was made to suffer martyrdom for having been responsible for such heretical printing.[2]

The Liesveldt Bible was dearly beloved by the common people. It was read and treasured during the darkest years of persecution. Tears were shed over it and martyrdom was braved because of it. For many years it played a leading role in the life of Protestants in the Netherlands. It was reprinted as late as 1585 and 1608.

Nevertheless dissatisfaction with the Liesveldt Bible was also expressed already at an early time. This can easily be understood if one considers that this Bible was a translation of a translation, and that the translation from which it had been made, i.e., the Luther Bible, could hardly lay claim to being a literal translation from the original languages of the Bible. The Reformed and Calvinistic views concerning Scripture, current in the Lowlands, seemed to demand a translation effort more in keeping with the original tongues than was now available.

Utenhove and His Successors

An important attempt in the direction of a more widely accepted translation of the Bible suitable for the Reformed churches of the Netherlands was made by the gifted Flemish nobleman, Jan Utenhove. This highly educated and refined Christian played a prominent role in the early phases of Reformed church life, both on the continent and in England, where a Dutch emigrant church had established itself. Prior to his efforts in the area of Bible translation Utenhove had already distinguished himself by preparing a metrical version of the Psalms in Dutch. Utenhove's Psalms enjoyed great popularity. They were sung by many refugees during their wanderings in search of a hospitable lodging place where they could practice the Reformed faith.[3]

Forced to leave England because of Bloody Mary's persecution, Utenhove took refuge in Emden. It was there that he produced a new translation of the New Testament. His collaborator in this venture was Godfried van Wingen, a Reformed minister in the city of Emden. The new translation appeared in Emden in the year 1556. Contrary to Luther's approach to the translation of the Bible, Utenhove believed that the time had come to take the people to the Bible as it actually was, rather than to make the Bible accessible to people who did not know it, as had been Luther's desire.

Although Utenhove's work was to bear fruit indirectly, the acceptance of his translation of the New Testament was disappointing. The reason for this lack of popularity lay in the fact that Utenhove's approach had been rather utopian in nature. One of these utopian features was the attempt to knead the Dutch language into the mold of Greek constructions. Utenhove believed that by doing so he would actually restore the Dutch to a more original purity than it presently possessed. A further feature barring ready acceptance of this version was the fact that Utenhove had attempted to create something like a national language out of the many regional accents spoken by the refugee groups in Emden. In order to accomplish this purpose, however laudable by itself, Utenhove was led to tone down his own native Flemish and to incorporate into the translation elements from other regions of the Netherlands. A concrete example of this attempt to create a national Dutch is Utenhove's use of the word "holden" instead of the variant "houden," used in the western regions of the country.

Nevertheless, Utenhove's translation opened the eyes of the people to the defects of the more commonly accepted translation. And so it was that in the year 1562 another translation was readied in which Utenhove's principles were applied, though with greater moderation than had originally been the case. The 1562 translation included the entire Bible. The Old Testament was prepared by Godfried van Wingen, Utenhove's helper. This was done on the basis of a revision of the Liesveldt Bible, with the further aid of a later edition of the Luther-Bible, the so-called Magdeburg edition. Other translations such as those of Zürich and Geneva had also been consulted. The New Testament was prepared by Johannes Dyrkinus,[4] another minister from the Emden region.

It was the combination of these two translation ventures, that of van Wingen and that of Dyrkinus, that produced in 1562 the standard translation of the Bible for the Reformed community in the Netherlands. This translation continued to be used until gradually it was replaced by the *Staten-Bijbel*, prepared upon the authority of the Synod of Dort and ready for publication in 1637.

The name whereby the 1562 translation came to be known popularly was *Deux Aes Bible*. This name was based on a footnote appended to Nehemiah 3:5. The note reads as follows: "the poor must bear the cross, the rich do not give anything, '*deux aes*' do not have, '*six cincque*' do not give, '*quater dry*' help freely." The three expressions left untranslated are taken from a game of dice. "*Deux aes*" (two and one) was the lowest, "*six cincque*" (six and five) was the highest. Freely translated, therefore, the footnote says: "The poor do not have, the rich do not give, the middle class pays."

Between 1562 and 1618

The Bible of 1562 was far from perfect. Improved editions were prepared in order to satisfy the demands for a more correct translation of God's Word. The first such edition appeared in 1567. An important feature of the new edition was the use that was made of the notes of a Reformed minister, Augustus Marloratus, who in 1562 had been killed during the capture of Rouen. These notes were thoroughly Calvinistic and had previously been printed in the Geneva Bible of 1565.

Various synods of the Reformed churches dealt with the important matter of Bible translation. The very first synod to be held was that of Emden in 1571. At this Synod the refugees from Cologne introduced the subject of Bible translation because they did not feel that the existing version was satisfactory. From this moment on one finds a long series of ecclesiastical gatherings devoting their attention to this topic. Of these we only mention the national Synod held in 1586 in the Hague. This Synod requested the well-known Philip Marnix of St. Aldegonde,[5] best known as "Marnix" among the Dutch, to prepare a translation of the Bible. Marnix had excellent qualifications. He knew the original languages and had given proof of his ability to translate. But Marnix declined originally. Not until the year 1594 could he be persuaded to undertake the work. His own dissatisfaction with the existing version was well-known.[6] But he was unable to carry the work beyond the book of Genesis. He died in 1598. From that time on, the doctrinal disputes of the Remonstrants and the Contra-Remonstrants absorbed most of the attention of the church.

Continued Efforts Preceding the Synod

Also after Marnix's death, other efforts were made to improve the translation of the Bible. One of these was by Wilhelmus Baudartius, a Reformed minister of the city of Zutphen, well versed in the Hebrew language that he had studied under such competent scholars as Bucerus in Leiden and Drusius in Franeker. Baudartius, impatient with the slow progress made by the official church gatherings, was of the opinion that the so-called Piscator Bible was the immediate answer to the needs of the Dutch Reformed Church. Piscator, a Reformed scholar in Herborn, Germany, had been commissioned by the count of that region to prepare a new translation of the Bible. For this purpose he had been freed from all teaching duties at the University of Herborn. The result of his efforts was the publication of a four-volume annotated Bible, published in 1602–1604. The general quality of the translation by Piscator was stiff and wooden. It found no general acceptance in Germany, where the Luther Bible had gained immense popularity, also among the Reformed. However, Baudartius believed that his Piscator Bible was the solution to the problem faced by the Dutch churches, and he exerted considerable effort to gain acceptance for his point of view among the Dutch churches.

At the Synod of Dort

In the meantime the long-expected national synod of the Dutch Reformed churches convened in Dordrecht in 1618. As was noted above the Synod gave first consideration to the pressing question of Bible translation. Its president, the venerable Johannes Bogerman,[7] himself a highly trained linguist and expert in the languages of the Bible, introduced the matter to the delegates.

Bogerman's Plea and Its Results

Bogerman pointed out that other countries were now in the possession of good translations of the Bible. He mentioned with a special word of praise the recently prepared English translation (generally known as the King James version, dating from 1611). He also referred to recent Protestant translations in Italy and Spain. It is important to note that at the time of the Synod of Dort the interests of the Reformed fathers ranged as widely as they did. This points to the true catholicity of concern that has always characterized the Reformed faith at its best. Neither should it be forgotten that the successor of Beza at the University of Geneva was the Italian scholar Giovanni Diodati. Diodati was a precocious Hebrew scholar. In the year 1607 he had prepared a widely acclaimed Italian translation of the Bible. Along with his excellent knowledge of Hebrew Diodati also had a good grasp of the Greek. His native Italian as used in this Bible translation was both lucid and vigorous.[8]

In the light of these noble examples, Bogerman urged the delegates to action. His pleas were eminently successful. Having begun the discussion in the sixth session, the Synod decided in the eighth session, by unanimous vote, to proceed to the production of a new translation of the Bible.

Subsequent sessions were devoted to a variety of basic questions. It was decided that the Hebrew and the Greek should form the basis of the new translation. The objective would be the production of a new translation, not the revision of an existing one. Nevertheless, it was felt that no needless offense should be given. Hence, where possible, the translators should preserve what was good in the existing versions. A literal translation was to be prepared even if this might mean at times the introduction of Hebraisms and Graecisms into the Dutch. If, however, at a certain point a free translation was deemed necessary, then a more literal translation should be included in a note. It was also decided that whenever the Dutch needed some additional words by way of explanation, these words should be inserted into the text in brackets and printed with a special letter type.

A lively debate developed around the question whether the apocrypha were to be included in the new translation or whether they would be omitted altogether. Both Gomarus and the Geneva delegate Diodati, mentioned earlier, argued strongly against inclusion of the apocrypha. The advocates of inclusion based their arguments on practical grounds. They pointed to the usefulness of these books, to the example of other Reformed churches, and to the possibility of creating offense among the unlearned if suddenly an established practice were to be discontinued. Especially the last two considerations swayed the opinion in favor of inclusion of the apocrypha. However, the points of principle adduced by Gomarus and Diodati were not as such denied. Gomarus had argued that these books consisted of fanciful fables and were full of dogmatic errors. Inclusion in the new Bible would be an attack upon God's honor. Already the Jews had kept these writings separate from the canonical books. There was now absolutely no reason to retain them, especially since the church of Rome had placed them on one line with the canonical books. Diodati likewise declared that most of these books belonged to the realm of Jewish fable, with the exception of First Maccabees, Baruch, Wisdom and Jesus Sirach. They conflicted with the truth and majesty of Holy Scripture, and hence they were harmful and dangerous to the reader.

Synod decided that less effort would be made in the translation of the apocrypha than in that of the canonical books, and that separate type and pagination would be used in printing them.

It also decided that a preface would be prepared in which attention would be called to the errors that the apocrypha contained.[9]

Translation-Organization

After some of these leading principles had been set down, the Synod proceeded to create the machinery to implement its decision. Six men were to translate the Bible, three for each Testament. These would reside in a well-known city in which there was an institution for higher learning. Leiden was chosen to be that city. Next to the translators there would be revisers, two for each provincial synod, to be appointed by the national synod. It was felt that within four years' time the project could be completed, but no binding limits were set. The translators were to begin with Genesis and Matthew respectively, and after that they were to follow the common arrangement of the Bible. This would give due experience for the translation of the more difficult books.

The following were chosen for the important task of translating the Old Testament: Johannes Bogerman, minister at Leeuwarden; Guilhelmus Baudartius, minister at Zutphen; Gerson Bucerus, minister at Veere. Each of them also had a substitute. The New Testament translators were: Jacobus Rolandus, minister at Amsterdam; Hermannus Faukelius, minister at Middelburg; Petrus Cornelii, minister at Enkhuizen.

Execution of the Decision

While it had been hoped that the translation work could begin three months after the adjournment of Synod, things turned out quite differently. This was largely due to the delay with which the civil government acted on the Synod's request for official support. Not until May 11, 1624, was the decision reached to begin with the work of translation. At first the government decided against the request to designate a certain city in which the translators could reside. But finally, July 18, 1625, this request was granted, and Leiden was designated. In the meantime two of the originally appointed translators, Cornelii and Faukelius, had died. Their place was taken by their respective substitutes, Walaeus and Hommius.

The first meeting of the three translators of the Old Testament took place on November 13, 1626, at the house of Bogerman in Leiden. It was decided that Bogerman would chair the meeting, Baudartius would serve as secretary and Bucerus would defend the translation whenever a difficult passage would make this necessary. All these men were exceptionally well qualified for their task. Bogerman had studied with the renowned linguist Drusius in Franeker as well as at universities abroad. Baudartius had also studied with Drusius. Bucerus was renowned for his knowledge of Hebrew and of antiquity.

At the second meeting of the group, held on November 24, the three men together worked through the book of Genesis in order to insure unity of language and style. At that same meeting it was decided that each of the three men would take one third of a given Bible book, would translate it at home and add the necessary marginal notes. They would then come together, read each verse in the Hebrew, and check the translation as to accuracy as well as the correctness of the notes. This procedure had a definite advantage. It insured rapid progress. This was necessary since the chief burden of translation rested on the heads of the Old Testament translators.

The Pentateuch was completed during 1628. The entire Old Testament was ready in manuscript form on the 4th of September 1632. The first proofs were ready early the next year.

During the translation process the revisers were in constant touch with the translators and offered their criticisms. The church assemblies likewise showed great interest in the progress of the work and continued to invoke the blessing of God's Spirit upon it.

The New Testament translators had less work to do, partly because of the smaller size of the New Testament and partly because much work in this area had already been done. By the end of 1628 they had completed Matthew and in 1634 they completed the entire translation.

Upon completion, both the Old Testament and the New Testament translations were submitted to the college of revisers. The first meeting of the Old Testament revisers took place on the ninth of July, 1633. The entire revision was finished on September 1, 1634. Bogerman had seen to it that no lengthy disputes were to be carried on, if at all possible. Yet the discussions often became more prolonged than he had hoped. The revisers did not just accept everything as originally submitted. They had power to introduce changes by majority vote, and they used this power upon occasion.

The New Testament revision took place between November 16, 1634 and October 10, 1635. During the year 1635 the city of Leiden was ravaged by a severe outbreak of the plague that took some 20,000 lives in that city alone. But after earnest prayer the company of translators and revisers decided to stay on rather than to leave the city.

It took until June 1637 before the proofs had been corrected. Just before his death on September 11, 1637, Bogerman, who had returned to Friesland exhausted from the strain of the preceding years, was privileged to see a copy of the completed Bible. Another copy of the first edition was solemnly presented to the States-General on September 17 of the same year. The official approval and authorization of the translation had taken place on July 29. This official recognition accounts for the name *Staten-Bijbel*.

The *Staten-Bijbel:* A Chapter in the History of Reformed Biblical Scholarship

Having thus sketched in brief outline some of the main events in the history of the translation of the *Staten-Bijbel* the present writer wishes to devote the remaining part of this paper to a discussion of a particular aspect of the *Staten-Bijbel*, namely to what extent and in which way this monument of devoted Christian Bible-scholarship contributes to our understanding of the Reformed principles of Scripture interpretation as they were prevalent in the Netherlands in the first half of the seventeenth century.

The specific segment of the question just raised that will be pursued here is that which concerns the question of the sense of Scripture, the relation between Old and New Testament, and other related questions. The timeliness of this discussion for the present need hardly be emphasized. As is generally recognized, the beginnings of the modern phase of biblical scholarship can be traced back to the Reformation period. Especially the seventeenth century plays a leading role in this respect, as has recently again been confirmed.[10] Since it was during this crucial period that the translators of the *Staten-Bijbel* performed their monumental task, a look at the principles that guided them and the scholarship that informed them should be most instructive for understanding the modern scene.

Biblical Scholarship in the Netherlands in the Seventeenth Century

Linguistics in General

During the period in which the translators of the *Staten-Bijbel* did their work, the first half of the seventeenth century, the Netherlands was an internationally renowned center of biblical learning. The scholarship of the Reformed churches in the Netherlands was significantly ahead of that in Lutheran countries both in linguistic ability and in the knowledge of antiquity.[11]

Two well-known linguistic authorities, both connected with the university of Franeker, were Johannes Drusius (Dutch: Van den Driesche), mentioned earlier, and his pupil and successor, Sixtinus Amama. Drusius lived from 1550 till 1616.[12] Amama published a book in 1628 entitled *Antibarbarus biblicus*, in which a strong plea was made in favor of the use of the original languages in the study of Scripture. Yet another scholar of great renown was the Leiden professor Ludovicus de Dieu. What these men had in common was a strong insistence on the literal sense of Scripture.

Reformed Hermeneutics

Hermeneutical questions were vigorously discussed in the Netherlands at this time. Andreas Rivetus, professor at the Leiden university, published his Introduction to Scripture in 1627, just one year after a beginning had been made with the actual translation work. In this work Rivetus develops his hermeneutical principles that have been called by Ludwig Diestel "*verstandig und meist treffend*" (showing insight and mostly to the point).[13] Rivetus defends the literal sense as the true sense, although he is not prepared to reject altogether the distinction between the two senses of Scripture, provided this be rightly understood. A similar insistence upon the essential oneness of the sense of Scripture can be found in the writings of Franciscus Gomarus, Arminius's chief opponent. Gomarus inserts much Old Testament exegetical material in his writing. Commenting on the meaning of the Nathan prophecy in 2 Samuel 7, Gomarus declares that the words of this prophecy refer both to Solomon (David's son) and to Christ (David's Son). Gomarus insists that, although the sense of Scripture is one, it nevertheless has two members, a historical and a prophetic member.[14]

The Arminian Grotius and His Influence

On Modern Biblical Scholarship

While thus in the orthodox camp the literal sense of Scripture was duly recognized as being the only true sense of Scripture, orthodoxy was not willing to divorce the Old Testament from the New as was done within the circles of the Arminians. A renowned example of the Arminian approach to Scripture is Hugo Grotius. In the year 1644 Grotius published an exegetical work entitled: *Annotata ad Vetus Testamentum* (Annotations on the Old Testament). Here, too, we have an insistence on the primary sense of Scripture. This primary sense, according to Grotius, lies in the Old Testament itself. Grotius seeks to "protect" the Old Testament against any intrusion on the part of either the New Testament or dogmatic theology. While Grotius occasionally, by way of concession, allows for a "mystical sense" by which certain Old Testament passages are seen to refer to Christ, this is not the leading principle of his exegetical work.[15]

As has been rightly pointed out, Grotius's understanding of the Old Testament represents in a nutshell the approach of eighteenth and nineteenth century criticism. No wonder that Abraham Kuenen, one of the leading exponents of nineteenth century criticism, hailed Grotius as the outstanding pioneer of the position he himself held.[16]

There was, of course, a formal similarity between what Grotius was trying to do and that which the reformers had done in their handling of Scripture. Calvin and also Luther in most of his commentaries, had broken with the idea of a multiple sense in Scripture, as this had been held during the Middle Ages. The reformers insisted that the literal sense was the only sense. This, as we have seen, was also the opinion of the orthodox leaders in the Netherlands during the days of the Bible translation. Yet the difference between Grotius on the one hand and the translators of the *Staten-Bijbel* on the other was a fundamental one, as fundamental as is the modern difference between those who still adhere to the Reformed principles of interpretation and those, who, while claiming to do justice to the Reformation principle of the literal sense, are nevertheless separated by a deep abyss from the real Reformation understanding of Scripture.[17]

Kraus points out that the approach followed by Grotius is informed by the principles of humanism. His hermeneutics is historico-anthropocentric. The authority of the speaking God has been eliminated from Grotius's "exegesis." Grotius not only opposed the orthodox concept of Scripture-inspiration. He not only sought to guard against undue encroachments from the realm of dogmatic theology. He also effectively withstood the possibility that in these texts God himself would be speaking. Kraus correctly indicates that this is the great division of spirit that humanism has brought about.[18]

Today we see the full fruition of the position that Grotius so ably developed. The authority of the speaking God who speaks in and through Scripture does not enter meaningfully into the study of the Bible as presently conducted. Atheists, agnostics, Christians, Roman Catholics, Jews, Protestants, all are said to have equal access to the primary sense of Scripture.[19] While the need for a faith commitment is recognized by some, and while others speak of the inevitability of some ideology influencing the biblical scholar,[20] all these admissions are carefully prevented from affecting the actual work of "biblical" scholarship.

The present phase of biblical studies is the fruition of the humanistic science ideal with its rigorous insistence on the historical sense. Of this humanistic ideal Grotius was an outstanding champion. His method, as Kraus so well points out, prevents the very possibility of the speaking of God through the sacred texts. The result of this method in the present is that the claim is made that in order to understand the mind of the Ultimate Author of the Bible, one must cease being academic.[21] This spells the end of truly biblical scholarship, with emphasis on both the "biblical" and the "scholarship." He who says "Bible" says "divine revelation." He who says "scholarship" says "scientific method that weighs objectively all the data at its disposal." If there is no academic method for the understanding of the mind of the Bible's Ultimate Author, then by that very admission biblical scholarship has dug its own grave as a scholarship that is truly biblical. Then faith must be reduced to ideology; acceptance of the objective truth of God's Word must be transformed into a mere subjective "commitment"; then there is no way anywhere of breaking out of the circle of an endless and boundless subjectivism.[22]

The Canons of Dort on the Agreement and the Diversity of the Testaments

The translators of the *Staten-Bijbel* did not do their work in isolation. They were part of the intellectual and spiritual ferment that characterized their country in the first half of the seventeenth century. They were faced with the option that the Socinians earlier and the Arminians subsequently had proposed for the understanding of Scripture.[23] This option they consciously rejected. Already in the Canons themselves one can find some admirable examples of the continued esteem that the orthodox had for the total agreement of all the various parts of Scripture; and yet one also finds an equally admirable awareness of the difference between the Testaments. Concerning the agreement between the Testaments, the Canons teach that the ministry of reconciliation that is needed to bring about conversion is "the glad tidings concerning the Messiah." By means of these glad tidings, they go on to assert, God was pleased to save those that believe "as well under the Old as under the New Testament" (III–IV, 6). At the same time they show an appreciation for the difference between the two Testaments. For in the following article they state that the mystery of God's will, which God revealed to but a small number under the Old Testament, was revealed to many under the New, and they attribute this greater diffusion of the gospel to the removing of the distinction between the various peoples.

Thus it would seem that the Canons do not treat the two Testaments as being completely on the same level. Nevertheless, they quote freely from the Old Testament in support of their doctrinal contentions (cf. III–IV, Rejection of Errors, par. 3, 6, 7). The Old Testament prophets as well as the New Testament gospels and epistles could be used equally well for the illumination and the support of the various heads of Christian doctrine. A similar wholesome regard for both the unity and the diversity between the Testaments pervades the translation of the Bible that came into being by decision of the Synod that drew up the Canons.

Application of Reformed Principles of Understanding Scripture

2 Samuel 7

A good example of the understanding of Messianic prophecy in the *Staten-Bijbel* is found in the marginal note added to 2 Samuel 7:11. This passage deals with the well-known Nathan prophecy. This prophecy was spoken in response to David's intention to build a "house," that is, a temple, to the Lord. David's desire to build such a house for God is not granted. Nevertheless, the event of his request becomes the occasion for one of the most fundamental Messianic passages that the Old Testament contains. But notice the restraint with which the annotators express their opinion. Commenting on the promise: "The Lord will build you a house" they state: "i.e., will make your kingdom durable in your descendants and (which is far greater) raise up out of your seed the Messiah (after the flesh) who will be an eternal king over his people." After this careful distinction between descendants on the one hand and the Great King on the other, both equally predicted by this prophecy, the annotators then proceed to spell out their principle of understanding this prophecy. This is what they state in carefully chosen words: "This prophecy must be understood in this way, that it has respect to Solomon on the one hand, as type (*voorbeeld*) of Christ, on the other hand to Christ, whose type he was." After this fine recognition of the more immediate and the more distant "horizon" of prophecy they then conclude by saying that "some things apply to Solomon only, some to Christ only, and some things apply properly (*eygentlick*) to both." At the end of their brief exposition they add a reference to 1 Kings 8:20. In this passage Solomon claims to have sat on the throne of Israel, "as Jehovah promised." Thus the annotators indicate that in their opinion Solomon's accession to the throne of David was a real fulfillment of the Nathan prophecy of 2 Samuel 7.

This keen sensitivity to the historical sense of an Old Testament Scripture passage does not lead the annotators to indulge in the kind of barren historicism of the type practiced by Hugo Grotius. For their comments on the phrase "for ever" (2 Sam. 7:13) (Dutch: *tot in eeuwighheyt*; Hebrew: *'ad 'olam*) they remark: "The kingdom of Solomon and of David's descendants lasted a long time, but this must properly (*eygentlick* again) be understood of the spiritual kingdom of Jesus Christ."

Here, then, the annotators show that they do not restrict the meaning of this prophecy to what it meant to its first recipients, although even that might have given some indication of the greatness of it (cf. e.g. David's being overwhelmed by the gracious words of promise, 2 Samuel 7:18 ff; and cf. 1 Peter 1:10). No, the annotators show an awareness that their task is not to transmit mere human understandings, but rather that their business is to convey the true meaning that the Spirit of inspiration has put into the words that he was pleased to use in the process of organic inspiration. Thus they felt that it was the "proper" sense of the words "for ever" to refer them to Christ's kingdom. One may even assume that they were fully aware that the Hebrew word *'olam*, which they translated "eternity," does not always have that precise meaning. While *'olam* is the word best suited for the expression of the notion of eternity, it actually suggests a long period of time reaching beyond the horizon of human perception, both backwards and forwards. Nevertheless, being duly impressed with the totality of the meaning of a given Scripture passage, the translators felt warranted to point out that this very use of the word *'olam* in 2 Samuel was "properly" understood as having reference to Christ and to his kingdom.

Other Examples of Historico-Prophetic Treatment of Old Testament Passages in the *Staten-Bijbel*

Psalm 16

Psalm 16 is quoted significantly in the New Testament in the context of Christ's death and resurrection (Acts 2:27, 34–35).

Modern biblical scholarship, following the footsteps of the Arminian Grotius and of the deists and rationalists who trace their lineage via him back to the Socinians, does not accept the appeal that Peter made to Psalm 16 at face value. Though the more "conservative" among the "biblical" scholars today are willing to concede that there is such a thing as the Holy Spirit's intention that somehow comes to expression in the words of Scripture, these same scholars are emphatic in stating that exegesis has no tools to get at the Holy Spirit's intention. Hence exegesis, in order to be scientific, must be content with the "primary" meaning; it must limit the understanding of a given passage from the Old Testament to the "limited vision" of the ones who first uttered and received it;[24] by necessary consequence, it must place question marks behind any such use of Old Testament materials as Peter is making of Psalm 16 on the day of Pentecost.

This approach places in jeopardy all truly scientific work on the biblical text as in any way contributing to the true and ultimate meaning of Scripture. It also places in jeopardy all Scripture proof as furnished in the Bible. If from an exegetical point of view these New Testament appeals to Scripture cannot really be condoned, then we no longer have a Christ who "according to the Scriptures" was born, lived, ministered, died and rose again. This, in turn, means that the Christ in whom we must believe for salvation ceases to be the Christ of the Scriptures. Herman Bavinck writes somewhere about the subjectivism that characterizes the movements of Socinianism and Anabaptism and points out that same spirit pervades the movement of Arminianism. This subjectivism is also rampant in "biblical" scholarship today.

Rejection of the adequacy of Scripture proof furnished in support of Christ's work and ministry is a direct contributor to the crisis of authority that besets our modern age. For this reason the work done by the Reformed translators of the Bible in the seventeenth century is still of great relevance for the present day. The translators of the *Staten-Bijbel* did not omit the historical dimension of revelation. But they refused to consider the meaning that an Old Testament passage had for the first recipients to be the only meaning about which they could legitimately speak in their comments and annotations.

In the heading of Psalm 16 the translators call this Psalm a prayer that David prays for safe-keeping uttered through faith in the Messiah. But they do not restrict the meaning of this Psalm to that horizon alone, for they openly state that "in the meantime Christ himself is introduced, speaking of his death, resurrection and eternal glory, for the good of his own." At some points in their marginal notes they allow for a more direct application to Christ while at the same time stating as their own conviction that the line from David to Christ runs via the typological significance of king David as type of Jesus Christ. On the other hand the fact that Acts 2:25 applies verse 8 to Jesus Christ is sufficient to make the annotators do the same. In the meantime the care with which the annotators seek to avoid a mere leveling off of revelation, as if all of this Psalm would only speak directly of Christ, becomes clear from the note added to the word "soul" in verse 10. According to this note the word "soul" should be understood as "person." After having made this significant point they add: " . . . by which furthermore [note this word! M.H.W.] the dead body of Christ is understood, cf. Leviticus 19:28 and Psalm 94:17 and compare for this Acts 2:31 and 13:35."

This is showing an admirable awareness of the intricacies of the Messianic understanding of this Psalm. Yet it is entirely different from the modern critical and existential approach to the question of prophecy and fulfillment.

Excellent is also the comment made on the word *Sheol* in verse 10, translated "hell" by the *Staten-Bijbel*. A footnote immediately explains "i.e. grave, or understand with some of the hellish agony which Christ for our sakes has borne." Of similar excellence is the exposition given of Peter's application of this word on the day of Pentecost (Acts 2:31).

The Virgin Birth Prophecy

As could perhaps be expected, the translators of the *Staten-Bijbel* translate the Hebrew word *'almah* in Isaiah 7:14 by *maagd* (virgin). However, it should be kept in mind that the denial of the Messianic application of this prophecy is very old and that therefore the choice of the word "virgin" was by no means an automatic one.

While thus safeguarding the understanding of this word in the sense in which the gospel of Matthew would subsequently understand it, the translators nevertheless attempted by means of their marginal notes to alert the reader to the necessity of seeing some of this prophecy in the context of Isaiah's own times. That is why they state that according to the opinion of many (*na veler gevoelen*) the words spoken in verse 16 no longer continue the thought of the preceding verses inasmuch as the deliverance promised to Ahaz must be measured first of all in terms of an actual child of his own time, be this Shear-Jashub, Isaiah's son, or some other child, already born or shortly to be born. At the same time—and this shows the moderation and the breadth of exegetical consideration shown by the annotators—the possibility of applying even these words of verse 16 directly to the time of Christ is mentioned. In general the annotators are of the opinion that the promise of the virgin birth, being a spiritual one and pertaining to the blessings of salvation, *a fortiori* guarantees to Ahaz and his contemporaries the physical deliverance from the political enemies of his own day.

Again we see that the translators do not in any way commit the mistake of a mere "leveling off" of the revelation process, a crime that, if one wishes to believe the current critical evaluation of past exegetical procedure, older orthodoxy altogether too often perpetrated.

Conclusion

The new *Staten-Bijbel* gradually became accepted by the Dutch. One of the difficulties that had to be overcome was the opposition of certain book-dealers who still had some 80,000 copies of the earlier Bible. The Remonstrants eagerly inspected the new version in order to discover whether dogmatic considerations might have adversely influenced the objectivity of the "universalist" passages and those dealing with conditionality in grace. But no such bias could be detected anywhere, a remarkable testimony to the scrupulousness with which men like Bogerman and his fellow-translators had done their work.

The original documents pertaining to the translation work were deposited for safe-keeping in the Hague and Leiden. A special commission was appointed for a regular inspection of these documents. Every three years this commission would first inspect the acts of Synod, kept in the Hague; then they would then go by boat to Leiden where the chest containing the thirteen original volumes constituting the translation work were kept. After this inspection the commission was entertained at dinner at the expense of the provincial government, the city government furnishing eight jugs of wine for the occasion. At night the gentlemen would return homeward. The secretary would render the following report: " . . . that the inspected pieces have been found pure and undamaged by worm, moth or mouse."

Also outside of the Netherlands the merits of the *Staten-Bijbel* were duly recognized. The well-known pietist and mystic Jung Stelling (1740–1817) had a copy of the *Staten-Bijbel* with its marginal notes open in his study. Czar Peter the Great of Russia had copies printed of the Dutch Bible in two columns. The left column was used for the Dutch translation. The right column was left open for a translation in the Slavic tongue. The Russian clergy, however, feared from this venture an abridgment of its rights and its faith. It had the Bibles stored in a damp room so that they disintegrated.

The *Staten-Bijbel* is generally considered to be one of the best translations of the Reformation period. The claim made on the title page: "Faithfully translated from the original languages" is fully justified. The 1637 version is still in use in the Netherlands, although a new version, produced in the 1950s, has found wide acceptance.

The marginal notes of the *Staten-Bijbel* will continue to have a permanent significance for the correct understanding of the passages commented upon. In the present writer's opinion these notes, as well as the translation that they accompany, stand as a monument to a crucial chapter of Reformed biblical scholarship. Current biblical scholarship might well consider whether the moderation and enlightened judgment with which the difficult question of the relation between the Testaments was handled by the men of 1637 may not be a better guide toward the truth than the boundless subjectivism and the abandonment of Scriptural authority that characterize much biblical scholarship today. The legitimate line from Calvin to the present in the area of biblical scholarship does not run via Grotius and his fellow-Arminians; it runs via the reverent and enlightened scholarship that lies expressed in the pages of the Bible produced at the behest of the Synod of Dort.

6 PREACHING AND THE SYNOD OF DORT

Peter Y. De Jong

Few creeds formulated by the Christian churches have received either such fulsome praise or bitter criticism as the Canons of Dort. To a large degree these judgments evidence the spiritual sympathies of those engaged in evaluating what has been widely recognized as the greatest of all ecclesiastical assemblies held by the Reformed churches.

Strikingly, the criticisms direct themselves primarily against Synod's formulation of the doctrine of predestination. The argument is pressed that the controversy between Calvinism and Arminianism was simply one of theological definition that need not or at least should not be regarded as having much personal and practical consequence for the Christian believer. After all, is it not presumptuous for man to claim that he can say anything definitive about the profound mysteries of God? And were it not better for theologians to keep their opinions to themselves or at least tolerate each other's constructions, rather than to disturb and hopelessly divide the allegiance of church members who cannot grapple with such subtleties?

Such critics patently ignore the fact that predestination is of immense practical consequence for Christian faith and conduct.

It has rightly been called the heart of the gospel. It deals with the foundation, nature and assurance of salvation. If salvation is solely of God, then preaching as the chief calling of the church will have quite another content than if salvation is viewed as a venture in which God and man in some sense cooperate.

It should come as no surprise, therefore, that Dort, in dealing with predestination and points related to this profound and much misunderstood theme, turned attention time and again to Christian preaching.

More than any other aspect of the church's life, preaching sets its stamp on individual believers, congregations and communities.

Hence with great and grave deliberation the church has upon occasion reflected on the unique character of preaching. Certain limits have been imposed with respect to its nature, form and content. What remains surprising is that so little direct, specific attention has been expressed in the official creeds.[1] Often it is alluded to, but usually in passing. Seemingly the churches in formulating their official position supposed that everyone knew what constituted sound preaching. In this respect the Canons of Dort constitute somewhat of an exception. Interwoven with all the doctrines here defined are statements concerning the necessity, nature, message, efficacy and consequences of gospel proclamation. Because the Dutch churches of that day were deeply concerned with preaching, this Synod deliberated and decided as it did.

This concern is evident in three ways: in the circumstances that precipitated the convening of Synod, in the several matters presented in the form of gravamina for its consideration, and most important of all in the statements of doctrine that it adopted together with the pastoral exhortations of the "Conclusion."

Preaching as a Precipitant of the Synod

Deep concern on the part of many within the churches for sound teaching and preaching concerning the way of salvation contributed to the assembling of the Synod of Dort. Repeatedly the Calvinists had insisted that those who embraced Arminian (Remonstrant) opinions deviated seriously from the gospel. By substituting their own opinions and formulations for the creedal affirmations of the churches they were misleading many.

From their inception the Dutch churches aimed at being a confessional and confessing church.

Early synods had adopted and thereupon reaffirmed the Belgic Confession and Heidelberg Catechism as the Forms of Unity.[2] Every preacher was required to deliver one sermon each Sunday on the "sum of doctrine" set forth in its consecutive Lord's Days. Professors chosen to train men for the ministry at universities and academies were obliged to demonstrate their loyalty to the Reformed creeds. All admitted to the ministry were to express wholehearted agreement with this teaching, pledging themselves to defend it against all opposition. And when "strange notions" began to alarm the churches, several classes, following the lead of Classis Alkmaar, adopted specific Forms of Subscription. Only by such means, so the churches believed, could some assurance be gained that among them the "pure Word" would be preached.

Intimations of the coming conflict arose in connection with the preaching of Arminius himself.[3] At an early date some of his pulpit statements aroused suspicion and doubt as to his soundness. This came into the open in connection with sermons on the epistle to the Romans. He raised eyebrows when in dealing with the first chapter he claimed that the Reformed, by repudiating the meritorious quality of good works, actually denied their necessity. Nor were fears allayed when he taught that death resulted from man's humanity and finiteness, since God alone is immortal. Much more serious were doubts as to his orthodoxy when in connection with Romans 7:14b he taught that the "natural" or unregenerate man, be it under influence of the Spirit, could rightly know and assess his own spiritual plight. To the orthodox this sounded like Coornhert, who had propagated an incipient Socinianism.

In a gathering of preachers Peter Plancius led the attack against such unwarranted exegesis. During the ensuing discussion Lydius together with Uytenbogaert and Jean Taffin managed to still the storm, especially after Arminius solemnly affirmed his agreement with the creeds.

Thereafter little more is heard about his preaching. For some time he continued to serve the Amsterdam congregation but avoided the crucial issues that he had raised earlier. It was widely known, however, that he had "some reservations" with respect to creedal statements and desired that these be reformulated.

The struggle entered its second phase when, despite objections, Arminius was appointed to teach theology at Leiden in 1602. He had sent 27 theses to Junius on certain doctrinal issues. These fell into the hands of Plancius who regarded them as heretical. Now suspicions as to his orthodoxy increased. Even his uncle, the regent Kuchlinus, maintained that his nephew was infected with the libertine notions of Coornhert. Yet the consistory of Amsterdam was willing to release him for teaching upon condition that he could satisfy Gomarus who was teaching at Leiden. After an interview the latter admitted that in so far as Arminius had explained himself, his position could be reconciled with the creeds.

It did not take long, however, before the churches became deeply disturbed. Students began to propagate opinions stemming from the teaching of the new professor. Usually he was critical of Calvin, Beza, and Zanchius on predestination while praising Castellio and Coornhert for their open-mindedness. For a brief period two ministers of Leiden attended his classes and warned him. Thereafter the controversy broke out anew, when Vander Borre, a friend and disciple of Arminius, preached on the Feast of the Three Kings that the heathen could be saved apart from knowing Christ and the gospel. A conference was held at Delft without satisfactory consequences. Deputies of the synods of North and South Holland went to Leiden to complain to Arminius that at classical examinations his students championed heretical notions. He replied that he had given no occasion for this; also that he would submit to questioning only by a national synod. At last Classis Dordrecht forwarded a complaint to the Synod of South Holland concerning sharp disagreements between Gomarus and Arminius that were disturbing the church at Leiden.[4] At this the curators of the university and the city magistrates took great offense, refusing thereupon to deal with the matter. Towards the end of his life, when suspicions against him appeared to be increasingly well-founded, Arminius sought the aid of the civil magistrates and expressed willingness to confer only under their guidance. From that time the political authorities became much more deeply and directly involved in the dispute.

Throughout this period of some twenty years it was exceedingly difficult for the churches to know precisely what Arminius did believe. Time and again he expressed agreement with the creeds. Yet he forbade his students to reveal what he discussed with them behind closed doors. Meanwhile he did not retract his reservations with respect to the creeds. Thus when his followers drew up the Gouda Catechism,[5] consisting solely of direct quotations from Scripture and thus demonstrating a radically different methodology from that of the Heidelberg Catechism, it was evident to the churches that more was at stake than revising a few formulations.

In 1610 the disciples of Arminius drew up their Remonstrance.[6] Here for the first time the opinions that they embraced were publicly set forth. Schaff has summarized the radical differences between the two parties as their convictions came to increasingly clearer expression thus,

> It started with the doctrine of predestination, and turned round the five articles or 'knotty points' of Calvinism; hence the term 'quinquarticular controversy.' Calvinism represented the consistent, logical, conservative orthodoxy; Arminianism an elastic, progressive, changing liberalism . . . [7]

Precisely this fluidity in conviction on the part of the Arminians was feared and resented by the Calvinists. If this could be tolerated in the churches, then soon one doctrine after another would become suspect.[8] Such an approach to Scripture and the creeds would subject preaching to repeated and far-reaching changes with respect to its content. This would at first confuse, then mislead and in the end divide Reformed congregations into hostile camps.

Conferences between the two parties were held at the Hague (1611) and Delft (1613). The Arminians insisted that the way to peace lay in allowing their opinions to be preached. The Calvinists expressed a willingness to tolerate the opinions in the Remonstrance until a national synod could decide the issues in the light of Scripture and upon condition that the Arminians in their preaching would express no other deviations from the creeds than those discussed at the conference. But this condition the Arminians refused to accept. In their minds, so they insisted, several doctrinal matters were still unclear and thus unresolved. In this way the disciples showed great kinship of spirit with their mentor.

Such imprecision and ambiguity with respect to the doctrines formulated in the creeds led to more serious disturbances in the period immediately prior to the convening of Synod.

The Arminian party recognized that in the churches they constituted a minority, even in North and South Holland. Thus a national synod would be to their disadvantage. Everywhere Calvinists still were in ecclesiastical control. Only by increasingly filling the pulpits with young men sympathetic to creedal laxity could they hope to maintain themselves. Thus delay was to their advantage, the more so since they were openly favored by the political authorities. In nearly every instance these supported Arminian pastors against the wishes of congregations as well as the decisions of classes and provincial synods. Such assemblies might judge a man worthy of deposition from office; the magistrates would maintain him in the manse, pay his salary, enforce his preaching on the congregation, and even expel from the town his Calvinist colleague.

During this period, then, congregations were rent by schism.[9] Rather than attend the preaching of an Arminian pastor, many who knew and loved the Reformed confessions went for worship to neighboring villages and towns. In several instances such disaffected members met in homes and warehouses (often in great secrecy for fear of reprisals) to hear Reformed ministers who had been invited to preach for them. As the threat of secession assumed larger proportions, the consistory of Amsterdam, which was uncompromisingly devoted to Reformed doctrine and church polity, sought by every possible means to maintain official ecclesiastical contact with such groups.[10] Where the Arminians were upheld, the Reformed were not only subjected to ridicule but to fines and even banishment of the clergy. Repeatedly they requested permission to hold worship services in their own in church edifices, which had been turned to other uses. In every case this was refused, until at long last Prince Maurice cast his lot with the Reformed. During this period of suppression, which lasted some five years, thousands of Reformed believers were gathering for worship in separate assemblies.

Often it is insinuated that the Calvinists were rigid, unbending and intolerant, while the Arminians were champions of religious freedom. History gives the lie to this construction. With a rare exception members of both groups were children of their age. Both seemed ready to lean on the political authorities when this was to their advantage.

By now it should be abundantly evident that Synod was not convened simply to settle a theological dispute among the professors. People of all strata of society in the Reformed churches had been affected by the controversy. This threatened the disruption of the churches and, closely associated therewith, the unity of the Dutch nation. Large numbers recognized the difference between Arminian and Calvinistic preaching. Ears and hearts had grown increasingly sensitive to the issues. Men realized that two irreconcilable constructions of the way of salvation were presented from the pulpits. And not until from these pulpits the same language was again heard could peace return to the churches.

Preaching as a Concern of the Synod

Even today some think Dort spoke only on doctrine, chiefly the doctrine of predestination. This is not merely an oversimplification of the interests and actions of that Synod; it is a glaring misrepresentation.

That preaching in the churches constituted one of its chief concerns is patent to anyone who surveys even in a cursory fashion its many decisions.

After several delays Synod opened its sessions on November 13, 1618. Its work-program was divided into three parts: at early sessions dealing with matters pertaining to certain issues raised by the churches themselves; thereupon assisted by the foreign delegates dealing with the doctrinal conflict between the Arminians and the Calvinists; finally in the closing sessions dealing with matters that could not be settled earlier.[11] In this section we refer briefly to what Dort did with respect to preaching in the first and third periods of its labors.

Already at an early session Dort interested itself in instruction given by the churches according to the Heidelberg Catechism. The matter was discussed under two rubrics: preaching according to the catechism and instruction given to children, young people and others according to this catechism. With the first of these two we are concerned.

The custom of many Reformed churches to preach sermons according to the order of a catechism was soon followed in the Netherlands. As early as 1566 it was introduced in Amsterdam by the Rev. Pieter Gabriel. Although several synods referred to it, this practice was not made mandatory for all churches until 1586. Time and again, however, provincial synods felt constrained to remind pastors and congregations of this obligation. Now at Dort the synods of Friesland and Overijssel urged that this obligation be underscored. Much difficulty had been occasioned by having one minister serve two or more churches simultaneously. Many people also failed to attend the second service on the Lord's day. Synod decided to reiterate the earlier decision, adding that such sermons should "be brief and easy to comprehend for the sake of the uneducated."[12] Even if attendance was poor, the ministers were to continue with such preaching in order that the truth confessed by the Reformed churches might be clearly and systematically presented. Church visitors were required to inquire diligently into whether the rule was being observed and, wherever neglected, to admonish the pastors. After the foreign delegates had spoken on the subject, president Bogerman explained that these decisions were taken not because a rule had been lacking but because a more effective means of making it fruitful in the churches was desired. His address enabled the Synod now to direct attention specifically to the catechesal nurture of children, young people and those adults whose knowledge of Scripture was deficient.

The churches of several provinces were also much concerned about securing suitable candidates for the Christian ministry. Notably the synods of Zeeland and South Holland brought this matter in detail to Synod's attention. What seemed to weigh most heavily on the Zeeland churches was the inadequate education received at the four recognized universities. Not only was the academic preparation too brief (often not more than two years); the churches were especially perturbed that so little training of a practical nature was given. Hence they suggested that in each province a theological academy under ecclesiastical supervision be established "since too great a freedom has already corrupted many at the academies" (i.e. those associated with the existing universities). Several suggestions echo the deep disquiet that prevailed because of the entrance of Arminianism into the pulpits through those trained at the universities.

It is regrettable that discussion and decisions on this matter focused almost exclusively on the status of theological students in the churches—a question of purely church governmental dimensions. Should such men be allowed to exhort in the churches? If so, under which provisions? How carefully should this be supervised? Was it ever permissible for them to administer the sacraments? Should they be allowed to attend sessions of consistory and classis? Synod left most of these matters to the judgment of either the classes or provincial synods. With respect to establishing theological academies nothing was done. Although Synod may rightly be charged with failing to come to grips with the issues involved, the official requests and ensuing discussions do demonstrate the abiding interest of the churches in sound preaching.[13]

Similarly, two matters intimately connected with preaching were decided at the concluding sessions of Synod.

The first of these was the adoption of a church order. This was to replace earlier editions. Although similar to these, the church order of Dort included improvements and additions at significant points. Much of this church order concerned itself with obtaining for the churches ministers who would be sound in doctrine, able to edify the churches, and academically trained.[14]

The second related to the adoption of an officially-recognized edition of the Belgic Confession. For more than half a century this creed had been recognized as one of the Forms of Unity. Yet many editions published by the printers of the land contained erroneous readings. To counteract such carelessness, Synod subjected every article to a thorough investigation. What was finally adopted as the authentic text appeared in excellent Latin. This prevented the possibility of appealing to an erroneous or incomplete edition in an attempt to obscure what the Reformed confessed.[15] This in turn could contribute to a sound and thorough exposition of the faith as well as to the confessional unity of the churches.

Preaching as Defined by the Synod

In the light of the preceding it is possible to ascertain and somewhat evaluate what Synod declared officially with respect to preaching.

The Canons of Dort,[16] to be sure, nowhere offer a precise and succinct definition of preaching. Nor do they spell out exhaustively its content. This lay outside of the scope of Synod's work.

It should be remembered further that the Canons are couched in "confessional" rather than in scientific "theological" language. These two modes of expressing Scriptural teaching sustain an intimate and indissoluble connection to each other. The one should at no point contradict or even obscure the other. However, while the latter seeks to formulate more precisely and in greater detail the truth of the Christian gospel, often raising and seeking answers to questions not officially resolved in and by the churches, the former speaks the language of the man-in-the-street. Although creeds contain the broad range of Christian truth as it is to be proclaimed to men everywhere and should be acknowledged by all who love and serve Christ, they do not pretend to exhaust all that God has revealed in his Word as applicable to the church in every historical situation. This view of the limited and limiting character of ecclesiastical creeds was that of the Synod. Hence it spoke incisively only to those issues raised in connection with the Arminian controversy, issues that indeed confront the church in one form or another in every age. And one of these issues was that of Christian preaching. But also on this subject the Canons do not say everything that could be said.

What was at stake, according to the Calvinists, was sound biblical teaching and preaching concerning man's salvation. Thus each of the five points of doctrine that were adopted deals, either explicitly or implicitly, with some facet of preaching.

Here again the radical difference between the Arminian and Calvinistic views must be sharply seen. Since the days of the Reformation—a century earlier—the doctrine of salvation had been the paramount concern of all evangelicals. Early reformers like Luther, Zwingli and Calvin had been unwavering in their insistence on pure preaching. At the heart of all such preaching lay the clear, consistent proclamation of God's work of grace in Christ. Unitedly they acknowledged that this was *sola gratia* (by grace alone), *sola Christo* (through Christ alone), *sola Scriptura* (according to Scripture alone), and *sola fide* (by faith alone). As the Lutherans had experienced struggles with synergists who revived in a mild form some of the heresies of Pelagius, so now the Reformed faced the Arminians as those who dimmed the pure gold of the biblical doctrine of sovereign grace.

To be sure, the Reformed realized that not all their opponents deviated to the same degree from the officially endorsed positions of the churches. At times Arminius had seemed to do little more than question some statements in the Belgic Confession and the Heidelberg Catechism without clearly setting forth his own views. But these questions and doubts were developed by his immediate successors. At first this was done in mild form in the Remonstrance of 1610. But the Reformed rightly feared that the champions of the new way harbored more dangerous and deadly deviations that would in time completely corrupt the pulpits. Subsequent history has amply substantiated their fears. Soon after the Synod Episcopius and others veered sharply in the direction of a rationalistic and humanistic Pelagianism, while Vorstius exposed himself as a Socinian.

This inherent drift away from confessional orthodoxy is implicit in the description given by Platt.

> Theologically, Arminianism is a mediating system throughout. Its most characteristic feature is conditionalism. Absolutism is its most persistent opposite; moderation, the mark of its method . . . it sought to construct a system which should be dominantly ethical and human throughout. It contended, therefore, that moral principles and laws consistently condition the manward activities of the Divine will . . . But whilst the peculiarity of Calvinism is found in holding fast to the absolute idea of God in opposition to all 'idolatry of the

creature,' the center of gravity of the Arminian system is found in the sphere of anthropology.[17]

This disproportionate concern with and for man led consistently, so the Calvinists urged, to a man-centered and even a man-conditioned view of salvation.

William Cunningham has put the issue into even sharper focus.

> The fundamental characteristic of Arminianism [shows itself as] a scheme for dividing or partitioning the salvation of sinners between God and sinners themselves, instead of ascribing it wholly, as the Bible does, to the sovereign grace of God—the perfect and all-sufficient work of Christ—and the efficacious and omnipotent operation of the Spirit.[18]

This radical contrast gave rise to two divergent types of preaching within the Reformed churches for a decade or more. Now in the Canons Synod, both directly and by implication, circumscribed what it deemed to be sound biblical proclamation and thus judged the Arminian presentation of the gospel message as unbiblical and therefore illegitimate in any Reformed pulpit. Within the scope of this article only a few salient emphases of the Canons on preaching will be mentioned.

(1) Its Urgency: the Desperate Plight of Man

Preaching is the proclamation of God's Word to men.

Most Christians would likely agree with this statement. On its delineation, however, we soon discover the radical differences that spring from widely divergent views concerning man and his need as held by Arminians and Calvinists.

The Arminians, indeed, claimed that sin had so vitiated man that, left to himself, he would not attain salvation. Yet it urged that his depravity was partial rather than total. Within him there is some ability to respond to the gospel. Although spiritually sick and corrupt, he can and should cooperate with God's grace.

The Calvinists at the outset underscored in the Canons the serious, the fatal consequences of sin.

> As all men have sinned in Adam, lie under the curse, and are deserving of eternal death, God would have done no injustice

in leaving them all to perish and delivering them over to condemnation on account of sin, . . . (I, 1).

Man's only hope lies in God's grace. This is manifested first of all in providing Christ (I, 2) and thereupon in

> . . . mercifully send(ing) the messengers of these most joyful tidings to whom he will and at what time he pleases. . . (I, 3).

These opening statements set the tone for all that follows. The first section, indeed, deals with the doctrine of "Divine Election and Reprobation," but always in the light of God's mercy and man's need.

But what, more specifically, is man's plight as he needs to be addressed by the gospel? Key statements on this are found especially in the Third and Fourth Heads of Doctrine.

> Therefore all men are conceived in sin, and are by nature children of wrath, incapable of saving good, prone to evil, dead in sin, and in bondage thereto; and without the regenerating grace of the Holy Spirit, they are neither able nor willing to return to God, to reform the depravity of their nature, or to dispose themselves to reformation (III–IV, 3).

Here the sharp contrast between Arminianism and Calvinism on man's sinful condition and its consequences becomes clear. Man has enslaved himself to sin; not only to some vicious habits and deeds. At one and the same time he is unwilling and unable to be converted. Actually he is in a state of spiritual "death." Thus only the grace of God in Christ through the Spirit's operation can bring him to salvation.

The Calvinists did not deny that after Adam's fall there remained in man "glimmerings of natural light" that render him without excuse. Thus

> . . . he retains some knowledge of God, of natural things, and of the difference between good and evil, and shows some regard for virtue and for good outward behavior . . . (III–IV, 4).

But all this is insufficient to "bring him to a saving knowledge of God and to true conversion" apart from the special work of the Holy Spirit.

The contrast between the two positions cannot be reduced to Arminian over-emphasis of human responsibility and Calvinistic under-emphasis of this biblical truth. Rather, on the score of man's actual ability to respond to the overtures of grace the two positions are mutually exclusive. The Reformed insisted that man cannot respond rightly to the gospel apart from the regenerating grace of the Holy Spirit. Yet at the same time they insisted that he was also unwilling to do so. They refused to separate inability and unwillingness, urging that

> ... this light, such as it is, man in various ways renders wholly polluted, and hinders in unrighteousness, by doing which he becomes inexcusable before God.

Man is never the helpless victim of circumstances outside of himself; he is fully responsible for perverting the truth and corrupting himself in all his ways. Indeed, there is an opaqueness here, when the Canons affirm that on the one hand God does not give regenerating grace unto all men and on the other hand that every man remains fully responsible for what he does and how he reacts to the gospel. But rather than attempting to solve the apparent antinomies that they found in Scripture by means of an appeal to reason, feelings or experience, the Synod affirmed both truths in unequivocal language.

But why preach, if the "natural" man neither can nor will respond savingly?

Because the proclamation of God's love in Christ Jesus is the divine antidote to the deadly poison of sin that dooms men to death. Apart from the gospel none can or will come to a saving knowledge of God in Christ Jesus. It is this desperate plight that, according to the Canons, must continually be set before men's eyes and minds and hearts. In such preaching sinners are addressed by the God of all grace and justice.

(2) Its Character: Preaching as "Means of Grace"

According to the Reformed, preaching is far from a bare, neutral, impersonal announcement of something that God did in the past in order to provide man with the possibility of salvation. It is rather "the most joyful tidings," "the glad tidings," the means by which God makes known "the mystery of his will" to bring unto salvation all who believe. Throughout we hear reverberations of Paul's assertions that the gospel "is the power of God unto salvation to everyone that believeth" (Rom. 1:16).

Preaching is the active, dynamic, efficacious act of God confronting men with his message of grace. Never may it be reduced to a chance that God takes in the hope of gaining some; much less to an effort on the preacher's part that may well prove fruitless. Preaching is the God-appointed means unto salvation.

It is God who provides the gospel, having sent his only-begotten Son into the world to save sinners. It is God who commissions men to bring this glad news. It is God who sends his messengers when and where and to whom he wills. But—and here the contrast between Arminianism and Calvinism becomes even sharper—it is God who, as Holy Spirit, alone can and does make preaching efficacious. If the spiritually recalcitrant and dead sinner is to experience saving fellowship with God in Christ, then the Spirit must engage him in and with and through proclamation to accomplish his "true conversion."

The Reformed insisted on holding together Word and Spirit. They refused to debate at length the relative importance of these two, urging that Scripture plainly declares that the Spirit makes use of the Word. All minimizing or neglect of preaching was contraband. Hence when the Canons assert

> ... he not only causes the gospel to be externally preached to them, ...

they were making no half-hearted concession. Precisely because some among the Arminians did cast doubt on the indispensability of the gospel unto salvation, the Reformed maintained the urgency of proclamation. Yet preaching to them always included more than what the preachers did. It is also and always an act of God himself.

Here the Reformed knew where to draw the line at human speculation. What takes place in the preaching situation by the Spirit's presence and power, they urged,

> . . . cannot be fully comprehended by believers in this life. Nevertheless, they are satisfied to know and experience that by this grace of God they are enabled to believe with the heart and to love their Savior (III–IV, 13).

Here we find no psychology of "true conversion," much less any attempt to define precisely the correlation between Word and Spirit in the preaching situation. Nonetheless they sought to guard against two errors. Proclamation might never be reduced to a human activity that either might or might not attain the purpose for which God appointed it. Nor might it be regarded as mechanically or magically effecting salvation. The results were not in control of the hearers, nor were they in the hands of the preacher. Only the Spirit makes the Word effective to God's high purpose.

(3) Its Content: Reconciliation by and to God

Nowhere do the Canons provide a complete account of the contents of preaching. In the nature of the case this would be impossible. From the beginning the Reformed insisted that "the holy gospel" consists in all that God

> . . . first revealed in Paradise, afterwards published by the holy patriarchs and prophets, and foreshadowed by the sacrifices and other ceremonies of the law; and lastly fulfilled by his only-begotten Son.

Here a few observations are in order. Never may the gospel be reduced. Both Old and New Testament constitute the message to be proclaimed. Also, no part of Scripture is to be regarded as "law" devoid of the message of God's redeeming grace. Thus the unity and coherence of the sacred writings are to be underscored. As God's own Word, the Bible may not be thought of as containing a variety of perhaps conflicting theologies. Although inspiring many men to write, God himself is its chief Author. Thus the message also is one—that of God reconciling the world unto himself in Christ Jesus. To them any sharp contrast between "God-centered" and "Christ-centered" preaching was unthinkable.

This unified message the Canons call "the mystery of his will." It is his plan of salvation, with no aspect of which any tampering might be tolerated. Possibly the closest approach to a summary of this "plan" we find in connection with the consideration that the Canons give to the efficacy of our Savior's death.

> For this was the sovereign counsel and most gracious will and purpose of God the Father that the quickening and saving efficacy of the most precious death of his Son should extend to all the elect, for the bestowing upon them alone the gift of justifying faith, thereby to bring them infallibly to salvation; that is, it was the will of God that Christ by the blood of the cross, whereby he confirmed the new covenant, should effectually redeem out of every people, tribe, nation, and language, all those, and those only, who were from eternity chosen to salvation and given to him by the Father; that he should confer upon them faith, which, together with all the other saving gifts of the Holy Spirit, he purchased for them by his death; should purge them from all sin, both original and actual, whether committed before or after believing; and having faithfully preserved them even to the end, should at last bring them, free from every spot and blemish, to the enjoyment of glory in his own presence forever (II, 8).

Preaching in the light of such a confession cannot be a hit-or-miss affair, using texts here and there according to the whims or insights of the people. Nor is it left to the preacher to decide what he deems essential for the welfare of his hearers. He must proclaim "the mystery of his will" as God had made this known. All preaching, then, centers in God's work of grace in Christ. It makes known the sure foundation of salvation in the eternal plan and purpose of God. It declares that the provision for our salvation is solely in Christ. Every benefit proceeds from the "saving efficacy of his most precious death." Through him men are redeemed out of all peoples and languages. Not only is their justification secured; also the daily purging of their lives.

Throughout all this work of grace God in Christ manifests faithfulness to his promise, bringing his own to everlasting felicity.

Thus also in preaching the issues between Arminianism and Calvinism are clearly stated. Is salvation solely of God? Or does man somehow add something essential by a response not wrought in him by grace? Only the first, so the Reformed declared without hesitation, is biblical. It is not man who reconciles himself to God, but God who restores man to faith-fellowship with himself in Christ Jesus.

(4) Its Approach: Preaching as "Unfeigned" Call

But how can God address men seriously and earnestly with the message, if salvation is a free gift not bestowed on all indiscriminately?

On this score the Arminians and all who make common cause with them have ceaselessly attacked the Calvinistic view. This, so it is claimed, makes God responsible for man's sin, leaves no room for moral responsibility, and makes mockery of gospel preaching. Usually the calumny is added that the Reformed were solely interested in constructing a logically consistent scheme, stressing only certain texts and neglecting or misinterpreting others.

These charges cannot stand the test of being scrutinized in the light of the Canons. Indeed, the Reformed did not attempt to resolve what seemed also to them quite incomprehensible. But they emphasized man's responsibility as taught in Scripture fully as much as God's sovereignty.

In gospel preaching God directs his "call" to all who come within its reach. And this call is "unfeigned" (*serio*). It is such precisely because

> God has most earnestly and truly declared in his Word what is acceptable to him, namely, that those who are called should come unto him. He also seriously promises rest of soul and eternal life to all who come to him and believe (III–IV, 8).

This call consists of both promise and command. The one is inextricably intertwined with the other. As stated earlier, it urges both repentance and faith.

> Moreover, the promise of the gospel is that whosoever believes in Christ crucified shall not perish, but have everlasting life. This promise, together with the command to repent and believe, ought to be declared and published to all nations, and to all persons promiscuously and without distinction, to whom God out of his good pleasure sends the gospel (II, 5).

All men, of whatever state and condition, must be so challenged by the preaching. To all the message comes urgently and unfeignedly. And because preaching is what it is—always an act of God through his Holy Spirit in serious address to the sinner in deep need of salvation—men cannot rightly blame God or Christ or the gospel for their unbelief. They refuse to come and be converted and "regardless of their danger, reject the Word of life."

But how, so the Arminians argued, could preaching be "means of grace" when so many apparently reject the message. Instead of appealing to reason or experience, the Canons urge what Scripture teaches on God's manner of dealing with mankind.

> As the almighty operation of God whereby he brings forth and supports this our natural life does not exclude but require the use of means by which God, of his infinite mercy and goodness, has chosen to exert his influence, so also the aforementioned supernatural operation of God by which we are regenerated in no wise excludes or subverts the use of the gospel, which the most wise God has ordained to be the seed of regeneration and food of the soul . . . (III–IV, 17).

Here is laid bare the nerve-center of Reformed conviction in its controversy not only with the Arminians but with all who differ from them in conceiving of the God-man relationship. For those who followed in the footsteps of Augustine and Calvin as did the fathers of Dort, God and man may never be regarded as in competition with each other. Whatever antagonism exists is due not to man's creatureliness but solely to his sinful rebellion. For the Reformed, man is truly free when he learns to live and respond within the created order according to the will of God. And in this created order God makes use of means, ordained and maintained by his gracious will, so that man may live in responsible obedience, which is his freedom.

This understanding of the Creator-creature relationship is in the Canons brought to bear upon the regeneration and renewal of man's life. Thus even as God in man's "natural" or "earthly" life apportions his gifts sovereignly, granting to the one more than to another, and yet always without in any way destroying man's responsibility, so in the sphere of "redemption" God works salvation as it pleases him but without diminishing man's obligation to make use of the means at his disposal. If there is "mystery" with respect of God's plan of salvation, so too the Reformed insisted there remains "mystery" with regard to the all-controlling providence of God with respect to man's "earthly" existence. To anyone sensitive to the biblical emphasis on man's responsibility under God's sovereignty with respect to daily life, the Reformed teaching concerning the necessity and propriety of making use of the "means" of grace is not at all incongruous.

In addition, true preaching takes seriously God's wrath against sin as well as his immeasurable love in Christ Jesus. Therefore all without exception are to be addressed as sinners in need of divine salvation. Men must be called to earnest self-examination. They must learn to pray "by the mouth of the prophet thus: 'Turn thou me, and I shall be turned.'" In this way man's pride and self-sufficiency are abased, so that he learns to live

> ... by the holy admonitions of the gospel, under the influence of the Word, the sacraments, and ecclesiastical discipline; For grace is conferred by means of admonitions, and the more readily we perform our duty, the more clearly this favor of God, working in us, usually manifests itself ... (III–IV, 17).

In this light we can understand why the Canons reject the notion of preaching as "only a gentle advising." It is rather God's call to true conversion that consists in

> ... that renewal, new creation, resurrection from the dead, making alive, which God works in us without our aid ...

yet in such a manner that

> ... the will thus renewed is not only actuated and influenced by God, but in consequence of this influence becomes itself active.
>
> Wherefore also man himself is rightly said to believe and repent by virtue of that grace received (III–IV, 12).

(5) Its Aim: God's Glory in the Salvation of Sinners

Above all what was at stake with respect to preaching in the controversy with the Arminians concerned the aim or goal of preaching. Both parties, indeed, admitted that this was the glory of the grace of God in Christ Jesus. But their understanding of what constituted the reflection of that glory differed radically. It was on this score that the Reformed insisted that their opponents emasculated the biblical teaching of the true and living God. They confined their emphasis too exclusively to what they construed as the love of God, thus failing to do justice to what the churches confessed in article 16 of the Belgic Confession.

Often it has been charged, in response to the above, that the Reformed had a deficient view of God's love in Christ Jesus. Any careful reading of the Canons will demonstrate that this cannot be rightly maintained. Throughout we find doxological affirmations of this biblical truth. Nor, as some others have argued, did the Reformed fall into the unbiblical error of maintaining two coordinate aims for Christian preaching: the salvation of some and the condemnation of others. Too carefully had the Reformed listened to the Scriptures to permit the Arminians to drive them into such an unbiblical schematization. Whenever and wherever and to whomever the gospel is addressed, it comes as "the most joyful tidings." This accent on its inherently gracious character they stoutly maintained. And that gracious character was manifest especially herein: that the sovereign God guaranteed the efficacy of the message. He provided not only the means of salvation and the sending of his messengers, he also worked the saving response in ways past man's finding out.

But why, then, do not all men turn to God in repentance and faith?

Here the Reformed faced seriously the mystery of the sin-dimension in man's life. Repeatedly in the Canons they call attention to it, without ever attempting to solve it. They refused to go beyond Scripture. At the same time—therein differentiating themselves from the Arminians—they were constrained to declare all that the Word taught clearly. Not only in his self-revelation in Christ Jesus does God make known his great love; he also and at the same time displays his justice. In his justice he punishes all who continue in their impenitence and hardness of heart. Even as Christ and the apostles did not camouflage God's wrath against the sinner's unbelieving resistance to the gospel, so the Canons refuse to mute this biblical accent.

Actually, comparatively little is said on this in the Canons, although its statements are unambiguous. Also in the revelation of his just judgment against man's sin God is glorified. But the stumbling block for the opposition lay in Dort's insistence that God alone remains in full control of the outcome of every preaching situation. It has pleased him not to bestow the gift of faith on all. And instead of "vainly attempting to investigate the secret ways of the Most High," (Acts 20:27; Rom. 11:33, 34; 12:3; Heb. 6:17, 18) (I, 14), the Canons outline the response that should characterize believers.

> . . . Hence they to whom so great and so gracious a blessing is communicated above their desert, or rather notwithstanding their demerits, are bound to acknowledge it with humble and grateful hearts, and with the apostle to adore, but in no wise curiously to pry into, the severity and justice of God's judgments displayed in others to whom this grace is not given (III–IV, 7).

Should the doctrine of divine election from which springs the whole of our salvation be preached in the churches? May, perhaps, this profound mystery be regarded as outside the scope of what truly constitutes the gospel of our Lord Jesus Christ?

To this question an unambiguous negative is given. Here Dort followed Calvin in his response to Bullinger. He had urged that since election was clearly revealed in Scripture, man may not attempt to be wiser than God in deciding what should and what should not be proclaimed. True faith, on the part of preacher as well as people, rejoices in this teaching that magnifies the God of all grace, humbles sinful human pride, and provides an inestimable consolation for believers.

Synod, however, was well aware that this doctrine could be and at times had been presented in the wrong way. Hence with pastoral concern it declared that the doctrine of divine election

> . . . is still to be published in due time and place in the Church of God, for which it was peculiarly designed, provided it be done with reverence, in the spirit of discretion and piety, for the glory of God's most holy Name, and for enlivening and comforting his people, . . . (I, 13).

As for those in whom a strong faith-assurance was not yet felt, it affirmed that they

> . . . ought not to be alarmed at the mention of reprobation, nor to rank themselves among the reprobate, but diligently to persevere in the use of means, and with ardent desires devoutly and humbly to wait for a season of richer grace . . . (I, 16).

In even greater detail the "Conclusion" directed its attention to the proper manner of speaking on divine election. Here Synod affirmed:

> Finally, this Synod exhorts all their brethren in the gospel of Christ to conduct themselves piously and religiously in handling this doctrine, both in the universities and in the churches; to direct it, as well in discourse as in writing, to the glory of the divine Name, to holiness of life, and to the consolation of afflicted souls; to regulate, by the Scripture, according to the analogy of faith, not only their sentiments, but also their language, and to abstain from all those phrases which exceed the limits necessary to be observed in ascertaining the genuine sense of the Holy Scriptures, and may furnish insolent sophists with a just pretext for violently assailing, or even vilifying, the doctrine of the Reformed churches.

Much more could and, perhaps, should be said about Dort on preaching. Yet the above demonstrates abundantly the deep concern that Synod manifested for this central activity in the churches. Nor should the relevance of what was there declared escape our attention.

Today, as so often in the past, preaching has become subjected to illegitimate pressures. Man incessantly seems to want a gospel tailored to his own intellectual insights and emotional satisfactions. Such compromise Dort refused to make, and that on unassailable grounds.

Preaching is not man's work. Neither is its content or consequence at his disposal. Since the church is "pillar and ground of the truth" by God's appointment, it devolves upon all preachers individually and collectively to declare no more and no less than what God has revealed in his Word. Only then are they truly messengers of reconciliation and peace. God has pledged to honor his own Word, which so calls men to repentance and faith in Christ crucified that

> ... such as receive it and embrace Jesus the Savior by a true and living faith are by him delivered from the wrath of God and from destruction, and have the gift of eternal life conferred upon them (I, 4).

The salvation that the Reformed churches in God's name proclaim to all men everywhere is not a mere possibility; it is reality, the gracious and glorious possession of everyone that believes.

Such preaching alone is relevant. It speaks truly to the need of man. It humbles the proud. It warns the impenitent. It encourages those who sorrow for their sins and seek after God. It begins and ends with the God and Father of our Lord Jesus Christ, to whom be praise, honor and adoration forever and ever.

7 THE SIGNIFICANCE OF THE CANONS FOR PASTORAL WORK

Edwin H. Palmer

To the uninformed pastor, the "Five Points of Calvinism" seem harsh, cold and spiritually deadening. The terms Calvinism, total depravity, election, reprobation, limited atonement and irresistible grace give him the shivers. As he views it, the God of Calvinism is arbitrary and his decree of reprobation is "horrible." Such "fatalistic" teachings, he believes, make men morally lazy, give a false sense of security, hinder missions, and deaden human responsibility. Therefore, instead of utilizing these teachings in his pastoral work, he may oppose them or at least ignore them.

Even some pastors who are Calvinists theoretically are Arminians practically. Such ministers agree that Dort is biblically sound but they manage to keep its teachings camouflaged enough so that no one will know them. They fear that the Five Points are unedifying or dangerous or apt to be misunderstood. Therefore, they hide their beliefs.

Such an attitude is unbiblical. A pastor should preach and teach all the Bible. Not to do so is to do despite to the Holy Spirit, for all the Bible is the Spirit's book and all of it was written for our welfare. As Paul wrote: "All Scripture is God-breathed and is profitable for teaching, for reproof, for correction, for instruction in righteousness in order that the man of God may be complete, equipped for every good work" (2 Tim. 3:16–17). All Scripture, says Paul—not parts of it. Man's responsibility, yes; but, also, God's sovereignty. Not only the free offer of salvation, but also divine election.

In the same vein Paul told the Ephesian elders that he preached to the Ephesian church "the whole counsel of God" (Acts 20:28). He did not select just what he thought was pleasant and profitable. He preached the whole, not a part.

We, too, should never deem ourselves wiser than the Holy Spirit, choosing and picking from all his revelation what we want to preach. What the Spirit has revealed, the minister is obliged to preach. It is a lack of true Spirit-filled humility, and it is the height of presumption, purposely to neglect what the Spirit has inspired. God knows what is best for us and has said that his whole Word is profitable for us. As Calvin wrote: "Therefore we must be on our guard against depriving believers of anything disclosed about predestination in Scripture, lest we seem either wickedly to defraud them of the blessing of their God or to accuse and scoff at the Holy Spirit for having published what it is in any way profitable to suppress" (*Institutes*, III, xxi, 3).

The rule for pastoral counseling should be the same as for preaching: *Scriptura tota* and *Scriptura sola*, all the Scriptures and nothing but the Scriptures.

First of all, the pastor should never run ahead of God, probing, inquiring, speculating where God has not revealed. There are certain problem areas concerning God's ways that are and forever will be incomprehensible and mysterious, just because he is God and we are finite creatures. The pastor must learn to control his curiosity and humbly refrain from entering where angels fear to tread. He must humbly accept *Scriptura sola*.

Secondly, however, he must learn to keep up with God. He must refuse to put on a false mask of piety by neglecting anything that God has revealed. *Scriptura tota*.

The Holy Spirit has neither included useless, harmful teaching, nor has he omitted what is profitable for the believer. Therefore, the pastoral counseling rule is: Go just as far as the Bible does, but do not go any further.

Encouragements

Not only should the minister teach all the doctrines in the Bible—including the teachings of Dort—but also he should understand how profitable they are in his pastoral work. Instead of being a stumbling block, they are a stepping stone. Instead of being a barrier, they are a ladder to greater heights. In place of being water that douses enthusiasm, they are water that refreshes. Instead of being deadening and cold, they are stimulating and exhilarating. When properly understood, the Canons of Dort will give the parishioner great comfort and encouragement.

1. Belief in God's Irresistible Grace Gives Hope in Hopeless Cases.

The pastor is confronted continually with rebellious people who refuse to believe. The unbelief of such a rebellious person does not stem from a lack of knowledge, for the recalcitrant has heard the gospel in many different situations from his childhood on. Neither does his resistance originate in a lack of attention and love, for the parents, pastor and friends have been very loving toward him, extending both small and large kindnesses to him. Nor are any of his excuses valid: they are only a rationalization of his conduct. Subconsciously, he knows he is wrong; but he will not go to Christ in humility.

Or the unsaved may simply be indifferent. He could not care less. Christ-talk neither turns him on or off. He is neither hot nor cold, but lukewarm. If he would only react! But he does not, except in search of financial security, thrills and novelty.

In such situations the pastor feels frustrated. What can he do? He has tried both the honey and vinegar methods. He has reasoned, pleaded, warned, commanded in the name of Jesus, laughed and cried: all to no avail.

Then he realizes more than ever—something he tended to forget before—that God must first of all touch him. For the man is spiritually dead. He cannot say Yes while he does not have life. He is totally depraved, that is, utterly unable to desire salvation unless the Spirit first of all makes him alive. The man must be born from above, born a second time, spiritually resurrected, made alive again in Christ Jesus. And how else can that be done except that God does it? The pastor knows he has tried every human means to no avail. But when he remembers that God in his electing love works irresistibly, then he can take hope. Although the pastor cannot touch the lost man's life, God can. If he could regenerate Paul, the Christ-hater, then he can touch today's hardened or indifferent man. God's election and the irresistible grace bring hope as the minister deals with the "hopeless" cases.

2. The Biblical Teachings of Dort are Conducive to Humility.

A father of four who attends church rather faithfully is an alcoholic. He loses his job, is put put under church discipline, is alienated from his friends and loses his self respect. A friend of his who is a Calvinist, knowing his own depraved inclination, instead of being censorious, says: There, but for the grace of God, go I.

A high school girl who has been brought up in a Christian home and who professes to be a Christian is a nymphomaniac. For her the beginning, high point, and end of life is sex. Looking at her, many a Christian girl will humbly say: here, but for the grace of God, go I.

A boy who has had all the advantages of a Christian upbringing rebels against authority in the home and church. He repudiates God with a vengeance. Going to college, he presents rational evidences that it is illogical to believe in the Christian God. He thinks that an all-powerful, yet loving God would not allow evil, sin and misery. So he repudiates God and Christianity. Other college students, who do believe, recognize themselves in him and know that if God had not saved them, they would have fallen into the same trap of unbelief.

A newspaper reporter flees God—avoids church and the Bible—but God pursues him until he pursues God.

Any pastor can multiply these experiences of human resistance to God and the good. Such personal evidence of the depravity of man and the irresistible loving grace of God is a humbling experience for the pastor. Coupled with the biblical teaching, they make the pastor depend upon God more.

And they enable him to point out these same humbling truths to his parishioners. Again and again, the biblical truth of man's total depravity induces humility in both the pastor and his flock by the consideration: Truly, Lord, except for thy grace, I would have done the same evil. Calvinism produces humility.

3. It Makes the Christian Praise and Thank God.

This is closely related to the preceding because praise and thanks arise out of humility.

The Arminian thanks God for partial salvation; the Calvinist, for total salvation. The Arminian thanks God for electing him after God has foreseen that he would believe (postdestination); the Calvinist thanks God for electing him unto faith and salvation (predestination). The Arminian holds that Christ did not first choose man, but that man chose Christ; whereas the Calvinist agrees with Christ's words, "You did not choose me, but I chose you" (John 15:16). The Arminian believes that man is sick in sins and trespasses; the Calvinist believes he is dead in sins and trespasses (Eph. 2:1). Accordingly, the Arminian believes that faith is partially from man and partially from God, whereas the Calvinist believes that faith is totally from God—a gift from God (Eph. 2:8). The Arminian believes that natural man has enough ability to believe on Christ before he is born again. But the Calvinist believes that natural man is totally unable to believe unless the Holy Spirit makes him alive spiritually and causes him to be born again.

Regardless of whether or not the Calvinist position is biblical—that is dealt with elsewhere—the fact is that if a man believes that he was once dead, he will thank God much more than a man who thinks he was only sick. He knows that if God had not irresistibly changed his heart, he never would have accepted Christ. He feels instinctively:

> "I sought the Lord, and afterward I knew he moved my soul
> to seek him, seeking me;
> It was not I that found, O Savior true;
> No, I was found of thee . . .
> 'Twas not so much that I on thee took hold,
> As thou, dear Lord, on me."

The knowledge of man's total spiritual inability and of God's unconditional election stir him to give unending praise to God. He will say: Why did God ever choose me? I am no better than anyone else. I do not know why, but I thank him for doing it; for if he had not, I would never have believed. Praise God from whom all blessings flow—not only the substitutionary sacrifice of Christ, but also my rebirth and my faith.

4. It Gives an Assurance of Salvation.

Pastors are constantly confronted with timid Christians who are fearful that they will not continue believing. Their current joy is great; but will it last, they ask themselves. Sometimes they are so distraught that they are not able to go on to more advanced kingdom work; they keep laying again the foundation of repentance toward God.

In such cases, it is comforting to point out that the Bible says: once saved, always saved. If salvation depended upon man's fickle nature, which is indeed corrupt and undependable, then Christians would have a real cause to worry. For their nature is inclined to all evil—even the sin of unbelief—and all men would lapse into apostasy.

The pastor, however, is able to show the timid that salvation depends ultimately not upon man's perseverance but upon God's love toward man. He can go on to demonstrate that this God is not chameleon-like, changing with man's varying moods. But rather, as he wrote, "I, the Lord, change not," (Mal. 3:6). Once the all-knowing God has sovereignly and lovingly determined to save a person, he will not change—Arminian-wise—because of an unforeseen wickedness in man. For he never chose a person in the first place because of any foreseen faith. And what God begins, God finishes. "I am persuaded of this one thing: he who started a good work in you will complete it by the day of Christ Jesus," (Phil. 1:6). If a person believes, the Bible says he has eternal life—eternal, that is, not temporary.

Therefore, a pastor can give real encouragement to his parishioners who worry continually about their future salvation. Such knowledge is of practical importance. Otherwise, fearful ones will concentrate so much on "laying again a foundation of repentance from dead works and of faith toward God" that they will not be able to go on to perfection (Heb. 6:1, 2). Such meek ones must be taught to rely on God's eternal, unchanging love and then to press on toward the goal of their high calling in Christ Jesus.

5. It Gives Confidence in Adversity.

What encouragement an under-shepherd can give to his troubled lambs through the biblical teaching of divine election! In the face of seemingly insurmountable obstacles—terminal cancer, the loss of the mother of a family, mental disturbances, unjust loss of a job, fear of violence—the child of God is able to find priceless strength in the knowledge that his heavenly Father has loved and chosen him from eternity unto salvation. He knows not only that Jesus died for his sins, but he knows, in addition, that in back of that death was the electing love of the Father—that the Father so loved him that he sent his only Son to go to hell for him. If, then, the Father spared not his own Son for those whom he loved, shall he not also with him freely give them all good things (Rom. 8:32)? Is it not the grand truth of Calvinism that all things—so-called evil as well as pleasant things—work together for good for those who are called according to God's purpose (Rom. 8:28)? Has not God promised to his elect to avert all evil or turn it to their profit? Shall anything be able to separate the child of God from God's love? Can tribulation, or hardship or persecution or famine or nakedness or peril or the sword (Rom. 8:35–39)? No, of course not. Therefore, the knowledge that God has eternally loved and chosen him for salvation gives the child of God boldness in prayer and the knowledge that in all circumstances God will also help him.

Misconceptions

Although the Canons of Dort are biblically founded, and although they give great encouragement when correctly understood, the pastor constantly finds misunderstandings about these comforting and encouraging truths. Such misapprehensions deprive the parishioners of much joy and comfort. Therefore, the following commonly-met misconceptions are listed along with a clarification of them.

1. **Misconception:** *"If I'm not elected, I cannot be saved; do what I may, I'm lost. It's no use to believe if God has predestinated me to hell."*

Clarification: People try to pry too much into God's business rather than stick to their own business. It is none of their business to figure out whom God has elected and whom he has not. The Bible does not give an answer. People should not curiously probe into the secret things of God: but the things that are revealed belong to them and their children to do them (Deut. 29:29). God gives us no answer about this problem—it is his secret. But he does tell us what we should do: Believe on the Lord Jesus. So, let us be done with putting our nose into God's business; and let us get on with our own work of believing.

Often those who raise the above objection are not really interested in being saved: rather, they are seeking an excuse to appear rational in their unbelief.

An effective way of answering such a person, and at the same time finding out if he is sincerely concerned about his lost condition, is to ask him what he wants. Does he want to be saved or not? Is he truly sorry for his sins or not? Does he truly love God and want to do his will or not?

If the answer is Yes, then he should be assured most heartily that he already is saved, already has eternal life; for the Bible says that whosoever believes—and that is what he is doing—has eternal life.

If his answer is that he is not sorry for his sins, but likes them and does not want to be saved, then he should be asked, why does he find fault? He has exactly what he wants. He loves his sins and does not want to be saved.

Each person who raises objections to election as if he were compelled to do something he does not want to do, should be delivered from his misconception. For God never forces anyone against his will. God does not drag into heaven a recalcitrant sinner who prefers hell to heaven: rather, he changes his heart of stone to a heart of flesh so that he cannot wait until he gets to heaven. Nor does God force anyone to hell who does not want to go there. If someone loves Jesus, and wants to go to heaven, then he goes there. He already is a believer and is saved. Everyone receives what he wants: heaven with the triune God or hell without him. Therefore, none should complain about divine compulsion.

2. Misconception: *The teaching of election and the perseverance of the saints tend to lead the Christian toward a false sense of security and toward a complacency in his faith in Christ.*

Clarification: It is true that if one is elected, he can never be lost; and that once saved, always saved. But how does a person know whether or not he is elected? He has no secret access into the hidden counsel of God. There is, however, a divinely ordained way for everyone to know: his present possession of faith. If one believes, such faith is an infallible sign that God loved and chose him, for faith is the gift of God's electing love.

If anyone should think that he was elected and should reason that it makes no difference whether or not he continues to believe, he would be rationalizing and departing from the clear teaching of Scripture. For although the Bible teaches eternal security, it never proclaims carnal security. Although Peter may write eloquently that the "elect" "are guarded by the power of God unto a salvation that is ready to be revealed in the last time," (1 Peter 1:5), he states that they are guarded "by means of faith." Here is the constant biblical combination: man's faith and God's electing power. God will certainly reserve salvation for his elect, but they will gain it only through faith—a faith that is not only past, but that is also present. Therefore, instead of lulling his readers into a false sense of security, Peter, by a striking combination of divine sovereignty and human responsibility, reminds his readers that they should make their calling and election sure (2 Peter 1:10). It is only by unbiblical, rationalistic deductions that one could conclude that the biblical teaching of election tends to minimize the necessity of trusting in Christ.

3. Misconception: *Perhaps the most common objection the pastor meets is that the doctrine of election causes one to become indolent, licentious and indifferent. If God has elected some, it is* *reasoned, why should they work hard for their sanctification and for God's kingdom? God's will will be done whether man works or not. Sin all you want. In other words, divine election treats man as a marionette and dulls his sense of responsibility.*

Clarification: Such popular sentiments are based on nothing but a caricature of the biblical teaching.

The Bible repeatedly associates election with holiness. Paul writes that God chose the Christian before the foundation of the world, not because he was holy, but in order that he "should be holy and without blemish" (Eph. 1:4). If a so-called Christian reasons that since he is elect, he can sin all he wants, the pastor should show him how faulty his reasoning is. For election always leads to holiness.

In 2 Thessalonians 2:13, Paul also informs us that God chose the Thessalonians "unto salvation in sanctification of the Spirit." God has a plan, a goal, in his election. It is not licentiousness, but holiness. Whomever God has foreloved, them he also foreordained to be conformed to the image of his Son, that is, to be holy. And those whom he foreordained, he also called and justified; and he will eventually glorify them (Rom. 8:29–30). Thus, there is a golden chain of salvation from election through sanctification to ultimate perfection. And if anyone says: I am elect and therefore I can sin all I want, he does not know what he is talking about. As a matter of fact, such a person—if he means what he says—is not a Christian. For an elect person cannot abandon himself to licentiousness: the all-powerful God who chose him has other plans—and his plans never fail.

Moreover, when correctly understood, the teachings of the Canons of Dort do not feed the flames of indolence and sin, but, on the contrary, induce one to be a better Christian. It is precisely the Calvinist who, knowing that by nature he has not an iota of a good thought, desire or deed; and realizing that he has been saved by grace all the way through, even to the extent of receiving the ability to believe on Christ—it is exactly such a Christian who will become more humble, increasingly filled with praise and more determined to live a holier life out of thankfulness. For he has more to be thankful for than one who thinks he is only partially bad.

Strikingly—contrary to popular opinion—the Bible reasons in the exact opposite way from those who think that the teaching of election leads to moral indifference. Paul appeals to election as a motivation for greater exertion!

He reminds the Colossians that God chose and loved them. Therefore, he says, they should put on compassion, kindness, humility, gentleness and patience (3:12). Similarly, he exhorts the Thessalonians to be sober and to put on the breastplate of love and salvation and the helmet of hope of salvation. Why? Because God has ordained them to obtain salvation (1 Thess. 5:8, 9). For Paul, divine election is not a motivation to be spiritually indolent, but to be active in holiness.

4. Misconception: *Some church members—especially those who are concerned about evangelism—labor under the false notion that "the doctrine of limited atonement . . . tends to inhibit missionary spirit and activity." They feel that in order to witness to an unbeliever, they have to say: "Christ died for you," even though they are not sure if he is going to heaven or hell.*

Clarification: Effective evangelism does not depend upon the statement: Christ died for you, i.e., Christ actually bore the guilt of the sins of everybody. (If that were the case, then no one would be guilty and all would go to heaven.) Instead, the Christian can tell the unsaved: "Christ died for sinners, and if you will turn from your sins and believe, he will save you. If you do not, you will be lost. Believe on the Lord Jesus Christ, and you will be saved." This is just as effective as making the untrue statement that God punished Christ for the guilt of every single person in the world.

Moreover, the knowledge of divine election, far from inhibiting missionary spirit and activity, actually stirs it up. For there is nothing more stimulating than the hope of certain victory. On the contrary, there is nothing more disheartening than the feeling of uselessness. If a missionary knows that all the unsaved are spiritually dead so that they cannot possibly turn to God, then his work is discouraging, and he feels, "What's the use? They cannot believe anyway." But if he also knows that God has elected some from every tribe and tongue, and that he will irresistibly open their hearts and cause them to believe, as in

Lydia's case (Acts 16), then the knowledge of certain results from his preaching buoys him up.

Misunderstanding of the Canons will inhibit missionary zeal: true perception will kindle it.

5. **Misconception:** *A natural reaction to the teaching of election is that God is arbitrary. The pastor will encounter this objection from both the non-Christian and the immature Christian who are not well versed in the Scriptures. To them it seems as if God is like a fireman who puts a ladder up on only one side of a burning hotel and thus arbitrarily favors only part of the hotel's clientèle.*

Clarification: This misconception is illustrative of a fundamental problem underlying all the Five Points of Calvinism. Repeatedly, the pastor will have to return to this issue. It will arise again and again, and it is of the utmost importance that this issue be squarely faced and biblically answered. Any thinking person will have serious questions, and if he is to receive joy and encouragement in these grand biblical truths, he must be able to meet this fundamental question head on.

The problem that the charge of God's arbitrariness raises is basic. It is the problem of the nature of man's final authority: Is the answer to be found in man's reason or God's Word? Every parishioner must answer this. Is he going to accept only that which makes sense to him, or what God's Word says, even if it sounds like nonsense? The pastor must first get this problem of authority settled. If the discussant answers: "Reason," then the discussion is closed. For the teachings of the Canons are unreasonable, ridiculous and foolish—to human reasoning. If, however, he answers "God's Word," then the pastor has a talking point. Now the pastor and the questioner can search the Bible to see what it does say. But first of all, both must be prepared to submit their reasoning to God's Word, even if the findings should turn out to be incomprehensible and against man's logic.

What then does the Bible say about the arbitrariness of God? It says that he is not arbitrary. He does not whimsically choose some and reject others. God is completely wise, holy and righteous. He does not unfairly discriminate against anyone. Yes, he does select, according to the good pleasure of his will,

(Eph. 1:5). The Bible is full of God's selection unto glorification. How can these two truths be reconciled? The Christian does not know. But the Bible says it is so, and therefore he believes it.

A similar problem of seeming contradiction arises with the free offer of the gospel. On the one hand, the Bible teaches that God desires and sincerely offers salvation to every man—Judas and the reprobate included. On the other hand, it teaches that Jesus did not die with the intent of removing the guilt of every person. How is it possible to harmonize these two apparently contradictory statements? The Bible gives no other answer than that God's ways are higher than man's ways as the heavens are higher than the earth.

Perhaps the antinomy that is the hardest for natural man to swallow centers on the problem of evil. God clearly foreordains sin. The selling of Joseph into Egypt (Gen. 45:5-8; 50:20) and the crucifixion of Jesus (Acts 2:23; 4:28) are the clearest examples, although the Bible, and especially the Old Testament, furnish many cases of God's foreordination of sin. On the one hand, there is this clear testimony of the Bible; yet, on the other, there are the repeated statements that God hates sin, that he will not listen to the prayers of the unrepentant, that he will punish sin either in eternal hell or in Jesus Christ, and that he is Holy, Holy, Holy. A reasoning person recoils from these two seemingly irreconcilable positions, yet the Christian believes because God had spoken.

In discussing these deep problems, the pastor must constantly lead his partner to the acknowledgment that God is incomprehensible. If they are faithful to the Word, they will end up with Paul's exclamation after a similarly great problem: "Oh, the depth of the riches both of the wisdom and knowledge of God. How unsearchable are his judgments and how incomprehensible are his ways" (Rom. 11:33).

The final question is: Do you believe God or not?

In conclusion, the pastor should always keep in mind the purpose of God's revelation about man's depravity and God's redemption. The purpose of such revelation is not to satisfy our intellectual curiosity about God's methods—not to give us a scholastic description of the process of salvation. Rather, his revelation was given for the practical purpose of inducing us to glorify God with all our being: i.e., of leading us to Christ, of causing us to thank him for so great a salvation, of moving us to holiness and to acknowledgment of him in all our ways. The pastor must be on his guard against academic discussions about God's electing grace, while at the same time the reality of the grace in one's life is missed. Too often, it is possible to get wound up in deep doctrinal discussions and meanwhile deny the power of God's grace in his life. As Paul expressed it, it is possible to have the form of godliness, but to deny the power of it (2 Tim. 3:5).

But when a person knows experientially the power of God's redemptive grace, then there is little that is more rewarding than to contemplate the unsearchable riches of his grace.

8 CALVIN, DORT AND WESTMINSTER ON PREDESTINATION — A COMPARATIVE STUDY

John
Murray

On December 4, 1646, the Confession of Faith, prepared by the Assembly of Divines meeting at Westminster, was completed. The date is more than a century later than that of the earlier editions of Calvin's masterpiece *Institutes of the Christian Religion* and also of the first edition of what is one of his most notable commentaries, the commentary on the Epistle to the Romans.

The century that intervened was one of prodigious theological output and intense controversy. Within the Reformed Churches the gravest issue was that focused in the Arminian Remonstrance of 1610, and it was this issue that gave occasion for the Synod of Dort in 1618 and 1619. It would be unhistorical and theologically unscientific to overlook or discount the developments in the formulation of Reformed doctrine that a century of thought and particularly of controversy produced. Study even of Calvin's later works, including his definitive edition of the *Institutes* (1559), readily discloses that his polemics and formulations were not oriented to the exigencies of debates that were subsequent to the time of his writing. It is appropriate and necessary, therefore, that in dealing with Calvin, Dort, and Westminster we should be alert to the differing situations existing in the respective dates and to the ways in which thought and language were affected by diverse contexts. In applying this principle, however, caution must be observed. This is particularly necessary in the case of Calvin. Too frequently he is enlisted in support of positions that diverge from those of his successors in the Reformed tradition. It is true that Calvin's method differs considerably from that of the classic Reformed systematizers of the seventeenth century. But this difference of method does not of itself afford any warrant for a construction of Calvin that places him in sharp contrast with the more analytically developed formulations of Reformed theology in the century that followed.

It would be expected that the vantage point occupied by the Assembly of Divines at Westminster, the unsurpassed care exercised in the composition of the documents that were the products of its labors, and the lengthy debates that characterized the Assembly would impart a precision scarcely equaled by earlier creedal formulations. This is conspicuously true in its Confession of Faith and Catechisms. In this essay we are concerned with the subject of predestination. No chapter in the Westminster Confession exhibits more of the qualities we might expect than Chapter III, "Of God's Eternal Decree." The chapter has eight sections. Sections I and II deal with the decree in its cosmic, all-inclusive reference, Sections III and IV with the decree as it has respect to men and angels in common, and Sections V–VIII with the decree as it applies to men distinctively. This order and the proportions of emphasis evince the competence that marks the Confession throughout.

The divines thought it meet to use the terms "predestinate" and "predestination" with reference to those appointed to everlasting life and the term "foreordain" for those appointed to everlasting death. "By the decree of God, for the manifestation of his glory, some men and angels are predestinated unto everlasting life; and others foreordained to everlasting death" (Sect. III). This variation is maintained in subsequent sections, (cf. Sects. IV, V, and VIII). It cannot be said that any difference is intrinsic to the terms such as would require this restriction, and it cannot be greater or less efficacy was intended to be expressed by the one term in distinction from the other. What consideration dictated the usage concerned it may not be possible to say. But it cannot be denied that in the structure of the chapter as a whole the interest of differentiating between the elect and non-elect is thereby promoted and the felicity of the expression "predestinated unto life" is made more apparent.

The doctrine of the Confession on predestination and foreordination is unequivocal. The differentiation involved and the diversity of destiny arising therefrom are clearly asserted. "These angels and men, thus predestinated, and foreordained, are particularly and unchangeably designed, and their number so certain and definite, that it cannot be either increased or diminished" (Sect. IV). It is worthy of note that this statement of the Confession includes both angels and men and is so framed that in respect of the doctrine set forth it has equal relevance to men and angels. This feature goes beyond what we find in the Canons of Dort. The Canons are concerned solely with the election and "reprobation" of men. The reason for this is obvious. The Remonstrant tenets against which the Canons were directed dealt with the decree of God with reference to mankind, and the issue would have been unnecessarily perplexed by introducing the subject of angels. But Dort enunciates the same position in respect of mankind. "And as God himself is most wise, unchangeable, omniscient, and omnipotent, so the election made by him can neither be interrupted nor changed, recalled nor annulled; neither can the elect be cast away, nor their number diminished" (Chap. I, Art. XI; cf. Art VI). In the Rejection of Errors, Articles II, III, and V, the reason for this emphasis upon definiteness is given. The opposing position is stated to be that "God's election to eternal life is manifold, the one general and indefinite, the other particular and definite . . . the one election to faith, the other to salvation . . . that the good pleasure and purpose of God, of which Scripture makes mention in the doctrine of election, does not consist in this: that God elected certain men above others but in this: that God from all possible conditions . . . elected faith, in itself unworthy, and the imperfect obedience of faith as the condition of salvation," a position pronounced to be pernicious error, prejudicial to the good pleasure of God and the merit of Christ. The Westminster

Confession is oriented against the same error, but the reference to angels in the same section is a reminder that the scope of its interest in Chapter III is more embracive than that of the Canons.

The parallelism of Sections V–VIII of the Confession with the First Head of Doctrine in the Canons is conspicuous, and comparison at various points will disclose not only the agreement of the two documents on what is germane to the doctrine of predestination, but also the debt the Assembly of Divines owed to the deliberations and conclusion of Dort. There is, of course, the marked contrast in proportions. Compact brevity is a distinguishing feature of the Confession. The four sections of the Confession comprise not more than one eighth of the space occupied by the eighteen affirmative and nine negative articles of the Canons. But the Canons are not to be accused of redundancy, and it should be kept in mind that there is in the text of the Canons copious quotation of Scripture in support of the doctrine asserted and in refutation of the errors rejected, a practice not adhered to in the Confession.

In contrast with the Remonstrant teaching, predestination to life and salvation is in both documents construed as unconditional, that is, as constrained by the sovereign good pleasure of God and not by any difference belonging to men themselves. This is expressed in the Confession in these terms: "Those of mankind that are predestinated unto life, God, before the foundation of the world was laid, according to his eternal and immutable purpose, and the secret counsel and good pleasure of his will, hath chosen in Christ, unto everlasting glory, out of his mere free grace and love" (Sect.V). The terms of the Canons are: "Election is the unchangeable purpose of God, whereby, before the foundation of the world, he has out of mere grace, according to the sovereign good pleasure of his own will, chosen from the whole human race . . . a certain number of persons to redemption in Christ" (Art. VII); "The good pleasure of God is the sole cause of this gracious election" (Art. X; cf. also Arts. XV and XVIII). So there is not only an identity of doctrine but also to a large extent of language.[1]

The negative counterpart of the emphasis upon mere free grace and the sovereign pleasure of God is, in contrast likewise with

Remonstrant teaching, that election is not determined by any foresight of faith or of perseverance. "Without any foresight of faith, or good works, or perseverance in either of them, or any other thing in the creature, as conditions, or causes moving him thereunto" (Sect. V) says the Confession. "This election was not founded upon foreseen faith and the obedience of faith, holiness, or any other good quality or disposition in man, as the prerequisite, cause, or condition on which it depended" (Art. IX) say the Canons (cf. also Rejection of Errors, Art. V).

That redemption by Christ and all the grace necessary to the fruition of God's electing purpose should flow from election rather than be the determinants of it is a correlate of the positive and negative declarations just noted. Both documents are careful to state this expressly. "This elect number . . . God has decreed to give to Christ to be saved by him, and effectually to call and draw them to his communion by his Word and Spirit; and having powerfully preserved them in the fellowship of his Son, finally to glorify them for the demonstration of his mercy, and for the praise of the riches of his glorious grace" (Canons, Art. VII; cf. Art. IX). It can scarcely be denied, however, that the formulation of Westminster excels in not only tying up the fruits with election but also in stating the certainty of effectuation in both redemption and application. "As God hath appointed the elect unto glory, so hath he, by the eternal and most free purpose of his will, foreordained all the means thereunto. Wherefore, they who are elected, being fallen in Adam, are redeemed by Christ, are effectually called unto faith in Christ by his Spirit working in due season, are justified, adopted, sanctified, and kept by his power, through faith, unto salvation" (Sect. VI).[2]

The section just quoted from the Confession requires comment from another angle. On the question of the order of the divine decrees the Canons of Dort are infralapsarian. This would appear to be the purport of Article VII when it says that election is that whereby God hath "chosen in Christ unto salvation a certain number of men from the whole human race, which had fallen by their own fault from their original integrity into sin and destruction, neither better nor more worthy than others but with them involved in common misery." But it is clearly set forth in

Article X when it is said that God was pleased "out of the common mass of sinners to adopt some certain persons as a peculiar people to himself." The Confession might seem to have the same intent. "Wherefore, they who are elected, being fallen in Adam, are redeemed by Christ." This would not be correct. The words, "being fallen in Adam," do not imply that the elect when elected were contemplated as fallen in Adam. The words simply state a historical fact that explains the *necessity* of redemption by Christ and the other phases of salvation. The Confession is non-committal on the debate between the supralapsarians and infralapsarians and intentionally so, as both the terms of the section and the debate in the Assembly clearly show. Surely this is proper reserve in a creedal document.

No paragraph in the whole compass of confessional literature excels for precision of thought, compactness of formulation, and jealousy for the various elements of truth in the doctrine concerned than Section VII of the Confession. "The rest of mankind God was pleased, according to the unsearchable counsel of his own will, whereby he extends or withholds mercy, as he pleases, for the glory of his sovereign power over his creatures, to pass by; and to ordain them to dishonor and wrath for their sin, to the praise of his glorious justice." Several observations should be noted.

The section deals with what has often been called the decree of reprobation. In distinction from Dort (cf. Arts. VI, XV, and XVI)[3] the Confession does not use this term. This restraint must be commended. Although the Scripture uses the term that is properly rendered "reprobate" (cf. Rom. 1:28; 1 Cor. 9:27; 2 Cor. 13:5, 6, 7; 2 Tim. 3:8; Tit. 1:16), yet its use is such that the elements entering into the decree of God respecting the non-elect could not legitimately be injected into it. The presumption is that Westminster divines hesitated to employ it for this reason. *Biblical* terms should not be loosely applied.

The precision of the formulation is evident in the distinction drawn between the two expressions "to pass by" and "to ordain them." The former is not modified, the latter is. No reason is given for the passing by except the sovereign will of God. If sin had been mentioned as the reason, then all would have been passed by. The differentiation finds its explanation wholly in God's sovereign will, and in respect of this ingredient the only reason is that "God was pleased . . . to pass by." But when ordination to dishonor and wrath is contemplated, then the proper ground of dishonor and wrath demands mention. And this is sin. Hence the addition in this case, "to ordain them to dishonor and wrath for their sin."

A third observation, however, is all-important. It might be alleged that the Confession represents judicial infliction and ill-desert as the only factor relevant to the ordaining to dishonor and wrath, that what has been called "reprobation" as distinct from preterition is purely judicial. The Confession is eloquent in its avoidance of this construction, and only superficial reading of its terms could yield such an interpretation. The earlier clauses, "God was pleased, according to the unsearchable counsel of his own will, whereby he extends or withholds mercy, as he pleases, for the glory of his sovereign power over his creatures," govern "to ordain them to dishonor and wrath" as well as "to pass by." So the sovereign will of God is operative in ordaining to dishonor and wrath as well as in passing by. And careful analysis will demonstrate the necessity for this construction. Why are some ordained to dishonor and wrath when others equally deserving are not? The only explanation is the sovereign will of God. The *ground* of dishonor and wrath is sin alone. But the reason why the non-elect are ordained to this dishonor and wrath when others, the elect, are not, is sovereign differentiation on God's part, and there is no other answer to the question.

The genius of the fathers of Dort did not lie in the direction of such compact and yet adequate definition. And the situation confronting them required more expanded treatment. But Dort was likewise alert to the need for these same distinctions and to the diverse factors entering into what it called the doctrine of reprobation (decretum reprobationis). "What peculiarly tends to illustrate and recommend to us the eternal and unmerited grace of election is the express testimony of sacred Scripture that not all, but some only, are elected, while others are passed by in the eternal decree; whom God, out of his sovereign, most just, irreprehensible, and unchangeable good pleasure, has decreed to leave in the common misery into which they have willfully plunged themselves and not to bestow upon them saving faith and the grace of conversion; but, permitting them in his just judgment to follow their own ways, at last, for the declaration of his justice, to condemn and punish them forever, not only on account of their unbelief, but also for all their other sins" (Art. XV; cf. also Art. VI).

The Canons are at this point careful to guard against the inference that the decree of reprobation makes God the author of sin. "And this is the decree of reprobation, which by no means makes God the Author of sin (the very thought of which is blasphemy), but declares him to be an awful, irreprehensible, and righteous Judge and Avenger thereof" (Art. XV). The Confession reiterates the same caution. Although God ordains "whatsoever comes to pass: yet so, as thereby neither is God the author of sin, nor is violence offered to the will of the creatures" (Sect. I).

On the distinction between the sovereign and judicial elements in foreordination to death Calvin likewise is cognizant. He draws the distinction in terms of the difference between "the highest cause" (*suprema causa*) and "the proximate cause" (*propinqua causa*).[4] The highest cause is "the secret predestination of God" and the proximate cause is that "we are all cursed in Adam." "But as the secret predestination of God is above every other cause, so the corruption and wickedness of the ungodly affords a ground and provides the occasion for the judgments of God."[5] Thus for Calvin, as for Dort and Westminster, the *reason* for discriminating is "the bare and simple good pleasure of God" (ad. Rom. 9:11) and the *ground* of damnation is the sin of the reprobate, a damnation to which they have been destined by the will of God (cf. ad. Rom. 9:20).[6]

It will be admitted that in "the decree of reprobation" the doctrine of God's absolute predestination comes to sharpest focus and expression. On this crucial issue, therefore, Calvin, Dort, and Westminster are at one. The terms of expression differ, as we might expect, and the Westminster Confession with inimitable finesse and brevity has given to it the most classic formulation. But the doctrine is the same, and this fact demonstrates the undissenting unity of thought on a tenet of faith that is a distinguishing mark of our Reformed heritage and without which the witness to the sovereignty of God and to his revealed counsel suffers eclipse at the point where it must jealously be maintained. For the glory of God is the issue at stake.

The abuses of the doctrine of predestination and the alleged conflict thereby instituted with other doctrines of Scripture are matters with which Calvin, Dort, and Westminster were compelled to deal. The Westminster Confession, with characteristic felicity, reads: "The doctrine of this high mystery of predestination is to be handled with special prudence and care, that men, attending the will of God revealed in his Word, and yielding obedience thereunto, may, from the certainty of their effectual vocation, be assured of their eternal election. So shall this doctrine afford matter of praise, reverence, and admiration of God; and of humility, diligence, and abundant consolation to all that sincerely obey the Gospel" (Sect. VIII). The situation Dort encountered demanded much more expansion of these same caveats, exhortations, and assurances pertaining to the doctrine. The first article of the Arminian Remonstrance required that Dort should give prominence to the universal sin and condemnation of mankind, to the love of God manifest in the giving of Christ, to the proclamation of the gospel, to the summons of men without distinction to repentance and faith, to the guilt and consequence of unbelief as well as to the saving effect of faith, and to the responsibility of men in the rejection of the gospel. It was necessary to show that these truths were not curtailed or negated by the doctrine of predestination, and the latter had to be set in proper focus in relation to them. Hence the first five articles of the Canons are devoted to such aspects of the gospel. But after the pattern followed by the Westminster Confession, and in greater fullness, Dort deals with the proper uses of the doctrine and warns against the distortions to which it is liable to be subjected. The way of attaining to the assurance of election is set forth in Article XII. The elect may attain to this assurance, "though in various degrees and in different measure . . . not by inquisitively prying into the secret and deep things of God, but by observing in themselves with a spiritual joy and holy pleasure the infallible fruits of election pointed out in the Word of God." The consolations of the sense and certainty of election and the corresponding responses in humiliation, adoration, and gratitude are reflected on in Article XIII, and the danger of carnal security, rash presumption, remissness in observing the commandments of God receives proportionate emphasis. Of particular and distinctive interest are Articles XIV and XVI, the former in setting forth the obligation to proclaim the doctrine of election constantly in due time and place to the glory of God's most holy name, and the latter for the concern that the proper response should be offered to the doctrine of reprobation. Those who do not yet experience living faith in Christ and its accompanying confidences ought not to be alarmed or terrified by the doctrine of reprobation or rank themselves among the reprobate, provided they persevere in the use of the means of grace and earnestly desire to be turned to God. But it is a terror to those who are forgetful of the claims of Christ and indulge the lusts of the flesh.[7]

In dealing with abuses of the doctrine of foreordination one objection that both Dort and Westminster found it necessary to controvert is that it makes God the author of sin and exculpates the human agent. No one has exposed the fallacies underlying this objection with greater effect than Calvin. A great deal of his argumentation in *Institutes,* Book I, Chapters XVI–XVIII is devoted to a refutation. With eloquent reiteration he develops the distinction between the motive, reason, and end by which men are actuated in the commission of sin, on the one hand, and the motive, reason, and end entertained by God, on the other. In Calvin there is no toning down of the fact that the will of God is the first and ultimate cause of all that comes to pass. But there is total disparity between the will of God and the will of man as these two wills are operative in the same event. When men sin they are not actuated by the design of fulfilling God's purpose but by evil passions in contravention of his revealed good pleasure. Here is the same principle asserted by both Dort and Westminster that the rule of our action is not foreordination but the will or commandments of God revealed in his Word. "From what source do we learn but from his Word? In such fashion we must in our deeds search out God's will which he declares through his Word. God requires of us only what he commands. If we contrive anything against his commandment, it is not obedience but obstinacy and transgression."[8]

In reference to election there is one other aspect that may not be overlooked. It is that election was in Christ. Calvin repeatedly stresses this. There are three lessons derived from it. First, it certifies that "the election is free; for if we were chosen in Christ, it is therefore not of ourselves."[9] Second, we cannot find assurance of our own election anywhere else than in Christ. Election is prior to faith but it is learned only by faith. Third, we learn thereby that election is discriminating; not all are members of Christ. It is noteworthy that both Dort and Westminster introduce this aspect in contexts where the sovereignty and freeness of election are set in the forefront (Confession, Sect. V and Canons, Art. VII). They are thus in accord with the position emphasized by Calvin. But in neither document is there reflection upon the more practical lessons mentioned by Calvin. We could scarcely expect the limits of creedal formulation to permit this. Both Dort and Westminster also speak of God's decree to give the elect to Christ to be saved by him (Confession, Chap. VIII, Sect. I and Canons, Art. VII). This decree from eternity must have been conceived of as distinct from and logically subsequent to election in Christ. No index is given, however, in either document as to how the framers conceived of this election in Christ. This is to their credit. The revelatory data do not warrant dogmatism as to the precise *character* of the "in Christ" although the Scripture makes apparent its manifold consequences.

The conclusion constrained by this comparative study is that although Calvin, Dort, and Westminster exhibit distinguishing features appropriate to their respective contexts and to the demands these contexts exacted, yet on the subject of predestination there is one voice on all essential elements of the doctrine. This is but one example of what is true in respect of the system of doctrine espoused by the Reformed Churches. There is what must be called the consensus of Reformed theology. Our debt is unmeasured. It is also one to humble us. In no doctrine is the *soli Deo gloria* more demanded of us than in our thought of predestination. Nowhere in the compass of theological formulation is the praise of God's glory more central than in the work of Calvin, Dort, and Westminster.

9 RECENT REFORMED CRITICISMS OF THE CANONS

Klaas Runia

This volume on the Synod of Dort and its doctrinal decisions would not be complete if it did not contain a chapter dealing with recent criticisms of the Canons. On purpose we confine ourselves to criticisms coming from theologians belonging to the Reformed tradition. Theologians coming from other traditions, especially from Arminians and Liberal backgrounds, naturally are critical of the Canons. But in their case it is usually not the Canons that are specifically criticized, but they reject the whole complex of doctrines dealt with in this statement. For theologians of the Reformed tradition the situation is different. In most cases they belong to churches that have accepted the Canons as one of their subordinate standards. These theologians therefore have subscribed to the Canons and will not easily criticize their own confession. Yet in recent years many critical voices have been heard, both in Europe and in the United States. In this chapter we shall briefly discuss these criticisms.

We begin with Karl Barth. To some it may seem strange that we include him among the *Reformed* theologians. Is it not true that on decisive points Barth has deviated from the theology of the reformers in general and from Calvin's theology in particular? Although the answer to this question is "Yes," it cannot be denied that Barth belongs to the Reformed tradition. He himself has stated this more than once and his theology, especially his *Church Dogmatics*, bears it out in many places.

Barth deals with the Canons in his doctrine of election.[1] During the discussion he refers several times to them. Right at the beginning he praises them for the fact that, in spite of the inclusion of reprobation in their doctrine of predestination, they formulated election itself in such a way that it really had "the character of evangelical proclamation."[2] This is particularly true of the formulation of Canons I, 7.

Yet Barth has a very serious objection against their doctrine. He believes that in the Canons we find the idea of a *decretum absolutum*, just as in the theology of all the reformers. Although they all maintained that our election is an "election in Christ" and spoke of Christ as the *speculum electionis* (Calvin)[3] or the *liber vitae* (Formula of Concord),[4] yet this "in Christ" was not the final word. Actually it referred only to the *ordo salutis* (Christ as the mediator and executor of our salvation). Behind this "in Christ" there was still deeper ground of election and reprobation: God's eternal decree, by which, in sovereign freedom, he decreed to save some in and through Christ and to leave others in their sin and perdition. The Arminians saw this serious defect, and over against the Calvinists they stated that "Christ, the mediator, is not only the executor of the election, but the foundation of the very decree of election."[5] Unfortunately their own understanding of the election was very faulty. With their doctrine of foreseen faith they themselves were the last exponents of medieval Semi-Pelagianism and at the same time the first exponents of Neo-Protestantism. Over against them the Calvinists of Dort were altogether right, when they maintained that our salvation is wholly a matter of divine election. Unfortunately they maintained this by taking recourse to the *decretum absolutum* idea. In this same connection Barth criticizes Canons I, 7, which before he had praised so highly.[6] Although Jesus Christ is mentioned, he is mentioned after the decision about election and reprobation has already been taken.

In all this we touch upon the very nerve of Barth's criticism. Again and again he returns to this point. In the section on "Jesus

Christ, Electing and Elected" he severely criticizes Calvin on this same point, and also the Canons.[7] The electing God of Calvin is a *Deus nudus absconditus,* and the same is true of the Canons. "Jesus Christ is not in any sense *the fundamentum electionis.* . . . but at very best he is only the *fundamentum salutis.*"[8] Later on, in his discussion of the "perseverance of the saints," Barth once more mentions the same point. Again he rejects the view of the Arminians, he even calls it "unspiritual, impotent and negligible—a feeble postlude to the Catholicism of the later Middle Ages and a feeble prelude to rationalist-pietistic Neo-Protestantism."[9] In principle he himself agrees with Calvin and the Synod of Dort. He even calls the doctrine of perseverance the "supreme statement of predestination." Yet there is again the old criticism. Although at this point the Synod "almost exclusively" referred to "Jesus Christ, the Word of God and his promises," yet the doctrine could not work properly, as appeared rather soon after the Synod, because *the decretum absolutum* remained the last background. This is clear from the fact that with regard to the "certainty" about our election, the Synod does *not* first mention the "constant promises of God" but "the marks proper to the children of God" (Rejection of Errors V, 5). Barth regards this as a necessary and unavoidable consequence of the *decretum absolutum* idea. If we have not been elected from all eternity "in Christ," then Christ cannot be the real *speculum electionis,* then we have to seek our last certainty somewhere else, and the only remaining possibility is that we seek it in the fruits of election in our own life.

It cannot be denied that Barth raises a very fundamental question regarding the Canons. If he is right in his criticisms, they would really stand condemned. The whole idea of a *decretum absolutum* is utterly foreign to the Bible. The real heart of the biblical doctrine of election is that we have been chosen "in Christ" before the foundation of the world (Eph. 1:4, cf. 1 Tim. 1:9). But is Barth right? Not all Reformed theologians agree on this point. For instance, C. Van Til states that "the Synod of Dort had no nominalist notion of a will of God to which a second decision of God had to be added in order to connect election properly with the love of Christ."[10] James Daane, on the other hand, says that "in its teaching about individual election the Canons do not even mention the Pauline expression "in Christ," except in the Rejection of Errors, and even there the "in Christ" is not even at issue."[11]

Unfortunately it is not possible within the limits of this chapter to examine this point at great length. We should not forget that Barth accuses not only the Canons but the theology of all the Reformers, especially of Calvin. For Calvin's view we may refer to G. C. Berkouwer's *Divine Election,* who declares that Barth's "dogmatical-historical judgment does not conform to Calvin's reflections on the *speculum electionis* and on Ephesians 1:4."[12] Berkouwer does not deny that Calvin did not always state the matter clearly and adequately, but at the same time adds that "at a decisive point he rejected precisely the penetration into *Deus nudus* (the Father alone, as Calvin puts it) by saying that the heart of the Father rests in Christ."[13] The same is true of the Canons. They too do not always state the matter clearly and adequately, but there is no doubt that the fathers of Dort would all reject the idea of a *decretum absolutum,* apart from Jesus Christ. Chapter I, 7 states that God has chosen from the whole human race "a certain number of persons to redemption in Christ, whom he from eternity appointed the Mediator and Head of the elect and the foundation of salvation." Unfortunately the English translation of this sentence is somewhat ambiguous. First, the phrase "He chose . . . to redemption in Christ" could be interpreted as meaning that Christ is only the *fundamentum salutis*. The Latin text, however, reads: "ad salutem elegit in Christo." In other words, the "in Christ" qualifies the act of choosing. Secondly, in the last clause of the above quoted sentence the word *"also"* has been left out. Both the Latin and the Dutch version read: "whom he *also* from eternity appointed. . . ." In other words, the article clearly distinguishes between our election in Christ (i.e., Christ as the foundation of election)[15] and Christ's appointment as Mediator (i.e., Christ as the foundation of salvation). The Canons do not see Christ only as the executor of the (previously decreed) election, but the election itself is in Christ.[16]

Yet it cannot be denied that in the Canons this central aspect of the biblical doctrine of election does not receive the emphasis it deserves. Because I, 7 is preceded by an article that speaks of a general double decree of election and reprobation, in which the "in Christ" aspect is altogether missing, the conclusion that there is a *decretum absolutum* behind the election-in-Christ could be drawn, and I am afraid that, unintentionally, the Canons thus have given occasion to later deterministic misunderstandings, which especially since the eighteenth century have plagued and still are plaguing large sections of the Reformed community. I am also sure that, if the Canons were to be rewritten in our day, the central affirmation of our election in Christ should be brought out more clearly and more unequivocally.

We now come to some publications of theologians belonging to the Dutch Reformed Church (Nederlandse Hervormde Kerk). In 1951 a booklet on *The Election* was published by Dr. J. G. Woelderink. This booklet is particularly interesting, because the author himself came from a strict-Calvinist background, with leanings towards hyper-Calvinism. In nearly all his writings, and in particular also in this booklet, he opposed all hyper-Calvinist tendencies while at the same time trying to remain faithful to the deepest intentions of Reformed theology.

What is Woelderink's view of the Canons? It is a combination of deep appreciation and of fundamental criticism. Fully agreeing with the teaching that our salvation is due to God's electing love, at the same time he sees two contrasting lines in the Canons. The first five articles of Chapter I take their starting point in the Gospel. But in article 6 they switch over to a second line of thought, which takes its starting point in the decree.[17] That this is the major point of criticism appears from the fact that time and again he returns to this same point.[18] To him this is the basic error of all Calvinist parties at Dort, both the supralapsarians and the infralapsarians. Because of their emphasis on the decree, they were necessarily thinking in terms of causality,[19] and consequently "election and rejection were no longer channels through which the stream of God's virtues broke forth, but they became springs that produced salvation and perdition."[20] It was no longer sufficient to ascribe faith to God's grace, and unbelief to man's sinful heart. No, God too had his share in unbelief, in as far as he had decreed "to leave the non-elect in his just judgment to their own wickedness and obduracy" (I, 6). The natural result of this "causal" way of thinking was that in I, 12 all emphasis is placed on man's inner spiritual life, where he can observe "the infallible fruits of election."

Woelderink's own solution is to see election primarily and essentially as *an act of God in time*. His main Scripture proof is taken from the Old Testament,[21] but he finds the same emphasis also in the New Testament. He does not deny that we are allowed to proceed from election as God's act in time to God's election from eternity, but this should not be done in terms of an abstract, eternal decree; instead we should see the eternal God himself who in his electing love guarantees the relationship of grace that he has established with us.[22] If one wants to speak of a decree, one should do this in the form of the "Covenant of Redemption," in which the triune God appointed the Son as Redeemer.

Rejection, too, is seen as an act of God in the history of the world and in the concrete lives of sinful people. In the case of rejection, however, we are *not* allowed to go back to an eternal decision of God "before the foundation of the world." Woelderink utterly rejects the idea of an eternal decree of reprobation.[23] At this point the Canons have gone beyond the limits of Scripture. It is not surprising, therefore, that they do not give any Scripture proof for this aspect of their teaching.

There are undoubtedly elements of truth in Woelderink's criticisms of the Canons. We too believe that there are traces of "causal" thinking. But at the same time we believe that Woelderink on his part has fallen into the other extreme and is virtually "historicizing" and "actualizing" election. Paul's statement that God chose us in Christ "before the foundation of the world" (Eph. 1:4) hardly plays any part in Woelderink's conception.[24] Election and rejection only "happen" in an "open situation." This is so much so that according to Woelderink election can change into rejection, and *vice versa*. [25] At this point he is very close to Barth's conception. Yet his position is also different from that of Barth, because he rejects the latter's objectivism of grace and its implied universalism.[26] The Bible knows not only of the light of the Gospel, but also of a shadow, the dark shadow of final rejection and therefore of final perdition.

Of great significance is a document on election adopted by and published on behalf of the Synod of the Dutch Reformed Church. This Pastoral Letter is particularly significant, because the Canons are one of the subordinate standards of this church. The Letter openly and joyfully confesses the miracle of *election*. "The congregation of Jesus Christ, drawn by the Holy Spirit from the darkness of guilt and lost-ness into the light of Christ's grace, confesses its faith in the electing God."[27] On the one hand, this is a humbling confession, for it means that we cannot redeem ourselves in any way. On the other hand, it is a comforting confession, for it means that our salvation rests on the faithfulness of God. This divine election becomes manifest in history. God gives faith to sinful people, through his Word and Spirit. But behind this divine act in history we may see God's eternal decree, which is fulfilled in this act. "In all this God is the decreeing, and deciding God, and he is such in his eternity, which is before, above, after and in our time."[28]

Rejection too is an act of God in history.[29] But in this case we may not infer an eternal decree of rejection. Although such a conclusion may seem to be natural and valid, Scripture itself never employs this logic.[30] Texts that have often been quoted in support of such an eternal decree of rejection (such as Prov. 16:4; Matt. 13:10–13; 22:14; Acts 13:48; Rom. 9:11–23; Pet. 2:8; Jude 4; Revel. 17:8) do not really teach this.

After all this it is not surprising to see that the Letter contains a number of criticisms of the Canons. In fact, not only the Canons, but the Belgic Confession as well is criticized, especially article 16, which speaks of God's *"leaving* others in the fall and perdition wherein they have involved themselves."[32] The Canons, I, 6, however, go beyond this and, in spite of what has been said in I, 5, suggest "that human guilt is not the last word about the ground of rejection."[33] Other points of criticism are that Word and Spirit are not always kept inseparably together,[34] that the certainty of election is too much sought in pious man himself,[35] that the election of the individual believer is onesidedly stressed,[36] and that the Scripture proof given is very weak.[37]

These last points, however, are only minor criticisms. The real criticism of this Letter is that the idea of "causality" is found in the teaching of the Canons. This idea, especially as it is applied to rejection, is the reason that the final responsibility of the sinner is obscured and God, somehow, seems to become the final "cause" of man's perdition. Again we feel inclined to agree with this criticism. yet we also believe that the Letter itself is in danger of actualizing the election. The doctrine of election seems to be nothing more than a confession of God's free grace in our life. But does the Bible not say more? There are, especially in the New Testament, many passages that speak of God's pre-determination (cf. Acts 4:28; Rom. 8:29, 30, Eph. 1:4–11, etc.). It is striking that in the Letter Ephesians 1:4 is discussed in connection with the realization of the election. At this point the Canons, in spite of their "causal" way of thinking, are closer to the fullness of the biblical message than this Letter.

Finally we come to recent criticisms of the Canons by theologians of the Reformed Churches (*Gereformeerd Kerken*) of the Netherlands. The one who started the new discussions on the Canons was G. C. Berkouwer, in his volume on *Divine Election*. Throughout the volume we observe his deep appreciation for the teaching of the Canons, against Barth's accusation of teaching a *decretum absolutum*.[38] He is of the opinion that Barth himself with his concentration upon Jesus Christ as the electing God transgresses the limits of God's revelation. Although he appreciates Barth's desire to banish all uncertainty from preaching by anchoring our election in the factuality of Christ, yet he believes that Barth falls into the other extreme. "If Barth's argument is that the consoling pastoral message misses its ontic foundation, we must reply that it is rather Barth's doctrine of election with its universality that evokes the problem that Barth thinks the Reformation left unanswered. For with Barth, Christ is not so much the mirror of election as the *manifestation* of the election of God, a universal manifestation that may be disregarded in unbelief, but which cannot be undone."[39] Likewise he defends the so-called *syllogismus practicus,* as found in the Canons, over against such theologians as Weber, Niesel, Klingenburg and others.[40]

Yet Berkouwer himself also sees "certain problems" in the Canons, especially in I, 6. While in I, 5 the Canons have clearly stated that the "cause or guilt of unbelief" is "in man himself," I, 6 seems to go beyond this. "One's first impression is that this is a simplistic way of explaining causality."[41] Berkouwer, however, tries to defend the Canons. "When we read I, 6, we see that it directs our attention to the acts of God in the life of man." A connection is laid "between sinfulness and stubbornness on the one hand, and the judicial acts of God on the other hand, not in the sense that either belief or unbelief become an independent and autonomous power over against the counsel of God, but in the sense that non-granting is evidently meant as the judicial act of God toward man in sin."[42] In spite of this defense, Berkouwer is well aware of the fact that there are certain difficulties in the formulation of the Canons. Cautiously he admits that "it could be wished that also in I, 6 the light of the epilogue had been shining more clearly and that therefore the criticism of the *eodem modo* had been more explicit." It is indeed "difficult to indicate completely and clearly the harmony between I, 6 and I, 5." But then he immediately adds, more or less as an excuse for the Canons that this same "opaqueness" is noticed wherever these things are discussed. "It is not the opaqueness of paradoxical irrationality, but the opaqueness which is due to (the nature of) unbelief, and which can be described from two sides: from the side of God's judgment and from the side of man's sin." "The imbalance of the *causa*-concept which we observe in Calvin and in the Canons is, on the level of human insight, a proof of the inexplicability of sin and unbelief. We prefer this imbalance rather that any synthesis from the point of view of the *praescientia* of determinism."[43]

In the foregoing paragraph the Conclusion of the Canons was mentioned. This epilogue plays a dominating part in

Berkouwer's interpretation. Two statements from the epilogue are mentioned again and again. The Synod rejects the idea that its doctrine teaches "that God, by a mere arbitrary act of his will, without the least respect or view to any sin, has predestinated the greatest part of the world to eternal damnation, and has created them for this very purpose" and "that in the same manner (Latin: *eodem modo*) in which the election is the foundation and cause of faith and good works, reprobation is the cause of unbelief and impiety."[44] We are not saying too much, when we call the *non eodem modo* in particular the master key that Berkouwer uses to open the door to the real teaching of the Canons, especially its teaching about reprobation.

In the chapter on "Election and Rejection" Berkouwer more than once emphatically states that "Scripture repeatedly speaks of God's rejection as a divine answer in history, as a reaction to man's sin and disobedience, not as its cause."[45] In this connection he points to such texts as 1 Samuel 15:23, 2 Kings 17:20; Deuteronomy 28:15ff.; Lamentations 5:22; Psalm 51:13; 78:67; Isaiah 50:1ff.; etc. He then asks the question: is there any reason to add anything to this Scriptural testimony?[46] Is there still a "plus," the "plus" of God's eternal decree? Is there a double cause, one in man's sin and guilt, and a second and deeper one in God's predestination? According to Berkouwer, Calvin at times wrote as if there were such a second *causa* in God. He even writes that "Calvin has seen the actual *causa* in predestination."[47] Berkouwer's own view is that the concept of cause is altogether insufficient. "One can never come to an acceptable solution by means of the concept of cause."[48] It leads inescapably to some form of determinism. This does not mean that Berkouwer chooses for indeterminism as the solution. The struggle between determinism and indeterminism in the doctrine of election is a futile one. As we are not allowed to make the divine counsel the abstract principle of explanation of sin and unbelief and perdition, so we are not allowed either to withdraw sin and unbelief from God's counsel. Quite often it has been tried to do this by speaking of autonomy, synergism, *praescientia, nuda permissio, liberum arbitrium*, over against God's election.[49] But this is an impossible solution. "Nothing can be made independent of the counsel of God." Berkouwer himself believes that we should stop at the well known words of Augustine: *contra*, but not *praeter voluntatem Dei*.

He interprets the Canons in the same light. "When the Church, in the Canons, for example, speaks of God's decree, it does not mean that we are confronted with an impersonal, iron law, *a fatum* of causal determination."[51] Reformed theology has always realized that neither determinism nor indeterminism provide a solution. Hence it maintained both that the *decretum Dei* is *Deus decernens* and that this *Deus decernens is* the God who reveals to us his sovereignty and freedom in the powerful "before" of his revelation.[52] The Preacher understood this well, when he said: "I know that, whatsoever God doeth, it shall be for ever; nothing can be put to it, nor anything taken from it; and God hath done it, that men should fear before him," (Eccl. 3:14). The question must be asked here, whether there is still a place left for *a decree of reprobation*. Berkouwer is very cautious. H. Berkhof of Leiden, in a review of Berkouwer's volume on election, wrote: Berkouwer is silent on I, 15 and this is significant![53] Although Berkouwer a few times does speak of a decree of reprobation, he usually puts the word "decree" between inverted commas. I believe that we may say that there is virtually no place for such a "decree" in Berkouwer's theology. He himself stops at the two statements from the epilogue, quoted before, and at the fact that in Scripture God's rejection is always a reaction against man's prior rejection of God. He is and remains very cautious, but I believe that H. N. Ridderbos was right, when he wrote that although Berkouwer is in full agreement with the basic motifs of the Canons, the emphases are definitely somewhat different from those in the Canons.[54]

More than ten years after the publication of his book on *Divine Election* Berkouwer touched again upon the Canons in a long article on "Questions around the Confession."[55] This time he speaks of "tensions" in the Canons.[56] On the one hand, there is I, 5, which clearly speaks of man's own guilt, on the other hand, there is I, 6, which speaks of God as the cause behind receiving and not receiving faith. At this point there is something problematical in the formulation. Berkouwer tries to solve the problem by distinguishing between the basic motif and the framework of the Canons. The basic motif is quite clear and fully scriptural. The central intention of the Canons is to speak of "the undeserved election, the sovereignty of grace in the way of salvation, the election as fountain of every saving good. Clearly and continually we hear the voice of the Gospel in the references to the 'golden chain of our salvation' and the 'in Christ.'"[57] But the framework within which this basic motif is expressed, is not always clear and pure. It is the framework of "causality." There is a "causal" approach, which is strongly influenced by a certain *exegesis of Romans 9*.[58] The sovereignty of God is apparently seen as something deeper or higher than the "*ekloge*" of Romans 9:11. One gets the impression that there are two themes: on the one hand, the merciful purpose of election; on the other, the absolute sovereignty of God "in general." Renewed study of Romans 9–11 in recent years, however, has convincingly shown that there is not such a double theme. The only theme Paul deals with is that of the "*ekloge*," the purpose of election, which God works out in the history of Israel. The emphasis is on God's acts of election in history and not on a pre-temporal decree that in a causal way determines all things.

There is no need here to go any further into the details of the article. The central question Berkouwer discusses is whether one can still be faithful to the confession, if one is critical of its "framework" but fully agrees with its basic motif. His answer is in the affirmative, for faithfulness to the confession is not a matter of certain terms, but rather of the total structure of the confession. There is therefore no need to lodge a gravamen against the Canons at this point.

This new approach of Berkouwer has been rather influential. Several Reformed theologians in the Netherlands have openly stated that they agree with Berkouwer's criticism of the Canons. I am thinking here in particular of A.D.R. Polman, for many years professor of systematic theology in the Reformed Seminary at Kampen. In his earlier publications he fully upheld the views of the Canons, but gradually, mainly under the influence of Barth and Berkouwer, he has changed his mind.[59] He summarizes his own view as follows. There are *two dangers* that continually threaten the biblical doctrine of God's election and rejection: *causal determinism* and (often as a reaction against the first) *synthetic synergism*. Causal determinism is the result of taking one's starting point in an abstract, sovereign decree, based on the concept of "absolute power." The consequence of this starting point is that election and rejection become two parallel, symmetrical lines, which both proceed from the absolute decree. But this is nothing else than causal determinism. In reaction, synthetic synergism overemphasizes man's responsibility and then projects this back into God's decree in the form of *praescientia* or *praevisio*. According to Polman the Bible does not know about a pre-temporal decree that in causal way determines all things, but it only speaks of a gracious election in Christ before the foundation of the world. When it mentions rejection, it is always a rejection in history, in which God's reaction against man's rebellion becomes manifest. This does not mean that man's sinful activity becomes autonomous over against God's counsel. The Bible sets the two aspects side by side, and leaves it at that. We have to respect these limits of our reflection. But it is quite clear that every one who objectivizes the elect and the reprobate in two fixed groups, can no longer do full justice to the serious call of the Gospel, which also comes to the reprobate.[60]

Polman is well aware of the fact that he deviates from the Canons. Somewhere he writes that the real problem is not God's free, sovereign good pleasure in the life of the believers, but the *partial symmetry* between the *decree* of election and rejection, in which from all eternity God has elected *and rejected* certain persons. "The latter is confessed in the Canons (I, 6 and 15) and this is *not* accepted by us." The fathers of Dort never produced scriptural evidence for this view, but based it on a mere logical conclusion. If some people call this a valid and necessary conclusion, then they should realize that the Bible itself never draws this conclusion.[61]

Reformed theologians of the Netherlands, however, are not the only ones who have followed this new line of thought. Also in the Christian Reformed Church of the U.S.A. there are similar voices. I am thinking here in particular of some articles by H. R. Boer and H. Pietersma in *The Reformed Journal*.[62] Boer summarizes the "ambiguities" in the context in which the decree of reprobation stands in the Canons follows: "1. That man alone is responsible for his unbelief. That lack of faith arises from the decree of reprobation. 2. That God is in no wise responsible for the unbelief of man. That the decree withholds the gift of faith and the grace of conversion. 3. That God unfeignedly calls all men to faith. 4. That in the reprobate the response of faith is impossible. That election and the promise of the gospel must be preached. That reprobation in its very nature appears not to be capable of being preached." Boer does not openly attack the Canons. Neither does he speak of a "causal" way of thinking, but it is quite obvious that his criticism is along the same lines as that of Berkouwer and Polman.[63]

It is evident that for all these theologians the doctrine of an eternal decree of reprobation is the *pièce de résistance*. To see the problem in its proper perspective, however, we wish to draw the attention to three things.

First, none of these theologians wants to limit God's power and sovereignty. All of them reject every form of synergism, which is so characteristic of all Semi-Pelagianism, including that of the Arminians. When these theologians question or reject an eternal decree of reprobation, they are not motivated by the desire to give some place to even a partial autonomy of the human will. On the contrary, they all fully agree with the Canons when the latter teach that we have been chosen by God in Christ before the foundation of the world. Or to put it in the formulation of I, 5: "Faith in Jesus Christ and salvation through him is the free gift of God."

Secondly, we should remember that most Reformed confessions of the Reformation period are either silent on reprobation or speak of it in very cautious terms. Even Calvin himself did not mention it in the Catechism of Geneva, the Confession of the Schools and in his draft for the French Confession. For a further survey we may refer to Berkouwer's *Divine Election*, Chapter VI, where he discusses and rejects Warfield's interpretation of this silence and caution; Berkouwer's own view is that "in the Reformed confessions there is an intuitive and reflexive understanding of the Scriptural message of election."[64]

Thirdly, at the Conference of Arminians and Calvinists at the Hague in 1611, the Dutch Calvinists more than once stated that their controversy with the Arminians did *not* concern the latter's view of reprobation. They declared "that they would have left the Arminians free in their view of reprobation, if only they (i.e. the Arminians) had been willing to confess that God out of mere grace, according to his good pleasure, had elected some to eternal life, without any regard to their faith as a preceding condition."[65] At the close of the conference they reiterated: reprobation is not a matter of controversy, if only election out of pure grace is maintained.[66]

I believe it is important and necessary to keep these three points clearly in mind when we discuss the matter of reprobation. It undoubtedly helps us to see the problem in its real proportions.

When we now turn again to the Canons, we must admit that there are indeed two lines of thought. On the one hand, the Canons take their starting point in the Gospel. Here all emphasis is laid on the "*ekloge.*" Salvation is wholly and fully God's work. It is God who has chosen those who believe in the Gospel. He has chosen them in Christ before the foundation of the world "out of mere grace, according to the sovereign good pleasure of his own will" (I, 7). Their faith is not their good work, but it is the "free gift of God" (I, 5). At this very point we find the real controversy with the Arminians,[67] who in their defense of man's free will made election conditional upon foreseen faith.

In addition to the above the Canons equally emphasize that unbelief is man's fault. "The cause of guilt of this unbelief as well as of all other sins is no wise in God, but in man himself" (I, 5). This too is part of the clear teaching of Scripture. Man is always seen as responsible for his own sin, and the blame for his unbelief is always put squarely upon the sinner himself. In no respect can God ever beheld responsible for it, not even in an indirect sense.

God is holy. "God is light and in him is no darkness at all." (1 John 1:5) But there is also a second line of thought in the Canons, namely, the line of "causality." We find this in particular in I, 6, which opens with the following words: "That some receive the gift of faith from God, and others do not receive it, proceeds from God's eternal decree." Reading this, one cannot help wondering whether there were some traces of the idea of "absolute power" in the minds of the author. At any rate it was at this point the Arminians always concentrated their attack. Time and again they repeated the accusation: you make God responsible for unbelief. At the conference of the Hague in 1611 they described the views of the Calvinists as follows: "those who are predestinated unto perdition (being by far the majority) must be damned necessarily and unavoidably, and they cannot be saved."[68] The Calvinists, on the other hand, always rejected this view as a caricature. They were firmly convinced that this was unbiblical and repudiated it as a statement of their own position. Yet the question may be asked whether the conclusion of the Arminians was not valid, if one takes I, 6 and I, 15 seriously. Is it really possible to avoid this conclusion? Of course, we gratefully notice that the fathers of Dort rejected it, but was it not a valid implication of their second line of thought?

The main question, however, is whether Scripture itself speaks of an eternal decree of reprobation. It is indeed very remarkable that the main "proof" in Reformed theology has always been the "logic" of the situation. At the Conference of the Hague the Calvinists stated: "When we posit an eternal decree of election of certain particular persons, it clearly follows that we also posit an eternal decree of rejection or reprobation of certain particular persons, for there cannot be an election without a rejection or reprobation. When from a certain number some persons are elected, then by this very act others are rejected, for he who takes them all does not elect."[69] A similar line of argument we find in the judgments given by the various groups of delegates at Dort. In fact, the argument appears in several forms. Some say that, if there is a decree, "It is a fixed rule: what God does in time, he must have, from eternity, decreed to do."[71] Others again say that if unbelief were the sole cause of rejection, all would have been rejected. Reformed theologians of our twentieth century still use the same kind of argument. When L. Berkhof gives his proof for the doctrine of reprobation, he begins with the following statement. "The doctrine of reprobation naturally follows from the logic of the situation. The decree of election inevitably implies the decree of reprobation. If the all-wise God, possessed of infinite knowledge, has eternally purposed to save some, then he *ipso facto* also purposed not to save others. If he has chosen or elected some, then he has by that very fact also rejected others."[73] And L. Boettner opens his discussion of "Reprobation" with these words: "The doctrine of Predestination of course logically holds that some are foreordained to death as truly as others are foreordained to life. The very terms 'elect' and 'election' imply the terms 'non-elect' and 'reprobation.' When some are chosen out others are left not chosen."[74]

It is of course true that "logic" does play an important part in theology. Reformed theology has always freely acknowledged its good right. The Westminster Confession states that "the whole counsel of God concerning all things necessary for his own glory, man's salvation, faith and life, is either expressly set down in Scripture or *by good and necessary consequence,* may be deduced from Scripture," (Ch. 1, vi). By this very means the church has developed its doctrine of the Trinity and also its Christology, yet the question must always arise: is a particular consequence "good and necessary"? In general we must say that especially at the point of an eternal decree of reprobation we have to be most careful. And one should ask oneself: why does Scripture itself not draw this conclusion, if it is so natural and so logical?

It is very striking indeed that the Canons themselves, in I, 15, do not mention any Scripture proof at all. In other articles, which touch upon the same matter, the Scripture proof given is very weak, to say the least.[75] The same is true of Reformed theology in general. The texts that are usually mentioned are all ambiguous and they all allow a different and better interpretation.[76]

This criticism of the Canons by some Reformed theologians in recent years, does not mean that these theologians themselves wish to derogate from the sovereignty of God or that they deny

God's eternal counsel. Polman, for instance, says: "God elects a man without any ground in this man. God rejects the man who rejects him, *without becoming dependent* on the negative decision of this man."[77] Rejecting the solution of the Calvinists at Dort, they equally reject the Arminian solution, namely, God's *praevisio* of unbelief that would precede his decree.[78]

They cannot accept these solutions for two reasons. First, they refuse to accept a "causal" connection between God's decree and that which happens in history. They believe that the whole concept of causality is out of place here. Causality would mean that there is no place for human responsibility, which is clearly depicted on nearly every page of Scripture. In addition, history would lose all its significance. It would only be a mechanical, pre-determined outworking of a divine decree. Secondly, they also refuse to change the biblical asymmetry between election and rejection, into a symmetrical, logical system, in which salvation and perdition evolve from the one decree in two parallel lines. "He who wants to be 'logical' here, must either make faith the work of man alone or unbelief the work of God."[79] But both conclusions are evidently unscriptural.[80] The Synod of Dort has clearly seen this, as appears from the Conclusion, in which it declares that the expression "that in the same manner *(eodem modo)* in which the election is the fountain and cause of faith and good works, reprobation is the cause of unbelief and impiety" is one of the many things "which the Reformed Churches not only do not acknowledge, but even detest with their whole soul!" If it is objected that the Synod did not always adhere to this in the formulation of the Canons, especially in I, 6 and 15, we immediately grant this. But Berkouwer is undoubtedly right when he says that the real intention of the Synod is found in this rejection of the *eodem modo* and not in the causal framework that we find in I, 6 and 15.

It is obvious that there are many unsolved problems left. The Synod of the Dutch Reformed Church (Ned. Herv. Kerk) rightly demands of its theologians that they must try to penetrate deeper into this "paradox," namely, that faith is God's gift and that unbelief has its sole cause in man's own heart.[81] At the same time it adds that "the Church has to call a halt to every one who wants to weaken or remove this paradox."

The only correct starting point for all our thinking about election and rejection, I believe, lies in the Gospel itself. We are very happy to note that the Synod of Dort has seen this too (I, 1–5). Unfortunately it has not adhered to this one starting point. In I, 6 it has added another line of thought, namely, one that starts from the counsel of God. Taking into account the whole pattern of thinking at that time (cf. the controversy between the supralapsarians and the infralapsarians) this is not surprising. As a matter of fact, the Synod was right when it saw an inseparable connection between the Gospel of Jesus Christ, as preached by the church, and the divine counsel. The problems can definitely not be solved by a mere historicizing and actualizing of election and rejection. But at the same time, we must say that the Gospel may not be robbed of its power by a method of thinking that takes its starting point in an eternal counsel and then proceeds to draw logical conclusions from this counsel. I often wonder whether the "solution" is not to be sought in a deeper study of what we mean by the word "eternal," when we speak of God's eternal counsel. Did Reformed theology perhaps overemphasize the pre-temporal nature of the divine counsel? Did it perhaps too simply identify the eternal nature of the counsel with the eternal nature of God himself? There are many questions here, and it is obvious that in many respects we in this twentieth century have not progressed much beyond the fathers of Dort. Perhaps we shall never get much further. But be this as it may, the depth of these problems remains a tremendous challenge for the future.

10 THE SIGNIFICANCE OF DORT FOR TODAY

Cornelius
Van Til

The Synod of Dort was concerned to defend the doctrine of the sovereign grace of God against the encroachment upon it by the doctrine of the free will of man. By the free will of man we mean the would-be autonomy of fallen man.

The apostle Paul tells us that there are two and only two kinds of people in this world. There are first those who, because of their fall in Adam, serve and worship the creature rather than the Creator. There are secondly those who, because of their redemption from the fall through Jesus Christ, have learned to serve God their Creator and Christ their Redeemer rather than the creature.

Men of the second group are not, of themselves, any better than men of the first group. It is not because of superior wisdom found in themselves that they of the second group have learned to serve and to worship God. It is, rather, because they have been born of the Spirit, born from above, that they would now dedicate themselves and their all to the Father, the Son and the Holy Spirit. This was the intent of Dort, and it can be understood and evaluated only against the centuries-old struggle of the true church for God's truth.

Dort and the Struggle for God's Truth

(1) The Roman Catholic Synthesis

The Roman Catholic church attempted to synthesize the worship of God and the worship of man. The genius of the Romanist position is that it combines an interpretation of man and his world as given by the method of the Greek philosophers, especially Aristotle, with an interpretation of man and his world as given by Christ in the Scriptures. In the nature-grace scheme of Rome the Aristotelian view of human autonomy and the biblical view of divine sovereignty are supposedly cooperating peacefully with one another for the welfare of man and for the glory of God.

In the Roman scheme of things the natural man is not told that he is a slave to sin because of his fall in Adam, and that only the grace of God in Christ applied to him by the regeneration of the Holy Spirit can set him free. The natural man is rather told that, although he is naturally free, he may have a greater degree of freedom through Christ. Through grace man may be lifted in the scale of being toward participation in the being of God. This largely metaphysical lifting in the scale of being is a gradual process. The church is therefore, in effect, a continuation of the incarnation of Jesus Christ. The mass is a non-bloody continuation of the sacrifice of Christ. The faithful who partake of it are moving, it is hoped, onward and upward toward the vision of and participation in the being of God.

(2) The Reformation Principle

By the gracious providence of God it was Luther and Calvin who brought to light the gospel of the grace of God, as of then buried beneath this false synthesis between the wisdom of man and the wisdom of God. For this reason Herman Bavinck speaks of the principle of the Reformation as being *ethical* rather than *meta-physical*. Man is and always will be a creature. The fall did not draw him toward non-being. Through the fall, man became a sinner. He hates his Maker. As such he is guilty and polluted. As such he is under the condemnation of his Creator and Judge. Through the atoning death of Christ, those who believe and therefore put their trust in Christ by the Spirit are, in principle, free from guilt and pollution and therefore free for the service of their Redeemer. By the testimony of the Spirit with their spirits they *know* that there is no longer any condemnation for them. They are not being gradually lifted in the scale of being, always fearful lest through their failure of determination to hold on to Christ they should, after all, slip back toward or into non-being again. The gates of hell cannot frustrate the work that Christ has done for them and the work that the Holy Spirit, in applying the work of Christ to them, has done and is doing within them.

What joy there was in the Reformed Churches of the Netherlands when the gospel of the sovereign grace of God, as recovered by Luther, and especially as recovered and restated by Calvin, ruled in the hearts of its members. In 1561 these Reformed Churches had adopted the Belgic Confession as their creed, and soon afterward they added the Heidelberg Catechism as a second ecclesiastical standard. Now to the glorious task of training the young and instructing the people to an ever deeper appreciation of the gospel of the sovereign grace of God!

(3) The Remonstrant Synthesis

It soon appeared, however, that a mixed multitude had come out of Rome. The biblical idea that through the fall man is corrupt in all the aspects of his personality was too much for some of them. Man could not be that bad! Did they and all the good people they knew deserve to go to eternal punishment for the sin that "Adam" had committed? Are we to take the Bible that literally? What of all the "heathen"? They have never even had an opportunity to hear the gospel. Are they "lost" too?

Why does God offer the gospel of salvation through Christ to us and not to others? Did not Christ die for all men? If it really takes the regeneration of the Holy Spirit for any one to accept the gospel then why does not the Holy Spirit regenerate all men?

The Remonstrants, who asked such questions, did not want to return to the Mother Church. They could not abide the idea of a pope to lord it over them. Besides, they said they believed in all the doctrines of the Reformed confessions.

They believed in the Bible as the final standard for teaching and practice. They believed, they said, in election and in the primacy of grace. But for all their opposition to Rome and her teachings, centering in the mass, they did not, so they said, want to go to opposite extremes. How can we defend ourselves against the Romanists when they tell us that in the theology of Calvin and especially in that of his follower, Beza, man is reduced to a puppet and God is made the author of sin? Are the teachings of the Reformation, especially the teachings with respect to God's election of some men to eternal salvation and his passing by of others to eternal death so clearly revealed in Scripture as the Reformers thought they were? Can we not have a *practical* rather than a theoretical combination of election and human responsibility?

In 1610 a number of followers of Jacobus Arminius expressed this type of opposition formally in a Remonstrance. It is the reply to this Remonstrance that we have before us in the Canons of the Synod of Dort. Of what relevance are these pronouncements for us today? To answer this question it is imperative that we think of the following facts.

(4) The Five Points of Calvinism

When we deal with the Canons of Dort we deal not, in the last analysis, with the so-called "five points of Calvinism." It is not the case that Reformed preachers preach exactly like Arminian preachers throughout the year except for the fact that perhaps once a year they preach one sermon or even five sermons on "the Five Points of Calvinism." Rather, the Canons of Dort presuppose the "system of doctrine" that had already been set out in the Belgic Confession and in the Heidelberg Catechism. The fathers of Dort were merely articulating this "system of doctrine" more carefully than had been done in these confessions at particular points that were attacked by the Remonstrants. The old heresy of human autonomy was raising its head anew within what was not only a church born of the principle of the Reformation but, more particularly, within a Reformation church that sought to be Reformed. The enemy was now within the gates. Using tactics similar to those that were used by the Viet Cong in the war in Vietnam, the Remonstrants pretended to be loyal to the Reformed confessions while they actually did all they could to destroy them.

The Remonstrants claimed the fullest right to operate within the Reformed Churches of the Netherlands. They sought to reform the Reformed Churches so that they would teach the sovereign grace of God in consonance with what they thought to be the obvious experiential truth of the free will of man. Only by doing this, they argued, could a Reformed church really be Reformed. Certainly the proper motto for a Reformed Church is that it must always reform itself. Is there not always new truth springing forth from the ever bubbling fountain of Scripture? Is not the Holy Spirit leading the people of God into an ever deeper and broader grasp of the truth as it is revealed to us by Christ the Son of God?

From what has been said it appears that the Remonstrant synthesis is not basically different from the Roman Catholic synthesis. The assumption of human autonomy underlies both of them. With the assumption of human autonomy as an ultimate given of experience goes a purely rationalist principle of continuity and a purely irrationalist principle of discontinuity. In short, involved in the assumption of human autonomy is a comprehensive theory with respect to the nature of all reality, including God and man.

We may illustrate this point by a reference to Socrates. Socrates answers the question whether the holy is holy because it is holy or whether it is holy because God says it is holy, by saying that he does not care what the gods say about the holy. He wants to know what the holy is in itself. In other words, he assumes absolute human autonomy. By saying this he, at the same time, answers the question asked. The holy is holy not because a god says it is holy; the holy is a concept and a reality that stands above the gods as well as above men. This is rationalism. But involved in this rationalism is the notion that holiness is an idea that is wholly beyond the reach of human definition. This is irrationalism. Instigated by Satan, Adam introduced the notion of human autonomy, and with it the rationalist-irrationalist synthesis that has marked all human thought that is not redeemed by Christ. Socrates exemplifies this fact clearly.

There are two purely contradictory statements that must, on this apostate view, be made about reality as a whole. In the first place all reality must be *one* in the sense that it is a static whole. If this were not so then man would not *understand* his own freedom. To understand is, on this view, to penetrate exhaustively by logical insight. But if man understood himself and therefore his freedom exhaustively then he would not be *free* any longer. He would not exist at all in any individuality. For to understand is, on this view, to be absorbed in being. Being and understanding are one. To understand himself man must, on this view, destroy himself. He must be absorbed into the "wholly other" reality above him. Yet he has no knowledge of a God that is wholly above him. Therefore he cannot, though he must, be absorbed into God.

The only possible escape for man from thus seeking to understand himself by absorption into abstract being is by destroying the very idea of understanding by means of the notion that reality, including gods and men, is wholly contingent. Only if reality is wholly contingent is man wholly free. By the same token he is then, at the same time, wholly indeterminate. As wholly contingent he cannot distinguish himself from other wholly contingent men any more than a drop of water in a bottomless and shoreless ocean can distinguish itself from any other drop in the same ocean.

The former idea, that of pure or blank identity, was defended by Parmenides, and the latter idea, that of pure or blank differentiation, was defended by Heraclitus. For Parmenides all reality is static and for Heraclitus all reality is flux. Seeking to escape the obvious contradiction between these ideas, Aristotle said that reality is inherently both continuous and discontinuous. This is what he meant when he spoke of the inherently analogous character of being.

This Aristotelian concept of the analogy of being is utterly destructive of the Christian scheme of things. The Greek way of thinking in general, and the Aristotelian way of thinking in particular, destroys the whole distinction between God as man's Creator and of man as the creature of God. In the place of the idea of Creation the Greeks substituted the notion of participation. Herewith the principle of apostasy is owned as legitimate. There can, on this view, be no revelation of God to man, either "natural" or "supernatural." There can, on this view, be no "fact revelation" and there can be no "word revelation."

Man is, on this view, not the image-bearer of God and therefore cannot sin against God. If he could sin and if he had sinned, there could be no redemption from sin for him through the incarnation and atoning death of the Son of God. There cannot be a Son of God, for God is the changeless and stationary one. There could be no son of man who was also the Son of God in distinction from other men, for *all* men as men would be participant in the being of God.

However, for all the obvious incompatibility of Christianity and Greek philosophy, the Church of Rome forced them into an artificial union. The principle of "free will" was so precious to the Church of Rome that it was willing to make an evil alliance with Greece in order to defend it. Loving Christ, the Church of Rome loved Aristotle—almost as well.

(5) The Reformation Principle Again

It was the fatal union between Christ and Aristotle that was broken by the reformers. For them it was Christ alone whom the redeemed from sin must serve.

It was the fatal union of Christ with Aristotle that constituted for Luther the Babylonian captivity of the Church. It was the principle of the Reformation—the principle of Christ alone, Scripture alone, and faith alone—that the Reformed Churches were seeking to work out in its full implications.

Granted they did not yet see the full implication of their own position; they did at least understand and set forth the gospel in its essence.

This precisely is where the Remonstrants failed. They did not grasp or did not want to live exclusively by the principle of the Reformation. Like the Church of Rome, the Remonstrants too loved the freedom or autonomy of man almost as well as they loved Christ. Like the Church of Rome, the Remonstrants were blind to the fact that with their commitment to their notion of the freedom of man they were, in effect, also committing themselves to a view of reality as a whole that excludes the truth of the whole Christian scheme of things.

(6) The Remonstrant Synthesis Again

In replying to the five points of the Remonstrance the way it did, the Synod of Dort was therefore not merely defending certain points of doctrine. It was defending the whole Christian scheme of things. The men of Dort were defending the Christian scheme of things by maintaining that God must be the self-sufficient point of reference in all that man asserts about himself or about his world. God is the source of what can *possibly* happen in the world of space and time. Therefore God cannot, without denying himself, create a formal or abstract possibility of salvation for all men. If he did this, then no man would or could be saved. The idea of the abstract possibility of salvation being offered equally to all men is tantamount to the idea of the actual salvation of all men. However, this salvation would then amount to nothing but the absorption of all men into blank identity. One cannot assert that God is the source of all possibility and at the same time assert that possibility is back of God.

In short, by holding to the idea of human autonomy, the Remonstrants, following the lead of the Roman Catholics, were in effect committing themselves to a monstrous synthesis between one system of thought in which God—and another system in which man—is the final reference point in predication.

The Reformed Churches had already rejected such a monstrous synthesis in their first major confessions. Now at Dort they refused to return to the flesh-pots of Egypt. But this time they made their stand in opposition to those who were members and ministers of their own church.

Herein then, quite obviously, lies the relevance of Dort for today. Reformed Churches should not be surprised if the idea of human autonomy together with its false principle of universality and its false principle of individuality, should raise its head again and again within their own confines. In fact these churches should expect that such will be the case. They should, moreover, expect that the monstrosity of a theology that seeks to worship both God and man will take on ever increasingly subtle form. Reformed Churches must ever be ready to identify and exclude heresy from their midst.

Roman Catholic Critique of Dort

(1) Johann Adam Möhler

It was to be expected that Romanism would attack the theology of sovereign grace set forth in the Canons of Dort, and in the other Reformed confessions. In 1832 the learned Roman Catholic historian of doctrine, Johann Adam Möhler, published a work in which he instituted a comparison between the creeds of the Roman Catholic and of the Protestant churches. Its title is *Symbolism* or exposition of the *Doctrinal Differences between Catholics and Protestants.* Möhler refers to Dort only briefly, but his general criticism of the Reformed confessions is applicable to what Dort teaches either directly or by assumption.

Basic to Möhler's critique is, of course, the assumption of human freedom as an ultimate given of experience. He assumes that autonomous freedom is the prerequisite for the idea of human responsibility.[1] The fact that the reformers definitely and clearly teach responsibility on the ground that man is made in the image of God does not keep Möhler from asserting that the reformers practically teach determinism.

In all of their teaching, both with respect to sin and salvation the Protestants, says Möhler, have an externalist view of the relation between God and man. How could it be otherwise since "according to them, all the phenomena in the world of man are God's own work, and man is the mere instrument of God; everything in the world's history is God's invisible act, visibly realized by the agency of man. . . . All is referred to God—God is all in all."[2]

The reformers affirm indeed "that man can repel the divine influence, though he cannot co-operate with it; whereby, they think, his guilt is sufficiently established. But this solution of the difficulty is unsatisfactory, because every man can *only* resist; since all are in like degree devoid of freedom, and of every vestige of spiritual faculties."[3]

If there is anything defective in man, this must be ascribed to God who made him. Of course, Calvin will not allow such a conclusion. But it is, says Möhler, involved in his basic determinism.[4] For all their emphasis on the heinousness of sin their determinism compelled the reformers, "in despite of themselves, to deny the very existence of sin."[5]

Turning now to the Protestant view of justification by faith we see, says Möhler, that in spite of claims to the contrary, this too is conceived in mechanical, impersonal terms.[6] According to Calvin, justification is not regarded "as a morally renovating and vital principle, flowing from the spirit of Christ; but as standing in the same relation to Christ as an earthen vessel to the treasure."[7]

Thus since the reformers have no real place for human freedom and responsibility in their system of thought, even their God himself cannot uproot sin from man. Evil "necessarily adheres to everything finite."[8]

One more point needs to be mentioned. Though the burden of Möhler's criticism on the Protestant view of God's relation to man is directed against its supposedly unbearable determinism, the opposite criticism is not lacking. This applies particularly to Calvinism. The God of Calvin, Möhler says, is arbitrary. This is apparent in the very externalism of all of God's dealings with man. Men are merely puppets in his hands. Christ dies only for some men, not for all. In arbitrary fashion he withholds from others the light of salvation and sends them to their eternal death regardless of merit or demerit.

Summing up the matter Möhler says that "the Catholic Church views the whole system of Christianity, and the immediate objects of the Savior's advent, in a manner essentially different from the Protestant communities . . . According to the old Christian view, the Gospel is to be regarded as an institution of an all-merciful God, whereby through his Son he raises fallen men to the highest degree of religious and moral knowledge that he is capable of attaining in this life, proffers to each one forgiveness of sins, and withal an internal sanatory and sanctifying power."[9]

(2) Vatican II

We now ask whether the Roman Catholic church still takes as strongly negative an attitude toward the sovereign grace of God as it did formerly. How about the pronouncements of Vatican II? In it the word "anathema" is not found. The children of the

Reformation are now addressed as departed brethren, not as heretics. Moreover, a new interest in the Bible in manifest in its documents.

The answer must be that the attitude of the Mother Church to the sovereign grace of God as brought to men in Christ and as proclaimed in Scripture is essentially the same as it was at the time of the Council of Trent and of Vatican I.

In the first place the attitude toward Scripture remains essentially the same. The teaching magisterium of the Church of Rome is still said to be the final arbiter of doctrine.[10] This fact appears in the opening address to the Council and controls what is said throughout all of the documents of the council.

In the second place the very heart of the idea of sovereign grace as taught by the reformers and as defended by Dort is denied in the Council's teaching on the universality of the grace of God. "All men who are born were redeemed by the blood of Christ . . . but the greater part of the human race . . . does not yet participate in those sources of divine grace which exist in the Catholic Church."[11] Hence the church "whose light illumines all, whose strength of supernatural unity redounds to the advantage of all humanity" seeks to envelope all within her bosom.[12]

The entire teleology of history that confronts us in the documents of Vatican II is essentially the same as that which confronts us in the documents of Trent. To be sure, there is a difference. The teleology of history as developed officially by Trent was an amalgam between the form-matter scheme of Greek philosophy and Christian theology. Vatican II carries forth this Aristotle-Christ synthesis of Trent but adds to it the nature-freedom scheme of the modern philosopher Immanuel Kant. Existentialism is now mixed in with essentialism. Instead of an Aristotle-Christ synthesis, Rome now proposes an Aristotle-Christ-Kant synthesis.

By adopting existentialism into its structure the church has "solved" some of the problems of its past. How shall the church add new teachings to its irreformable system of doctrine? In the past this was a difficult problem. There was too much staticism in the church. But now all teaching is more dynamic. If Cardinal Newman sought to explain the progress of dogma by the notion of implication, this appears to be too logicistic now. We now see that all reality involves inherent change as well as inherent permanence. With this dialectical vision the church's exclusivism and her universal inclusivism are now seen to be supplementary instead of contradictory to one another.

All men may now rejoice in the fact that Mother Church dwells in her midst. For all her surface exclusiveness she now appears as "the universal sacrament of salvation." In her presence the Christ-Event is present.

The church reveals the "innermost realities of God" to men, and if these appear to coincide with the current existentialist patterns of thought, men should all the more readily return to her bosom.

Mother Church beckons the sons of Dort too. "You who were defending the sovereign grace of God at Dort meant so well. But in defending the grace of God you used causal, determinist categories. Together with the reformers you made God to be the first cause of all things on earth, including the will of man. But some of your own prophets, notably Karl Barth, have taught us, better even than our fathers have taught us, that if we are really to teach the sovereign grace of God we must reject the notion of an all-controlling God (*Alleinwirkzamkeit Gottes*). Your great philosopher, Kant, back of Barth, has taught all of us that God meets man in the realm of free person-to-person confrontation and not in the realm of causality. Why not return to the bosom of the church and there, with us, preach the sovereign-universal grace of God?"

The Confession of 1967 and Dort

If the children of Dort still hesitate to return to Mother Church, they may be ready to listen to what some of their Reformed brethren, the children of Westminster, have done. These have adopted what they call the Confession of 1967.

This confession has for its background the philosophy of Kant's freedom-nature scheme. In recent terminology this scheme is expressed in terms of a dimensional philosophy. There is first, the I-it dimension. It is the realm of science, the realm of causal relations. Then there is the I-thou dimension. It is the realm of freedom, the realm of person to person relations.

The Synod of Dort and the Westminster General Assembly did not know about this scheme. They thought that God could meet man directly in the causal dimension. They called God the first cause. Anyone who cherished his experience of freedom and therefore refused to accept the determinist scheme of these confessions was said to deny the sovereign grace of God.

For many years the determinist philosophy of the Westminster Confession was taught at Princeton Theological Seminary. Recently Dr. George Hendry and others, inspired by such men as Karl Barth, have seen how utterly wrong the causal method of theological thinking involved in this determinist scheme of theology was.

When the composers of the Westminster Confession wrote their creed they used, says Dr. Hendry, "a false model." When they wrote about the decrees of God they assumed "the cast of a deterministic philosophy, in which there is no real place for human freedom, despite verbal protestations to the contrary."[13] Worse than that, they left no freedom for God. They traced the sovereignty of God back to the absolute and inscrutable will of God. For no reason at all this God elected some men to salvation and passed others by. Accordingly the third chapter of this confession with its particularism breathes "an air of dread and doom," whereas the New Testament passages, on which its chief teaching is built, with their universalism, "breathe an air of exultant joy."[14]

The men of Westminster were Calvinists. Yet, though thinking to defend the sovereignty of God, they could not even come in sight of it. Some of their opponents were Arminians. These, thinking to defend the freedom of man, could not even come in sight of it. Such was the case because the Calvinists and the Arminians alike sought for a theoretical instead of a practical knowledge of God.[15] But now, since Kant, since Søren Kierkegaard, and especially since Karl Barth, we know how to speak properly of the freedom of God and of the freedom of man. We have now learned that grace is the all-controlling attribute of God. When God's righteousness requires the punishment of sinners, this righteousness is subject to grace. We may and must, says Barth, believe in election. We must even believe in reprobation.

All men are reprobate, but their reprobation is sublated in Christ so that the last, the final word to man is *yes*. To be man at all, man must be fellow-man with Jesus.

Calvin had no eye for this fact. He did not realize that Jesus Christ is the electing God and the elected man. For all his emphasis on divine election "he still passes by the grace of God as it has appeared in Jesus Christ."[16] The Synod of Dort "repeated more harshly if anything, the unsatisfactory answer already given by Calvin."[17]

It appears then that the "principle of Roman Catholicism" as expressed by Vatican II and the "principle of Protestantism" as expressed in the Confession of 1967 are, to all intents and purposes, the same. Both teach the sovereign universal grace of God in Christ. Both reject the historic Reformed view of the sovereign grace of God as expressed by the theologians of Dort and by the theologians of Westminster.

Klare Wijn and Its Evaluation of Dort

The composers of the Confession of 1967 write as those that have found a great treasure. They write with a sense of great release. Kierkegaard has led them into the land of promise. There are no more heretics now. The Calvinist-Arminian antithesis, the Reformed-Lutheran antithesis, and the Protestant-Catholic antithesis are overcome in principle. Barth has enabled them to see that it is the nature of God to turn wholly into the opposite of himself and then to take up all men into participation in his own being. In the Christ-Event all things in heaven and on earth and under earth are being united.

With similar lyrical enthusiasm the General Synod of the Netherlands Reformed Church (Hervormde Kerk) offers its members a statement of its newly-formed view of Scripture in a book with the appropriate title *Klare Wijn* (Clear Wine).[18] The composers of this new confession follow essentially the same pattern of reasoning that is followed in the Confession of 1967.

There is frequent reference to the position of orthodoxy. The orthodox theology of the time of Voetius and others was looking for knowledge as a theoretical system.[19] "Independent of the content of the Bible, they seek for proof that the Bible is the

Word of God."[20] Orthodoxy *identifies* the Word of God with Scripture. For orthodox theologians the Bible became one massive body of revelation truth for man's possession.[21]

Hence all the tears. Hence all the heresy charges. Hence all the irrational fears with respect to Bible criticism, to modern science and modern philosophy. Hence all the vain efforts of a misguided apologetic to defend the Scriptures and its teachings. The result was a condition of general distress.

But now in the twentieth century the Bible is "on the march again."[22] "Light is dawning."[23] As "our Reformed fathers" used to say, the Bible reveals its mystery afresh to us. We have done with the merely formal ascription to Scripture. When orthodoxy said the Bible *is* the Word of God, it had no eye for the teleology of Scripture.[24] We speak of the Scripture as the Word of God because it holds before us the gospel of the sovereign-universal grace of God.

The Bible speaks of the *event* of God's salvation.[25] We no longer speak of God's election as an eternal decree according to which some men are and some men are not chosen for life. When we speak of election we now speak of God's love for mankind.[26]

When we see the Bible in this way it speaks with force, with compulsion to all men. Only thus does the Bible become concrete.[27] "Only thus can the Bible bless us."[28]

The Challenge of the Emerging Neo-Protestant and Rome Synthesis

What has been said in the preceding four sections makes it evident that they who would today defend the sovereign grace of God must, as was the case at the time of Dort, be prepared to find the enemy within the church. The Remonstrants claimed to have every right to be considered as true believers in the gospel of Christ. They thought that their view of the freedom of man was a legitimate Christian view. They held that it was the Calvinist who, with his determinism, kept God from freely loving all men.

Today the situation is the same but with a difference. The view of human freedom that underlies the basic position of Roman Catholicism and of Neo-Protestantism today is virtually identical with the modern philosophical notion of human autonomy. On this view there is no such thing as sin that makes man justly subject to the wrath of God and that, therefore places him, as Calvin says, in "the way of death." Man has no need for the substitutionary death of Christ. Man may be evil. He may be *very* evil. To read a few pages of Freud, some one has said "is enough to shock any decent beast." Even so, man's inherent goodness is deeper than his evil.

More than that, and basic to it all, who can still believe all this abracadabra about an eternal ogre of a God arbitrarily pitching men into hell or taking his pets into glory? Modern philosophy has shown us that *nobody* knows or can know anything about a god existing in an eternity of bliss above the world.

We *know* therefore, that the historic Protestant position with respect to God and his relation to man is nothing but pure speculation.

What then shall we preach about? Well, let us *postulate* a good God as a practical device. True, we *know* nothing of such a God. But we must believe that *somehow* good people will be rewarded and evil people punished. We can *all* believe this. We can, accordingly, have one church. When we have organized this one church we shall send out missionaries to the ends of the earth to tell all men everywhere, not that they must believe what took place on a certain date of the calendar, in a certain little country called Palestine, but that they are already in Christ.

Theoretically there will then be no heretics. All men must, to be men at all, be in Christ. But practically there will be some heretics. The practical heretics are they who will not reconstruct their theology in accordance with the principle of human autonomy.

Among these remaining practical heretics some of the most stubborn will be the followers of Dort. They will be most stubborn because they alone are, in the last analysis, unwilling to compromise their view that it is on the basis of the presupposition of the self-determinate triune God of Scripture that any human predication has meaning at all.

Here then, in the last analysis, lies the significance of Dort for today. The followers of Dort, together with their brethren, the followers of Westminster, alone have the wherewithal to proclaim the gospel of the sovereign grace of God at all. Today the battle of Armageddon is on. It is up to those who prize their heritage as children of the Reformation and, more specifically, of the Reformed Reformation to lead all the true followers of the self-identifying Christ of Scripture against unbelief without and against unbelief within the church.

APPENDIX A – CHRONOLOGICAL TABLE

1517—Luther nails his theses to the church door in Wittenberg (Oct. 31)
1519—Count Edzard introduces the Reformation in East Friesland
1520—Charles V becomes ruler of the Netherlands
1522—Luther's Bible published
1523—First martyrs at Brussels, southern Netherlands
1525—First martyr at the Hague, northern Netherlands
1526—Liesveldt Bible published at Antwerp
1527—Beginnings of Anabaptism in the Netherlands
1534—Anabaptist revolt at Munster (Westphalia), Germany
1536—Calvin arrives in Geneva
1544—Pierre Bruly becomes first Reformed preacher in the Netherlands
1550—Reformed refugee congregation organized in London
1555—Accession of Philip II as sovereign of the Netherlands
1559—Treaty of Cateau–Cambrésis, ending the conflict between Spain and France
Final edition of Calvin's *Institutes*
Establishment of the Academy at Geneva
Creation of new bishoprics in the Netherlands
1561—Belgic Confession approved
1563—Heidelberg Catechism published
1566—Dathenus publishes his liturgy, psalter, and translation of the Heidelberg Catechism
Field preaching begun in the Southern Netherlands
Iconoclastic riots in the southern Netherlands
1567—Duke of Alva arrives in the Netherlands
de Brès and de la Grange martyred for the faith at Valenciennes
1568—Outbreak of the Eighty Years' War
Convent of Wesel, preparatory general assembly of the Dutch churches
1571—Synod of Emden meets

1572—Capture of the Brielle, turning point of the war for northern Netherlands
1573—William of Orange publicly professes the Reformed faith
1574—University of Leiden organized
1576—Pacification of Ghent
1579—Union of Utrecht
1581—Synod of Middelburg meets
  Repudiation of Philip II as sovereign of the united provinces of northern Netherlands
  Arminius appointed professor at Leiden
1584—William of Orange assassinated by Balthazar Gerard
1585—Leicester, as representative of Queen Elizabeth, becomes governor-general of the Netherlands
  University of Franeker founded
1586—Synod of the Hague meets
1591—Uytenbogaert becomes pastor of Walloon congregation at the Hague
1594—Gomarus appointed professor at Leiden
1598—Naval victory of the Dutch at Nieupoort
  First missionary efforts by the Reformed
1602—Organization of the Dutch East Indies Company
  Pestilence at Leiden
1607—Gouda Catechism written
1609—Twelve Years' Truce between Spain and the Netherlands
  Arminius dies
1610—Remonstrance drawn up
1611—Conference at the Hague
  Counter Remonstrance drawn up
1613—Conference at Delft
1614—Grotius prepares his "Resolution for Peace in the Churches"
1617—"Sharp Resolution" of Oldenbarnevelt passed by the States-General Prince Maurice chooses for the Reformed.
1618—Opening of the Synod of Dort (Nov. 13)
1619—States-General authorizes Synod to act as an ecclesiastical court to solve Arminian controversy (Jan. 1)
  Dismissal of the Arminians from the Synod (Jan. 14)
  Adoption of the Canons (April 23)
  Closing session of the Synod (May 29)

APPENDIX B – BIOGRAPHICAL NOTES

BEZA, Theodorus

Born 1519 at Vezelay, France; educated under Wolmar in law and literature. In 1548 he became Reformed, went to Geneva, and thereafter taught Greek at Lausanne. In the Servetus incident Beza defended Calvin and his doctrine of predestination in *De haereticis a civili magistratu puniendo* (1554). At Calvin's appointment he taught in the Academy at Geneva from 1558 until his death (1605) at the age of 85. Beza was deeply interested in the unity of all evangelicals, doing much to help the Waldensians in the Piedmont, the Reformed in France at Poissy (1561) and St. Germain (1561), and holding a colloquy with the Lutheran leader Andreae in 1585. Francis de Sales tried in vain to win back Beza to Rome in 1597. Beza is best remembered for his Greek New Testament and his *Life of Calvin*.

BOGERMAN, Johannes cf. chapter III, pp. 57–59

CASTELLIO, Sebastian

Born 1515 in the Savoy and became acquainted early with Calvin at Strasburg. For some years he served as rector of the school in Geneva, but when he called into question the doctrine of predestination and called the Song of Solomon "a spiritual song of adultery," he was compelled to leave in 1544. He blamed Calvin for the poverty that he suffered for some years in Basel before becoming professor of Greek there in 1553. During this period he attacked Calvin with bitterness. He died in 1563.

COORNHERT, Dirk Volkertszoon

Born at Amsterdam in 1522. Although he recognized the defects of Rome, he was equally antagonist to Lutherans, Anabaptists and especially Calvinists. As a well-educated humanist he opposed the doctrine of original sin, emphasized the "good life" as the essence of Christianity, held that man could prepare himself for salvation, and that one could be a Christian without attending church. His defense of liberty of conscience commended him to William of Orange. In 1572 he attacked Calvin and Beza on predestination, and thus prepared the ground for the Arminian controversy. He remained a Roman Catholic until his death in 1590. His signal contributions were in the field of Dutch language and literature.

DAMMANNUS, Sebastian

Born at Antwerp in 1578. After thorough education in Hebrew, Greek and theology, he became pastor at Zutphen in 1604. His influence in Gelderland and Utrecht during the Arminian struggle was unusually great, for which he was feared and hated by his opponents. With Hommius he served as clerk of the Synod of Dort. The *Acta Contracta* were prepared by him, and he was appointed one of the revisors of the translation of the New Testament. In 1638 he was imprisoned by the Spaniards and died at Zutphen in 1640.

DATHENUS, Petrus

Born at Mont-Cassel, Flanders, in 1531. Trained in a monastery in Ypres, he became Reformed in 1549 and the next year was compelled to flee to England where he associated closely with à Lasco, Delanus and Micron. In 1555 under Bloody Mary he again fled, this time to Frankfurt where he met Calvin. Lutheran opposition compelled him to leave for Frankenthal where he ministered to a growing congregation of Dutch refugees. Here he translated the Heidelberg Catechism and prepared the liturgy and Dutch Psalter for the churches. By 1565 he engaged in field preaching in southern Netherlands and became president of the Convent of Wesel (1568). Traveling repeatedly between the Palatinate and Holland, Flanders, and England, he often represented Elector Frederick of the Palatinate. His vehemence and lack of tact alienated many of the Reformed, including William of Orange. He died at Elbing, Prussia, in 1588.

DRUSIUS (Johannes van den Driesche)

Born at Oudenaarde, Flanders, in 1550. Studied theology and especially Greek at Louvain, London, and Cambridge. In 1572 became professor of Oriental languages and Greek at Oxford; in 1577 professor at Leiden; in 1585 professor at Franeker. So great was his renown in his field, that throughout Europe his services as well as his advice on Bible translations were repeatedly sought. In his last years some of his positions were attacked by Lubbertus. He died in 1616.

DUIFHUIS, Hubert

Born at Rotterdam in 1531. He served for years as Roman Catholic priest and fled when the Spanish soldiers devastated the land. By 1578 he settled in Utrecht, where with his congregation he claimed to have become Reformed. Duifhuis, however, refused to have the church organized with a consistory, which view was pleasing to the magistrates of the town, who were inclined to Erastian views. He opposed the doctrines of Calvin and Beza, and insisted on having no creed other than Scripture itself. He died in 1581.

EPISCOPIUS, Simon

Born at Amsterdam in 1583. After studying at Leiden and Franeker, he became pastor at Bleiswijk in 1610 by which time he openly espoused Arminius' views. As a Remonstrant he attended the Conference at the Hague (1611). His appointment to serve as professor at Leiden came the next year. When he refused to appear as theological advisor at the Synod, he was compelled to attend as one of the Remonstrants and served as their chief spokesman. His attitude and tactics soon rendered him and his party suspect in the eyes of the entire foreign delegation. After the Synod he fled to Antwerp where he organized the "Remonstrant Brotherhood." Returned to Rotterdam in 1625, helped organize the Remonstrant seminary, and served as professor until his death in 1643.

FAUKELIUS, Hermannus

Born at Bruges, Belgium, in 1560. Became pastor at Cologne in 1585 and in Middelburg in 1599, where he was soon recognized as an outstanding preacher and pastor. He served as a delegate to the Synod of Dort, was appointed as a translator of the New

Testament, and received the honor of having Synod take cognizance of his Compendium (1608), which has ever since been widely used in the Reformed churches. Faukelius died unexpectedly in 1625.

GOMARUS, Franciscus cf. chapter III, pp. 61–64

GROTIUS, Hugo (Huig de Groot)

Born at Delft as son of the mayor in 1583, Grotius was enrolled at Leiden when only 12 and entered a career in law at the court of Holland when 16. Grotius gained world-wide recognition in the field of international law by writing definitive works on the freedom of the seas and on the causes of war. Inspired by Erasmus and Coornhert, he espoused the Erastian views on church polity and early chose for Arminius. Because of political involvements he was imprisoned, only to escape. Thereafter he served Sweden as ambassador to France for ten years. He died in Rostock in 1645.

HOMMIUS, Festus

Born in 1576 at Jelsum in Friesland, he received an excellent education at Franeker, La Rochelle, and Leiden. In 1599 he became pastor at Dokkum and three years later at Leiden, where he taught homiletics and dogmatics. Known as an ardent opponent of unreformed views, he authored the Counter Remonstrance in 1611. In spite of his many gifts and recommendations, the curators refused to confirm him as professor. His popularity as a preacher was unexcelled in that time. Delegated to the Synod of Dort, he was elected first clerk and prepared the *Acta* and the *Libellus supplex*. Hommius died in 1642.

à LASCO, Johannes (Jan Laski, or Lasky)

Born in 1499 in Poland of a noble family, he prepared for a career in the Roman church. Was early influenced by the Reformation and felt strong kinship with Erasmus. Well educated and widely traveled (coming into contact with many Reformation leaders), he rejected an appointment as bishop in 1538 and was compelled to flee. For more than eight years he labored for the reformation of the church in East Friesland. Again an exile, he went to England and was befriended by Cranmer. Here he served the Reformed refugee congregation (Austin Friars) and wrote *Forma ac Ratio,* providing the church with a liturgy and church order. His large although indirect influence on the development of the Reformed churches in the Netherlands has been too long obscured. Forced to flee under Bloody Mary, he spent time on the Continent in exile and returned to Poland in 1556 which in those years appeared ripe for the Reformation. He died in 1560.

LUBBERTUS, Sibrandus cf. chapter III, pp. 64–66

LYDIUS, Balthazar

Born in 1577 at Umbstadt in the Palatinate, educated at Leiden, and became pastor at 's-Hertogenbosch (Bois le Duc) in 1602 and the next year in Dordrecht. Known as a zealous and popular preacher, his opposition to Arminius increased as his novel views were more fully expressed. Delegated to the Synod, he served on several committees, notably the one assigned to prepare suitable catechetical manuals for children, and also preached both the opening (Acts 15) and the closing (Isaiah 12:1–13) sermons for the Synod as pastor of the local church. He wrote on archeology and also a two volume work on the Waldenses (1616, 1617). Lydius died in 1629.

MACCOVIUS, Johannes (Makowsky)

Born in 1578 at Lobzenia, Poland, of a noble Reformed family, he studied at Danzig, Prague, Coblenz, Heidelberg, Marburg, Leipzig, Wittenberg, and Franeker. In 1615 he became professor at Franeker and drew, among others, many Polish and Magyar students. His ability, erudition, and popularity made him one of the greatest professors ever to teach at Franeker. As strong supralapsarian and champion of the scholastic method and ardent opponent of Socinians and Jesuits, he was involved in heated and even acrimonious debates. He died in 1644.

MARNIX OF ST. ALDEGONDE, Philip

Born in 1540 at Brussels, he became after 1561 a leading political, ecclesiastical and even theological leader in the Dutch churches. Was an intimate friend of William of Orange.

His literary gifts equaled those of Coornhert. He prepared a Dutch psalter, wrote the Dutch national anthem ("Wilhelmus van Nassau"), made preparations for the Convent of Wesel (1568), and was urged by the Synod of Emden (1571) to compile the history of the Reformation in the Netherlands. His *Bijencorf* (a satire on Roman Catholic theology) contains some of the finest early Dutch prose. Great difficulties with the States-General arose for him after 1586. He began with a new Dutch translation of the Bible, which project was cut short by his untimely death in 1599.

PISCATOR, Johannes

Born at Strasbourg in 1546, he served as professor with Olevianus at Herborn after 1577. His Bible translation, commentaries, and works on predestination, the Lord's Supper and justification (written especially against Bellarmine) won wide recognition for him among many of the Dutch Reformed. He died in 1625.

PLANCIUS, Petrus (Platevoet)

Born in 1552 at Dranoutre near Ypres, Flanders, he became Reformed pastor in 1576 after finishing his studies in Germany and England. He served the church at Brussels from 1578 to 1585, when he was compelled to flee because of the successes of the Duke of Parma. At Amsterdam he was welcomed with open arms and soon became the leading preacher. Here he vigorously opposed the Roman Catholics, who because of vigorous Jesuit activity were making headway, and also Arminius and his successors. Well versed in geography, navigation and astronomy, he encouraged Dutch commerce and became "the father of Dutch Reformed missions." Died in 1622.

RIVETUS, Andreas

Born in 1572 at St. Maixent (Poitou), France. Became a court preacher for the Duke of Thouars in 1572. Delegated by the French churches to attend the Synod of Dort, but prevented by political situation. Became professor at Leiden in 1620. Here he strongly opposed Grotius and Amyraut, whose unreformed theories had won a following. With other professors he wrote

Synopsis Purioris Theologiae (1625), the classic Reformed systematics of that time. Died at Breda in 1651.

ROLANDUS, Jacobus

Born in 1562 at Delft; served as Reformed pastor in Flanders, Frankenthal, and after 1604 in Amsterdam. Was present at the Conference at the Hague in 1611. Delegated to the Synod of Dort, he was chosen assessor and appointed as one of the translators of the New Testament. His son, Timothy, served as missionary. Rolandus died in 1632.

TRIGLANDIUS, Jacobus (Drie-eikels)

Born in 1583 at Vianen, he studied at Louvain and became Reformed about 1600. Ordained as pastor of Stolwijk in 1607, he went to Amsterdam in 1610 and soon was recognized as an ardent champion of Calvinism. He served the "secession" church at the Hague at the time when Prince Maurice chose for the Reformed versus the Arminians. Delegated to the Synod of Dort. Became professor at Leiden in 1634 and won renown for his detailed account of the Arminian controversy. Died at Leiden in 1654.

UTENHOVE, Jan

Born at Ghent in 1520. Because of persecution he fled to Germany in 1544, where he met Bucer, Peter Martyr, and other reformers. In 1548 he migrated to England, became well acquainted with Cranmer, and served as leading layman in the Dutch refugee congregation. His unusual linguistic abilities enabled him to provide the Reformed with translations of à Lasco's materials, as well as with versifications of some psalms and a Bible translation. Under Bloody Mary was compelled to flee, and spent some time in Lubeck and Poland. Returned to England in 1559 and died in London in 1565.

UYTENBOGAERT, Johannes cf. chapter III, pp. 66–68

VOETIUS, Gijsbertus cf. chapter III, pp. 68–69

VORSTIUS, Conrad cf. chapter III, pp. 69–71

WALAEUS, Anthonius

Born in 1583 at Ghent, he became Reformed pastor at Koudekerke in 1602, and was appointed as court preacher by Prince Maurice in 1604. In 1605 went to Middelburg until he was appointed professor at Leiden in 1611. He was delegated to the Synod of Dort and appointed to edit the final draft of the Canons. Also served as one of the authors of *Synopsis Purioris Theologiae*. Died at Leiden in 1639.

ZANCHIUS, Jerome

Born in 1516 at Alzano, Italy. While a monk in Lucca, he was influenced by the writings of Bullinger and Calvin. Forced to leave Italy for the faith, he came to Strasbourg where he taught. Returned as preacher to Chiavara, Italy, from 1567 to 1568. From 1568 to 1576 he taught systematics at Heidelberg, and thereafter until his death at Neustadt with Ursinus. His writings had wide influence among the Dutch. He died in 1590.

APPENDIX C – THE REMONSTRANCE OF 1610

By the time of Arminius's death in 1609 two parties had appeared within the Reformed churches. On January 14, 1610, more than forty who championed the views of Arminius met in the city of Gouda under the leadership of Uytenbogaert. Here they subscribed to the "Remonstrance," a petition to be forwarded to the political authorities in which their case was set forth and defended. The document begins by complaining how they had been falsely accused by the opposition. Thereafter it posits a view of church government that recognizes the authority of the State in ecclesiastical matters, proceeding then to describe the views of their Calvinist opponents which, according to the Remonstrants, differed radically from both Scripture and the creeds. These accusations provide the background against which the Remonstrants presented their convictions in a series of five articles. Hence the title often ascribed to the material, Articuli Arminiani sive Remonstrantia (The Five Arminian Articles). The ensuing discussions and debates, including the Canons of Dort drawn up by the Synod, follow the same pattern.

This material can be found in J. Uytenbogaert: Kerckl, Historie, fol. 524a–529a; J. Triglandius: *Kerckelijke geschiedenissen*, fol. 522a–535b; Bakhuizen vanden Brink et al.: *Documenta Reformatoria*, vol. I, pp. 290–293. An English translation, together with the Dutch and Latin versions, appears in Philip Schaff: *Creeds of Christendom*, vol. III, pp. 545–549.

In order that your Worships may know what the Remonstrants believe and teach concerning these same matters, we declare that our opinion on this is as follows:

1. That God by an eternal and immutable decree has in Jesus Christ his Son determined before the foundation of the world to save out of the fallen sinful human race those in Christ, for Christ's sake, and through Christ who by the grace of the Holy Spirit

shall believe in this his Son Jesus Christ and persevere in this faith and obedience of faith to the end; and on the other hand to leave the incorrigible and unbelieving in sin and under wrath and condemn (them) as alienate from Christ—according to the word of the holy gospel in John 3:36, 'He that believeth on the Son hath eternal life, and whosoever is disobedient to the Son shall not see life, but the wrath of God abideth on him,' and also other passages of the Scriptures.

2. That in agreement with this Jesus Christ the Savior of the world died for all men and for every man, so that he merited reconciliation and forgiveness of sins for all through the death of the cross; yet so that no one actually enjoys this forgiveness of sins except the believer—also according to the word of the gospel of John 3:16, 'God so loved the world that he gave his only-begotten Son that whosoever believeth in him shall not perish but have eternal life.' And in the first epistle of John 2:2, 'He is the propitiation for our sins; and not only for ours, but also for the sins of the whole world.'

3. That man does not have saving faith of himself nor by the power of his own free will, since he in the state of apostasy and sin cannot of and through himself think, will or do any good which is truly good (such as is especially saving faith); but that it is necessary that he be regenerated by God, in Christ, through his Holy Spirit, and renewed in understanding, affections or will, and all powers, in order that he may rightly understand, meditate upon, will, and perform that which is truly good, according to the word of Christ, John 13:5, 'Without me ye can do nothing.'

4. That this grace of God is the commencement, progression, and completion of all good, also in so far that regenerate man cannot, apart from this prevenient or assisting, awakening, consequent and cooperating grace, think, will or do the good or resist

any temptations to evil; so that all good works or activities which can be conceived must be ascribed to the grace of God in Christ. But with respect to the mode of this grace, it is not irresistible, since it is written concerning many that they resisted the Holy Spirit. Acts 7 and elsewhere in many places.

5. That those who are incorporated into Jesus Christ and thereby become partakers of his life-giving Spirit have abundant strength to strive against Satan, sin, the world, and their own flesh and to obtain the victory; it being well understood (that this is) through the assistance of the grace of the Holy Spirit, and that Jesus Christ assists them through his Spirit in all temptations, extends the hand, and—if only they are prepared for warfare and desire his help and are not negligent—keeps them standing, so that by no cunning or power of Satan can they be led astray or plucked out of Christ's hands, according to the word of Christ, John 10, 'No one shall pluck them out of my hands.' But whether they can through negligence fall away from the first principle of their life in Christ, again embrace the present world, depart from the pure doctrine once given to them, lose the good conscience, and neglect grace, must first be more carefully determined from the Holy Scriptures before we shall be able to teach this with the full persuasion of our heart.

These articles here set forth and taught the Remonstrants hold to be conformable to God's Word, edifying, and with respect to this matter sufficient unto salvation, so that it is neither necessary nor edifying to rise higher or to descend more deeply.

APPENDIX D –
THE COUNTER REMONSTRANCE OF 1611

Immediately after the Remonstrants held their conference in Gouda, Uytenbogaert as the leader presented the Remonstrance to van Oldenbarnevelt, in order that he might submit it officially to the States-General. This statesman, however, decided to withhold it from public presentation for a period of several months. Meanwhile Uytenbogaert published a treatise arguing the right of the political authorities to determine matters of doctrine for the Reformed churches. The States of Holland, determined to prevent the convening of particular synods, forwarded to the classes a copy of the five articles with their judgment that these might not be regarded as contrary to the creeds, and insisted that preachers desist from discussing these matters and tolerate each other's opinions.

On December 10 six deputies of the classes, under the leadership of Plancius, appealed to the political authorities and stated that they were prepared at any time to demonstrate to a properly constituted synodical assembly that the five articles of the Remonstrants were contrary to both Scripture and the creeds. Instead of convening a particular synod, the States of Holland arranged for a conference between six Arminians, led by Uytenbogaert, and six Calvinists, led by Plancius. The conference was scheduled for March 10, 1611, and continued until May 20. Permission was given each party to present only two written documents: the Counter Remonstrants one in refutation of the five Arminian articles and another in refutation of the objections which the Remonstrants would raise against the Calvinist position submitted to the conference; the Remonstrants one in defense of their own position and another in refutation of the Calvinist position outlined by said members of the conference. The proceedings of this conference were published in a sizable volume of 440 pages the next year.

In their Counter Remonstrance, the first document presented to the conference, the Calvinists responded to the charge of the Arminians that they were being continually slandered. Again the plea is made that this matter be submitted for adjudication to a properly constituted synod. Open disapproval is expressed of the Arminian tactic of presenting the doctrinal issues to the political authorities without having submitted them to consistories and classes. Then follows the Counter Remonstrance proper in the form of seven articles on the controverted points.

> This material can be found in *Schriftelicke Conferentie, gehouden in 'sGravenhaghe inden Jare 1611*, pp. 13–29; J. Triglandius: *Kerckelijke geschiedenissen*, fol 545a–552a; and Bakhuizen vanden Brink et al: *Documenta Reformatoria*, vol I, pp. 293–300.

With respect to the points of doctrine, when they present certain teachings which they claim are carried to extremes by us, we cannot find therein that they have dealt honestly and in good faith, since they begin with the profound point of predestination, concerning which we endeavor to speak with restraint and caution, solely for the sake of demonstrating God's undeserved grace and removing all human merits and worth. They ascribe to us such things to which we have never thought to consent, much less to teach. The articles wherein they claim that their opinion is set forth are stated in an ambiguous and dubious manner of speaking; in part they conflict with God's Word. In our churches the preaching is as follows:

> 1. As in Adam the whole human race, created in the image of God, has with Adam fallen into sin and thus become so corrupt that all men are conceived and born in sin and thus are by nature children of wrath, lying dead in their trespasses so that there is within them no more power to convert themselves truly unto God and to believe in Christ than a corpse has power to raise itself from the dead; so God draws out of this condemnation and delivers a certain number of men who in his eternal and immutable counsel he has chosen out of mere grace, according to the good pleasure of his will, unto salvation in Christ, passing by the others in his just judgment and leaving them in their sins.

Appendix D – The Counter Remonstrance of 1611

2. That not only adults who believe in Christ and accordingly walk worthy of the gospel are to be reckoned as God's elect children, but also the children of the covenant so long as they do not in their conduct manifest the contrary; and that therefore believing parents, when their children die in infancy, have no reason to doubt the salvation of these their children.

3. That God in his election has not looked to the faith or conversion of his elect, nor to the right use of his gifts, as the grounds of election; but that on the contrary he in his eternal and immutable counsel has purposed and decreed to bestow faith and perseverance in godliness and thus to save those whom he according to his good pleasure has chosen to salvation.

4. That to this end he has first of all presented and given to them his only-begotten Son Jesus Christ, whom he delivered up to the death of the cross in order to save his elect, so that, although the suffering of Christ as that of the only-begotten and unique Son of God is sufficient unto the atonement of the sins of all men, nevertheless the same, according to the counsel and decree of God, has its efficacy unto reconciliation and forgiveness of sins only in the elect and true believer.

5. That furthermore to the same end God the Lord has his holy gospel preached, and that the Holy Spirit externally through the preaching of that same gospel and internally through a special grace works so powerfully in the hearts of God's elect, that he illumines their minds, transforms and renews their wills, removing the heart of stone and giving them a heart of flesh, in such a manner that by these means they not only receive power to convert themselves and believe but also actually and willingly do repent and believe.

6. That those whom God has decreed to save are not only once so enlightened, regenerated and renewed in order to believe in Christ and convert themselves to God, but that they by the same power of the Holy Spirit by which they were converted to God without any

contribution of themselves are in like manner continually supported and preserved; so that, although many weaknesses of the flesh cleave to them as long as they are in this life and are engaged in a continual struggle between flesh and Spirit and also sometimes fall into grievous sins, nevertheless this same Spirit prevails in this struggle, not permitting that God's elect by the corruption of the flesh should so resist the Spirit of sanctification that this would at any time be extinguished in them, and that in consequence they could completely or finally lose the true faith which was once bestowed on them and the Spirit of adoption as God's children which they had once received.

7. That nevertheless the true believers find no excuse in this teaching to pursue carelessly the lusts of the flesh, since it is impossible that those who by a true faith are ingrafted into Christ should not produce the fruits of thankfulness; but on the contrary the more they assure themselves and feel that God works in them both to will and to do according to his good pleasure, the more they persist in working their own salvation with fear and trembling, since they know that this is the only means by which it pleases God to keep them standing and to bring them to salvation. For this reason he also employs in his Word all manner of warnings and threatenings, not in order to cause them to despair or doubt their salvation, but rather to awaken in them a childlike fear by observing the weakness of their flesh in which they would surely perish, unless the Lord keep them standing in his undeserved grace, which is the sole cause and ground of their perseverance; so that, although he warns them in his Word to watch and pray, they nevertheless do not have this of themselves that they desire God's help and lack nothing, but only from the same Spirit who by a special grace prepares them for this and thus also powerfully keeps them standing.

APPENDIX E –
POLITICAL COMMISSIONERS ASSIGNED BY THE STATES-GENERAL

The States-General of the United Republic of the Netherlands consented to and arranged for the convening of the Synod of Dort. It delegated a number of representatives to supervise the proceedings and report to it on behalf of the assembly. The credentials and instructions of the following were received and formally read by the Rev. Balthazar Lydius, pastor of the church of Dordrecht, at the first session of Synod, held on Tuesday morning, November 13, 1618:

From the *States of Gelderland*
Martinus Gregorius—doctor of law; chief justice of the provincial Court
Henricus van Essen—justice of the provincial Court

From the *States of Holland and West-Friesland*
Walraven van Brederode—baron of Vianen and Ameide, lord of Noordeloos, viscount of Utrecht, etc.
Hugo Muys van Holij—knight; sheriff of Dordrecht; bailiff of the lands of Strijen; mayor of the city of Dordrecht
Jacob Boelens—mayor of Amsterdam
Geraert Janszoon van Nyenburg—mayor of Alkmaar
Rochum vanden Honert—chief justice of the High Court of Holland, Zeeland, and West Friesland; curator of the academy of Leiden Nicolas Cromhout—lord of Werkendam; presiding justice of the Court

From the *States of Zeeland*
Simon Schotte—doctor of law; secretary of the city of Middelburg
Jacobus van Campen—doctor of law; member of the States of Zeeland

From the *States of Utrecht*
Frederick van Zuylen van Nyevelt—lord of Aartsbergen, Berkenwoude, etc.
Willem van Hartevelt—mayor of Amersfoort

From the *States of Friesland*
Ernst van Aylva—member of the states of Friesland; chief officer ("grietman") of Oost-Dongeradeel
Ernst van Harinxma a Donia thoe Sloten—chief justice of the provincial Court; chief officer ("grietman") of Leeuwarderadeel

From the *States of Overijssel*
Henricus Hagen—nobleman of Vollenhove
Johannes van Hemert—mayor of Deventer

From the *States of Groningen en Ommelanden*
Hieronymus Ysbrants—doctor of law; syndic of Groningen
Edzard Jacobs Clant—lord of Ezinge and Landeweer

The Political Commissioners appointed as their secretary Prof. Dr. Daniel Heinsius of Leiden. Jacob Corneliszoon de Witt, of Dordrecht, served as treasurer. All expenses, also for the foreign delegations, were paid by the States-General.

APPENDIX F – DELEGATES TO THE SYNOD OF DORT

This list is taken from *Acta ofte Handelinghe des Nationalen Synodi . . . tot Dordrecht, Anno 1618 ende 1619* printed at Dordrecht by Isaack Jansz. Canin (1621) "Met Privilegie der H.M. Heeren Staten Generael." Names of cities and provinces have been slightly altered to conform with modern use.

The following credentials were presented at the second session of Synod, held on Wednesday morning, November 14, 1618:

From *Gelderland*
  Wilhelmus Stephani—minister of Arnhem, doctor of theology
  Eilhardus van Mehen—minister of Harderwyk
  Sebastianus Dammannus—minister of Zutphen
  Johannes Boulietus—minister of Warnsveld
  Jacobus Verheyden—elder of Nijmegen, rector of the school
  Henricus van Hel—elder of Zutphen, mayor of the city

From *South Holland*
  Balthazar Lydius—minister of Dordrecht
  Henricus Arnoldi—minister of Delft
  Festus Hommius—minister of Leiden
  Gisbertus Voetius—minister of Heusden
  Arnoldus Muys van Holij—elder of Dordrecht, bailiff of South Holland
  Johannes Latius—elder of Leiden

From *North Holland*
  Jacobus Rolandus—minister of Amsterdam
  Jacobus Triglandius—minister of Amsterdam
  Abrahamus van Doreslaer—minister of Enkhuizen
  Samuel Bartholdus—minister of Monnikendam
  Theodorus Heyngius—elder of Amsterdam
  Dominicus van Heemskerc—elder of Amsterdam, doctor of law

From *Zeeland*
   Hermannus Faukelius—minister of Middelburg
   Godefridus Udemans—minister of Zierikzee
   Cornelius Regius—minister of Goes
   Lambertus de Rijcke—minister of Bergen-op-Zoom
   Josias Vosbergen—elder of Middelburg, doctor of law
   Adrianus Hofferus—elder of Zierikzee, member of the city council

From *Utrecht*
   (delegated by churches holding the Counter Remonstrant position)
   Johannes Ibbetzius—minister of Dordrecht, but delegated by the provincial Synod of Utrecht
   Arnoldus Oortcampius—minister of Amersfoort
   Lambertus Canterus—elder of Utrecht, member of the city council
   (delegated by churches holding the Remonstrant position)
   Isaacus Frederici—minister of Utrecht
   Samuel Naeranus—minister of Amersfoort
   Stephanus van Helsdingen—elder of Utrecht, doctor of law and member of the Provincial Court

From *Friesland*
   Johannes Bogermannus—minister of Leeuwarden
   Florentius Ioannis—minister of Sneek
   Philippus Dannielis F. Eilshemius—minister of Harlingen
   Meinardus ab Idzerda—elder of Leeuwarden, member of the States of Friesland
   Kempo van Harinxma van Donia—elder of Leeuwarden, member of the Provincial Court
   Johannes vander Sande—elder of Leeuwarden, doctor of law and member of the Provincial Court

From *Overijssel*
   Casparus Sibelius—minister of Deventer
   Hermannus Wiferdingius—minister of Zwolle
   Hieronymus Vogelius—minister of Hasselt, serving for a time the church at Kampen
   Johannes Langius—minister of Vollenhove
   Guilielmus van Broeckhuyzen—elder of Zwolle
   Johannes van Lauwick—elder of Kampen, mayor of the city

Appendix F – Delegates to the Synod of Dort

From *Groningen*
  Cornelius Hillenius—minister of Groningen
  Georgius Placius—minister of Appingedam
  Wolfgangus Agricola—minister of Bedum
  Johannes Lolingius—minister of Noordbroek
  Egbertus Halbes—elder of Groningen
  Johannes Ruffelaert—elder of Stedum

From *Drenthe*
  Themo van Asscheburge—minister of Meppel
  Patroclus Rommelingius—minister of Ruinen

From the *Walloon churches*
  Daniel Colonius—minister of Leiden, regent of the Walloon college in that city
  Johannes de la Croix—minister of Haarlem
  Johannes Doucher—minister of Vlissingen (Flushing)
  Jeremias de Pours—minister of Middelburg
  Everardus Becker—elder of Middelburg
  Petrus du Pont—elder of Amsterdam

Professors of Theology
  Johannes Polyander—doctor of theology and professor at Leiden; delegated by the States of Holland and West-Friesland
  Franciscus Gomarus—doctor of theology and professor at Groningen; delegated by the States of Groningen en Ommelanden
  Anthonius Thysius—professor at Harderwyk; delegated by the States of Gelderland and the duchy of Zutphen
  Antonius Walaeus—minister of Middelburg and professor in the academy in that city; delegated by the States of Zeeland
  The following credentials were presented at the third session of Synod, held on Wednesday afternoon, November 14, 1618

Delegated as representatives of the church in *Great Britain* by James I
  George Carleton—bishop of Llandaff
  Josephus Hall—doctor of theology; dean of Winchester
  Johannes Davenantius—doctor of theology; professor at Cambridge

Samuel Wardus—doctor of theology; archdean of Taunton and regent of Sidney College at Cambridge

Delegated by the Elector of *the Palatinate*
Abrahamus Scultetus—doctor of theology; professor at Heidelberg and court preacher
Paulus Tossanus—doctor of theology; member of the Consistory of the lower Palatinate
Henricus Altingius—doctor of theology; professor at Heidelberg and regent of the Collegia Sapientiae

Delegated by the Landgrave of *Hesse*
Georgius Cruciger—doctor of theology; professor and rector of the Academy of Marburg
Paulus Steinius—court preacher; professor of Theology in the College of the Brethren at Cassel
Daniel Angelocrator—minister of Marburg; superintendent of the churches along the Laen and Eder rivers
Rudolphus Goclenus the Elder—dean and professor of Philosophy in the Academy of Marburg

Delegated by the four Reformed republics of *Switzerland*
Johannes Jacobus Breytingerus—minister of Zürich
Marcus Rutimeyerus—minister of Berne; doctor of theology
Sebastianus Beckius—doctor of theology; professor of New Testament at Basel and dean of the theological faculty
Wolfgangus Meyerus—minister of Basel; doctor of theology
Johannes Conradus Kochius—minister of Schaffhausen

Delegated by the republic and churches of *Geneva*
Johannes Deodatus—minister of Geneva; professor of theology
Theodorus Trochinus—minister of Geneva; professor of theology

Delegated by the republic and churches of *Bremen*
Matthias Martinius—rector and professor of the Illustrious School
Henricus Isselburgius—minister of the church of the Virgin Mary; doctor of theology and professor of New Testament
Ludovicus Crocius—minister of the church of St. Martin; doctor of theology and professor of Old Testament and Philosophy

Delegated by the republic and church of *Emden*
  Daniel Barnhardus Eilshemius—oldest minister of Emden
  Ritzius Lucas Grimershemius—minister of Emden

The Synod of the Reformed churches of France, meeting in Cevennes, had delegated the following to be its representatives at the Synod of Dort:
  Pierre Dumoulin—minister of Paris
  Andre Rivet—minister of Thouars
  Jean Chauve—minister of Sommieres
  Daniel Chamier.

On October 2, 1618, notice was received that the king refused to grant permission to these men to leave the country. Later efforts to persuade him failed. Hence the seats allotted to the French delegation were not filled.

The following credentials were presented at the thirty fourth session of Synod, held on Monday morning, December 17, 1618.

Delegated by Duke John of Nassau for the churches of *Nassau-Wetteravia*
  Johannes Bisterveldius—court preacher; superintendent at Siegen
  Johannes Alstedius—professor of theology at Herborn (Bisterveldius passed away at Dordrecht on March 11, 1619, and his seat was taken by Georgius Fabricius—minister of Windeck.)
  Margrave Georg Wilhelm had also delegated two men to represent the Reformed churches of Brandenburg, who were prevented from attending because of intense Lutheran opposition. The two appointed were:
  Johannes Bergius—professor at Frankfurt-on-the-Oder
  Christoph Storch (also called: Pelargus)

APPENDIX G –
REMONSTRANTS CITED TO APPEAR AT SYNOD

One of the chief issues facing the opening sessions of Synod was how to deal with the Remonstrants both fairly and definitively. It was well known to all the delegates that many in the churches leaned towards the Remonstrant position. What both the Political Commissioners and the accredited delegates of the churches in the several provinces sought to avoid was the appearance of a delegation selected in some unofficial assembly of Remonstrant pastors. This would have given the impression that the Reformed churches in official synodical session would countenance and deal with what would appear to be a counter-synod. Hence at the fifth session of Synod, held on Friday morning. November 16, 1618, the Political Commissioners together with the officers of Synod decided with the approval of the entire assembly to call in the following Remonstrants who were to present themselves within two weeks:

From *Gelderland*
    Henricus Leonem—minister of Bommel
    Bernerus Vezekius—minister of Echteld
    Henricus Hollingerus—minister of Grave

From *South Holland*
    Simon Episcopius—professor at Leiden
    Johannes Arnoldi Corvinus—minister of Leiden
    Bernardus Dwinglo—minister of Leiden
    Eduardus Poppius—minister of Gouda
    Nicolas Grevinckhoven*—minister of Rotterdam
    Theophilus Rijckewaert—minister of Brielle

From *North Holland*
    Johannes Geesteranus*—minister of Alkmaar
    Dominicus Sapma—minister of Hoorn

From *Overijssel*
  Thomas Goswinus—minister of Kampen
  Assuerus Matthysius—minister of Kampen
From the *Walloon churches*
  Carolus Niellius—minister of Utrecht
  Simon Goulart—minister of Amsterdam

*Because Grevinckhoven and Geesteranus had been deposed from the ministry, they were not cited to appear in the assembly. Instead, a place was given to Philippus Pijnacker as minister of Alkmaar.

APPENDIX H – THE OPINIONS OF THE REMONSTRANTS

Only with difficulty did the Synod obtain from the Remonstrants, who had been charged by the political authorities to appear before Synod, a statement of their convictions on the points in dispute. After appearing a day later than scheduled and holding conferences among themselves, they presented their opinions on the first article at the 31st session, on December 13, and on the other articles at the 34th session, on December 17. The *Sententia* are essential to a proper understanding and evaluation of the Canons, since at many points the latter are so phrased as to show clearly wherein the Synod was convinced that the Remonstrants erred.

The Latin edition of this material can be found in *Acta Synodi Nationalis, pp.* 113, 116–118; in Bakhuizen vanden Brink: *De Nederlandsche Belijdenisgeschriften, pp.* 283–288; and the Dutch edition in *Acta ofte Handelinghen des Nationalen Synodi* (ed. Canin, 1621), pp. 138–139; 152–158. For the translation provided here we are indebted to Dr. Anthony A. Hoekema, professor of Systematic Theology at Calvin Theological Seminary.

A. The Opinion of the Remonstrants regarding the first article, dealing with the decree of Predestination.

1. God has not decided to elect anyone to eternal life, or to reject anyone from the same, prior to the decree to create him, without any consideration of preceding obedience or disobedience, according to his good pleasure, for the demonstration of the glory of his mercy and justice, or of his absolute power and dominion.

2. Since the decree of God concerning both the salvation and perdition of each man is not a decree of the end absolutely intended, it follows that neither are such means subordinated to that same decree by which the elect and the reprobate are efficaciously and inevitably led to their final destination.

3. Therefore God has not with this plan created in the one Adam all men in a state of rectitude, has not ordained the fall and the permission of it, has not withdrawn from Adam the grace which was necessary and sufficient, has not brought it about that the Gospel is preached and that men are externally called, does not confer on them any gifts of the Holy Spirit by means of which he leads some of them to life, but deprives others of the benefit of life. Christ, the Mediator, is not solely the executor of election, but also the foundation of that same decree of election: the reason why some are efficaciously called, justified, persevere in faith, and are glorified is not that they have been absolutely elected to eternal life. That others are left in the fall, that Christ is not given to them, that they are either not called at all or not efficaciously called—these are not the reasons why they are absolutely rejected from eternal salvation.

4. God has not decreed to leave the greatest part of men in the fall, excluded from every hope of salvation, apart from intervening actual sins.

5. God has ordained that Christ should be a propitiation for the sins of the whole world, and by virtue of that decree he has determined to justify and to save those who believe in him, and to provide for men means necessary and sufficient for faith in such a way as he knows to be in harmony with his wisdom and justice. But he has by no means determined, by virtue of an absolute decree, to give Christ the Mediator solely to the elect, and through an efficacious calling to bestow faith upon, justify, preserve in the faith, and glorify them alone.

6. No one is rejected from life eternal nor from the means sufficient for it by an absolute antecedent decree, so that the merit of Christ, calling, and all the gifts of the Spirit can be profitable to salvation for all, and truly are, unless they themselves by the abuse of these gifts pervert them to their own perdition; but to unbelief, to impiety, and to sins, as means and causes of damnation, no one is predestined.

7. The election of particular persons is decisive, out of consideration of faith in Jesus Christ and of perseverance; not, however, apart from a consideration of faith and perseverance in the true faith, as a condition prerequisite for electing.

8. Rejection from eternal life is made on the basis of a consideration of antecedent unbelief and perseverance in unbelief; not, however, apart from a consideration of antecedent unbelief and perseverance in unbelief.

9. All the children of believers are sanctified in Christ, so that no one of them who leaves this life before the use of reason will perish. By no means, however, are to be considered among the number of the reprobate certain children of believers who leave this life in infancy before they have committed any actual sin in their own persons, so that neither the holy bath of baptism nor the prayers of the church for them can in any way be profitable for their salvation.

10. No children of believers who have been baptized in the name of the Father, the Son, and the Holy Spirit, living in the state of infancy, are reckoned among the reprobate by an absolute decree.

B. The Opinion of the Remonstrants regarding the second article, which deals with the universality of the merit of the death of Christ.

1. The price of the redemption which Christ offered to God the Father is not only in itself and by itself sufficient for the redemption of the whole human race but has also been paid for all men and for every man, according to the decree, will, and grace of God the Father; therefore no one is absolutely excluded from participation in the fruits of Christ's death by an absolute and antecedent decree of God.

2. Christ has, by the merit of his death, so reconciled God the Father to the whole human race that the Father, on account of that merit, without giving up his righteousness and truth, has been able and has willed to make and confirm a new covenant of grace with sinners and men liable to damnation.

3. Though Christ has merited reconciliation with God and remission of sins for all men and for every man, yet no one, according to the pact of the new and gracious covenant, becomes a true partaker of the benefits obtained by the death of Christ in any other way than by faith; nor are sins forgiven to sinning men before they actually and truly believe in Christ.

4. Only those are obliged to believe that Christ died for them for whom Christ has died. The reprobates, however, as they are called, for whom Christ has not died, are not obligated to such faith, nor can they be justly condemned on account of the contrary refusal to believe this. In fact, if there should be such reprobates, they would be obliged to believe that Christ has not died for them.

C. The Opinion of the Remonstrants regarding the third and fourth articles, concerning the grace of God and the conversion of man.

1. Man does not have saving faith of himself, nor out of the powers of his free will, since in the state of sin he is able of himself and by himself neither to think, will, or do any good (which would indeed be saving good, the most prominent of which is saving faith). It is necessary therefore that by God in Christ through his Holy Spirit he be regenerated and renewed in intellect, affections, will, and in all his powers, so that he might be able to understand, reflect upon, will and carry out the good things which pertain to salvation.

2. We hold, however, that the grace of God is not only the beginning but also the progression and the completion of every good, so much so that even the regenerate himself is unable to think, will, or do the good, or to resist any temptations to evil, apart from that preceding or prevenient, awakening, following and cooperating grace. Hence all good works and actions which anyone by cogitation is able to comprehend are to be ascribed to the grace of God.

3. Yet we do not believe that all zeal, care, and diligence applied to the obtaining of salvation before faith itself and the Spirit of renewal are vain and ineffectual—indeed,

rather harmful to man than useful and fruitful. On the contrary, we hold that to hear the Word of God, to be sorry for sins committed, to desire saving grace and the Spirit of renewal (none of which things man is able to do without grace) are not only not harmful and useless, but rather most useful and most necessary for the obtaining of faith and of the Spirit of renewal.

4. The will in the fallen state, before calling, does not have the power and the freedom to will any saving good. And therefore we deny that the freedom to will saving good as well as evil is present to the will in every state.

5. The efficacious grace by which anyone is converted is not irresistible; and though God so influences the will by the Word and the internal operation of his Spirit that he both confers the strength to believe or supernatural powers, and actually causes man to believe—yet man is able of himself to despise that grace and not to believe, and therefore to perish through his own fault.

6. Although according to the most free will of God the disparity of divine grace is very great, nevertheless the Holy Spirit confers, or is ready to confer, as much grace to all men and to each man to whom the Word of God is preached as is sufficient for promoting the conversion of men in its steps. Therefore sufficient grace for faith and conversion falls to the lot not only of those whom God is said to will to save according to the decree of absolute election, but also of those who are not actually converted.

7. Man is able through the grace of the Holy Spirit to do more good than he actually does, and to avoid more evil than he actually avoids; and we do not believe that God simply does not will that man should do more good than he does and avoid more evil than he does avoid, and that God has decreed precisely from eternity that both should so happen.

8. Whomever God calls to salvation, he calls seriously, that is, with a sincere and completely unhypocritical intention and will to save; nor do we assent to the opinion of those

who hold that God calls certain ones externally whom he does not will to call internally, that is, as truly converted, even before the grace of calling has been rejected.

9. There is not in God a secret will which so contradicts the will of the same revealed in the Word that according to it (that is, the secret will) he does not will the conversion and salvation of the greatest part of those whom he seriously calls and invites by the Word of the Gospel and by his revealed will; and we do not here, as some say, acknowledge in God a holy simulation, or a double person.

10. Nor do we believe that God calls the reprobate, as they are called, to these ends: that he should the more harden them, or take away excuse, or punish them the more severely, or display their inability; nor, however, that they should be converted, should believe, and should be saved.

11. It is not true that all things, not only good but also bad, necessarily occur, from the power and efficacy of the secret will or decree of God, and that indeed those who sin, out of consideration of the decree of God, are not able to sin; that God wills to determine and to bring about the sins of men, their insane, foolish, and cruel works, and the sacrilegious blasphemy of his name—in fact, to move the tongues of men to blasphemy, and so on.

13. To us the following is false and horrible: that God impels men to sins which he openly prohibits; that those who sin do not act contrary to the will of God properly named; that what is unrighteous (that is, what is contrary to his precept) is in agreement with the will of God; indeed, that it is truly a capital crime to do the will of God.

D. The Opinion of the Remonstrants with respect to the fifth article, which concerns Perseverance.

1. The perseverance of believers in the faith is not an effect of that absolute decree by which God is said to have chosen singular persons defined by no condition of obedience.

2. God provides true believers with as much grace and supernatural powers as he judges, according to his

infinite wisdom, to be sufficient for persevering and for overcoming the temptations of the devil, the flesh, and the world; it is never to be charged to God's account that they do not persevere.

3. True believers can fall from true faith and can fall into such sins as cannot be consistent with true and justifying faith; not only is it possible for this to happen, but it even happens frequently.

4. True believers are able to fall through their own fault into shameful and atrocious deeds, to persevere and to die in them; and therefore finally to fall and to perish.

5. Nevertheless we do not believe that true believers, though they may sometimes fall into grave sins which are vexing to their consciences, immediately fall out of every hope of repentance; but we acknowledge that it can happen that God, according to the multitude of his mercies, may recall them through his grace to repentance; in fact, we believe that this happens not infrequently, although we cannot be persuaded that this will certainly and indubitably happen.

6. The following dogmas, therefore, which by public writings are being scattered among the people, we reject with our whole mind and heart as harmful to piety and good morals: namely, (1) True believers are not able to sin deliberately, but only out of ignorance and weakness. (2) True believers through no sins can fall out of the grace of God. (3) A thousand sins, even all the sins of the whole world, are not able to render election invalid . . . (4) To believers and to the elect no sins, however great and grave they can be, are imputed; but all present and future sins have already been remitted. (5) True believers, having fallen into destructive heresies, into grave and most atrocious sins, like adultery and homicide, on account of which the church, after the justification of Christ, is compelled to testify that it is not able to tolerate them in its external communion and that they will have no part in the kingdom of Christ unless they are converted, nevertheless are not able to fall from faith totally and finally.

7. A true believer, as for the present time he can be certain about his faith and the integrity of his conscience, and thus also concerning his salvation and the saving benevolence of God toward him, for that time can be and ought to be certain; and on this point we reject the pontifical opinion.

8. A true believer can and ought indeed to be certain for the future that he is able, by diligent watchfulness, through prayers, and through other holy exercises, to persevere in true faith, and he ought also to be certain that divine grace for persevering will never be lacking; but we do not see how he can be certain that he will never afterwards be remiss in his duty but that he will persevere in faith and in those works of piety and love which are fitting for a believer in this school of Christian warfare; neither do we deem it necessary that concerning this thing a believer should be certain.

APPENDIX I –
THE CANONS OF DORT

On April 22, 1619, the Synod had adopted the Canons as setting forth the faith of the Reformed churches on the points of doctrine in dispute. The document was read in presence of all the delegates, including those from the foreign churches, and thereupon subscribed by them without any exception. This official document was thereupon forwarded to the States-General, which granted its approbation and ordered that it should be solemnly and publicly published on Monday, May 6. Although the Latin edition is the original, Synod itself provided for and approved translations into Dutch and French, so that these may likewise be regarded as official. The Latin edition may be found in Philip Schaff: *Creeds of Christendom,* vol. III, pp. 550–577, to which is appended the text without the Rejection of Errors as adopted by the Reformed Church in America, pp. 581–597. Here follows the official text adopted by the Christian Reformed Church as found in the Psalter-Hymnal, 1976 edition, pp. 92–116.

FIRST HEAD OF DOCTRINE –
Divine Election and Reprobation

ARTICLE 1

As all men have sinned in Adam, lie under the curse, and are deserving of eternal death, God would have done no injustice by leaving them all to perish and delivering them over to condemnation on account of sin, according to the words of the apostle: *That every mouth may be stopped, and all the world may be brought under the judgment of God* (Rom. 3:19). And: *For all have sinned, and fall short of the glory of God* (Rom. 3:23). And: *For the wages of sin is death* (Rom. 6:23).

ARTICLE 2
But in this the love of God was manifested, that he *sent his only begotten Son into the world, that whosoever believeth on him should not perish, but have eternal life* (1 John 4:9; John 3:16).

ARTICLE 3
And that men may be brought to believe, God mercifully sends the messengers of these most joyful tidings to whom he will and at what time he pleases; by whose ministry men are called to repentance and faith in Christ crucified. *How then shall they call on him in whom they have not believed? And how shall they believe in him whom they have not heard? And how shall they hear without a preacher? And how shall they preach except they be sent?* (Rom. 10:14, 15).

ARTICLE 4
The wrath of God abides upon those who believe not this gospel. But such as receive it and embrace Jesus the Savior by a true and living faith are by him delivered from the wrath of God and from destruction, and have the gift of eternal life conferred upon them.

ARTICLE 5
The cause or guilt of this unbelief as well as of all other sins is no wise in God, but in man himself; whereas faith in Jesus Christ and salvation through him is the free gift of God, as it is written: By *grace have ye been saved through faith; and that not of yourselves,* it is *the gift of God* (Eph. 2:8). Likewise: *To you it hath been granted in the behalf of Christ, not only to believe on him,* etc. (Phil. 1:29).

ARTICLE 6
That some receive the gift of faith from God, and others do not receive it, proceeds from God's eternal decree. *For known unto God are all his works from the beginning of the world* (Acts 15:18, A.V.). *Who worketh all things after the counsel of his will* (Eph. 1:11). According to which decree he graciously

softens the hearts of the elect, however obstinate, and inclines them to believe; while he leaves the non-elect in his just judgment to their own wickedness and obduracy. And herein is especially displayed the profound, the merciful, and at the same time the righteous discrimination between men equally involved in ruin; or that decree of election and reprobation, revealed in the Word of God, which, though men of perverse, impure, and unstable minds wrest it to their own destruction, yet to holy and pious souls affords unspeakable consolation.

ARTICLE 7
Election is the unchangeable purpose of God, whereby, before the foundation of the world, he has out of mere grace, according to the sovereign good pleasure of his own will, chosen from the whole human race, which had fallen through their own fault from their primitive state of rectitude into sin and destruction, a certain number of persons to redemption in Christ, whom he from eternity appointed the Mediator and Head of the elect and the foundation of salvation. This elect number, though by nature neither better nor more deserving than others, but with them involved in one common misery, God has decreed to give to Christ to be saved by him, and effectually to call and draw them to his communion by his Word and Spirit; to bestow upon them true faith, justification, and sanctification; and having powerfully preserved them in the fellowship of his Son, finally to glorify them for the demonstration of his mercy, and for the praise of the riches of his glorious grace; as it is written: *Even as he chose us in him before the foundation of the world, that we should be holy and without blemish before him in love: having foreordained us unto adoption as sons through Jesus Christ unto himself, according to the good pleasure of his will, to the praise of the glory of his grace, which he freely bestowed on us in the Beloved* (Eph. 1:4, 5, 6). And elsewhere: *Whom he foreordained, them he also called: and whom he called, them he also justified: and whom he justified, them he also glorified* (Rom. 8:30).

ARTICLE 8

There are not various decrees of election, but one and the same decree respecting all those who shall be saved, both under the Old and the New Testament; since the Scripture declares the good pleasure, purpose, and counsel of the divine will to be one, according to which he has chosen us from eternity, both to grace and to glory, to salvation and to the way of salvation, which he has ordained that we should walk therein (Eph. 1:4, 5; 2:10).

ARTICLE 9

This election was not founded upon foreseen faith and the obedience of faith, holiness, or any other good quality or disposition in man, as the prerequisite, cause, or condition on which it depended; but men are chosen to faith and to the obedience of faith, holiness, etc. Therefore election is the fountain of every saving good, from which proceed faith, holiness, and the other gifts of salvation, and finally eternal life itself, as its fruits and effects, according to the testimony of the apostle: *He hath chosen us* (not because we were, but) *that we should be holy, and without blemish before him in love* (Eph. 1:4).

ARTICLE 10

The good pleasure of God is the sole cause of this gracious election; which does not consist herein that out of all possible qualities and actions of men God has chosen some as a condition of salvation, but that he was pleased out of the common mass of sinners to adopt some certain persons as a peculiar people to himself, as it is written: *For the children being not yet born, neither having done anything good or bad, etc., it was said unto her (namely, to Rebekah), The elder shall serve the younger. Even as it is written, Jacob I loved, but Esau I hated* (Rom. 9:11, 12, 13). *And as many as were ordained to eternal life believed* (Acts 13:48).

ARTICLE 11
And as God himself is most wise, unchangeable, omniscient, and omnipotent, so the election made by him can neither be interrupted nor changed, recalled, or annulled; neither can the elect be cast away, nor their number diminished.

ARTICLE 12
The elect in due time, though in various degrees and in different measures, attain the assurance of this their eternal and unchangeable election, not by inquisitively prying into the secret and deep things of God, but by observing in themselves with a spiritual joy and holy pleasure the infallible fruits of election pointed out in the Word of God—such as, a true faith in Christ, filial fear, a godly sorrow for sin, a hungering and thirsting after righteousness, etc.

ARTICLE 13
The sense and certainty of this election afford to the children of God additional matter for daily humiliation before him, for adoring the depth of his mercies, for cleansing themselves, and rendering grateful returns of ardent love to him who first manifested so great love towards them. The consideration of this doctrine of election is so far from encouraging remissness in the observance of the divine commands or from sinking men in carnal security, that these, in the just judgment of God, are the usual effects of rash presumption or of idle and wanton trifling with the grace of election, in those who refuse to walk in the ways of the elect.

ARTICLE 14
As the doctrine of divine election by the most wise counsel of God was declared by the prophets, by Christ himself, and by the apostles, and is clearly revealed in the Scriptures both of the Old and the New Testament, so it is still to be published in due time and place in the Church of God, for which it was peculiarly designed, provided it be done with reverence, in the spirit of discretion and piety, for the glory of God's most holy Name, and

for enlivening and comforting his people, without vainly attempting to investigate the secret ways of the Most High (Acts 20:27; Rom. 11:33, 34; 12:3; Heb. 6:17, 18).

ARTICLE 15
What peculiarly tends to illustrate and recommend to us the eternal and unmerited grace of election is the express testimony of sacred Scripture that not all, but some only, are elected, while others are passed by in the eternal decree; whom God, out of his sovereign, most just, irreprehensible, and unchangeable good pleasure, has decreed to leave in the common misery into which they have willfully plunged themselves, and not to bestow upon them saving faith and the grace of conversion; but, permitting them in his just judgment to follow their own ways, at last, for the declaration of his justice, to condemn and punish them forever, not only on account of their unbelief, but also for all their other sins. And this is the decree of reprobation, which by no means makes God the Author of sin (the very thought of which is blasphemy), but declares him to be an awful, irreprehensible, and righteous Judge and Avenger thereof.

ARTICLE 16
Those in whom a living faith in Christ, an assured confidence of soul, peace of conscience, an earnest endeavor after filial obedience, a glorying in God through Christ, is not as yet strongly felt, and who nevertheless make use of the means which God has appointed for working these graces in us, ought not to be alarmed at the mention of reprobation, nor to rank themselves among the reprobate, but diligently to persevere in the use of means, and with ardent desires devoutly and humbly to wait for a season of richer grace. Much less cause to be terrified by the doctrine of reprobation have they who, though they seriously desire to be turned to God, to please him only, and to be delivered from the body of death, cannot yet reach that measure of holiness and faith to which they aspire; since a merciful God has promised that he will not quench the smoking

flax, nor break the bruised reed. But this doctrine is justly terrible to those who, regardless of God and of the Savior Jesus Christ, have wholly given themselves up to the cares of the world and the pleasures of the flesh, so long as they are not seriously converted to God.

ARTICLE 17
Since we are to judge of the will of God from his Word, which testifies that the children of believers are holy, not by nature, but in virtue of the covenant of grace, in which they together with the parents are comprehended, godly parents ought not to doubt the election and salvation of their children whom it pleases God to call out of this life in their infancy (Gen. 17:7; Acts 2:39; 1 Cor. 7:14).

ARTICLE 18
To those who murmur at the free grace of election and the just severity of reprobation we answer with the apostle: *Nay but, O man, who art thou that repliest against God?* (Rom. 9:20), and quote the language of our Savior: *Is it not lawful for me to do what I will with mine own?* (Matt. 20:15). And therefore, with holy adoration of these mysteries, we exclaim in the words of the apostle: *O the depth of the riches both of the wisdom and the knowledge of God! how unsearchable are his judgments, and his ways past tracing out! For who hath known the mind of the Lord, or who hath been his counselor? or who hath first given to him, and it shall be recompensed unto him again? For of him, and through him, and unto him are all things. To him* be *the glory for ever. Amen.* (Rom. 11:33–36).

REJECTION OF ERRORS

The true doctrine concerning election and reprobation having been explained, the Synod rejects the errors of those:

PARAGRAPH 1

Who teach: That the will of God to save those who would believe and would persevere in faith and in the obedience of faith is the whole and entire decree of election unto salvation, and that nothing else concerning this decree has been revealed in God's Word.

For these deceive the simple and plainly contradict the Scriptures, which declare that God will not only save those who will believe, but that he has also from eternity chosen certain particular persons to whom, above others, he will grant, in time, both faith in Christ and perseverance; as it is written: *I manifested thy name unto the men whom thou gavest me out of the world* (John 17:6). *And as many as were ordained to eternal life believed* (Acts 13:48). And: *Even as he chose us in him before the foundation of the world, that we should be holy and without blemish before him in love* (Eph. 1:4).

PARAGRAPH 2

Who teach: That there are various kinds of election of God unto eternal life: the one general and indefinite, the other particular and definite; and that the latter in turn is either incomplete, revocable, non-decisive, and conditional, or complete, irrevocable, decisive, and absolute. Likewise: That there is one election unto faith and another unto salvation, so that election can be unto justifying faith, without being a decisive election unto salvation.

For this is a fancy of men's minds, invented regardless of the Scriptures, whereby the doctrine of election is corrupted, and this golden chain of our salvation is broken: *And whom he foreordained, them he also called: and whom he called, them he also justified: and whom he justified, them he also glorified* (Rom. 8:30).

PARAGRAPH 3

Who teach: That the good pleasure and purpose of God, of which Scripture makes mention in the doctrine of election, does not consist in this, that God chose certain persons rather than others, but in this, that he chose out of all possible conditions (among which are also the works of the law), or out of the whole order of things, the act of faith which from its very nature is undeserving, as well as its incomplete obedience, as a condition of salvation, and that he would graciously consider this in itself as a complete obedience and count it worthy of the reward of eternal life.

For by this injurious error the pleasure of God and the merits of Christ are made of none effect, and men are drawn away by useless questions from the truth of gracious justification and from the simplicity of Scripture, and this declaration of the apostle is charged as untrue: *Who saved us, and called us with a holy calling, not according to our works, but according to his own purpose and grace, which was given us in Christ Jesus before times eternal* (2 Tim. 1:9).

PARAGRAPH 4
Who teach: That in the election unto faith this condition is beforehand demanded that man should use the light of nature aright, be pious, humble, meek, and fit for eternal life, as if on these things election were in any way dependent.

For this savors of the teaching of Pelagius, and is opposed to the doctrine of the apostle when he writes: *Among whom we also all once lived in the lusts of our flesh, doing the desires of the flesh and of the mind, and were by nature children of wrath, even as the rest; but God, being rich in mercy, for his great love wherewith he loved us, even when we were dead through our trespasses, made us alive together with Christ (by grace have ye been saved), and raised us up with him, and made us to sit with him in the heavenly* places, *in Christ Jesus; that in the ages to come he might show the exceeding riches of his grace in kindness towards us in Christ Jesus; for by grace have ye been saved through faith; and that not of yourselves,* it is *the gift of God; not of works, that no man should glory* (Eph. 2:3–9).

PARAGRAPH 5

Who teach: That the incomplete and non-decisive election of particular persons to salvation occurred because of a foreseen faith, conversion, holiness, godliness, which either began or continued for some time; but that the complete and decisive election occurred because of foreseen perseverance unto the end in faith, conversion, holiness, and godliness; and that this is the gracious and evangelical worthiness, for the sake of which he who is chosen is more worthy than he who is not chosen; and that therefore faith, the obedience of faith, holiness, godliness, and perseverance are not fruits of the unchangeable election unto glory: but are conditions, which, being required before hand, were foreseen as being met by those who will be fully elected, and are causes without which the unchangeable election to glory does not occur.

This is repugnant to the entire Scripture, which constantly inculcates this and similar declarations: Election is *not of works, but of him that calleth* (Rom. 9:11). *And as many as were ordained to eternal life believed* (Acts 13:48). *He chose us in him before the foundation of the world, that we should be holy* (Eph. 1:4). *Ye did not choose me, but I chose you* (John 15:16). *But if it is by grace, it is no more of works* (Rom. 11:6). *Herein is love, not that we loved God, but that he loved us, and sent his Son* (1 John 4:10).

PARAGRAPH 6

Who teach: That not every election unto salvation is unchangeable, but that some of the elect, any decree of God notwithstanding, can yet perish and do indeed perish.

By this gross error they make God to be changeable, and destroy the comfort which the godly obtain out of the firmness of their election, and contradict the Holy Scripture, which teaches that *the elect can not be led astray* (Matt. 24:24), that Christ *does not lose those whom the Father gave him* (John 6:39), and that *God also glorified those whom he foreordained, called, and justified* (Rom. 8:30).

PARAGRAPH 7

Who teach: That there is in this life no fruit and no consciousness of the unchangeable election to glory, nor any certainty, except that which depends on a changeable and uncertain condition.

For not only is it absurd to speak of an uncertain certainty, but also contrary to the experience of the saints, who by virtue of the consciousness of their election rejoice with the apostle and praise this favor of God (Eph. 1); who according to Christ's admonition rejoice with his disciples that *their names are written in heaven* (Luke 10:20); who also place the consciousness of their election over against the fiery darts of the devil, asking: *Who shall lay anything to the charge of God's elect?* (Rom. 8:33).

PARAGRAPH 8

Who teach: That God, simply by virtue of his righteous will, did not decide either to leave anyone in the fall of Adam and in the common state of sin and condemnation, or to pass anyone by in the communication of grace which is necessary for faith and conversion. For this is firmly decreed: *He hath mercy on whom he will, and whom he will he hardeneth* (Rom. 9:18). And also this: *Unto you it is given to know the mysteries of the kingdom of heaven, but to them it is not given* (Matt. 13:11). Likewise: *I thank thee, O Father, Lord of heaven and earth, that thou didst hide these things from the wise and understanding, and didst reveal them unto babes; yea, Father, for so it was well-pleasing in thy sight* (Matt. 11:25, 26).

PARAGRAPH 9

Who teach: That the reason why God sends the gospel to one people rather than to another is not merely and solely the good pleasure of God, but rather the fact that one people is better and worthier than another to which the gospel is not communicated.

For this Moses denies, addressing the people of Israel as follows: *Behold, unto Jehovah thy God belongeth heaven and the heaven of heavens, the earth, with all that is therein. Only Jehovah had a delight in thy fathers to love them, and he chose their seed after them, even you above all peoples, as at this day* (Deut. 10:14, 15). And Christ said: *Woe unto thee, Chorazin! woe unto thee, Bethsaida! for if the mighty works had been done in Tyre and Sidon which were done in you, they would have repented long ago in sackcloth and ashes* (Matt. 11:21).

SECOND HEAD OF DOCTRINE –
The Death of Christ, and the Redemption of Men Thereby

ARTICLE 1
God is not only supremely merciful, but also supremely just. And his justice requires (as he has revealed himself in his Word) that our sins committed against his infinite majesty should be punished, not only with temporal but with eternal punishments, both in body and soul; which we cannot escape, unless satisfaction be made to the justice of God.

ARTICLE 2
Since, therefore, we are unable to make that satisfaction in our own persons, or to deliver ourselves from the wrath of God, he has been pleased of his infinite mercy to give his only begotten Son for our Surety, who was made sin, and became a curse for us and in our stead, that he might make satisfaction to divine justice on our behalf.

ARTICLE 3
The death of the Son of God is the only and most perfect sacrifice and satisfaction for sin, and is of infinite worth and value, abundantly sufficient to expiate the sins of the whole world.

ARTICLE 4
This death is of such infinite value and dignity because the person who submitted to it was not only really man and perfectly holy, but also the only begotten Son of God, of the same eternal and infinite essence with the Father and the Holy Spirit, which

qualifications were necessary to constitute him a Savior for us; and, moreover, because it was attended with a sense of the wrath and curse of God due to us for sin.

ARTICLE 5
Moreover, the promise of the gospel is that whosoever believes in Christ crucified shall not perish, but have eternal life. This promise, together with the command to repent and believe, ought to be declared and published to all nations, and to all persons promiscuously and without distinction, to whom God out of his good pleasure sends the gospel.

ARTICLE 6
And, whereas many who are called by the gospel do not repent nor believe in Christ, but perish in unbelief, this is not owing to any defect or insufficiency in the sacrifice offered by Christ upon the cross, but is wholly to be imputed to themselves.

ARTICLE 7
But as many as truly believe, and are delivered and saved from sin and destruction through the death of Christ, are indebted for this benefit solely to the grace of God given them in Christ from everlasting, and not to any merit of their own.

ARTICLE 8
For this was the sovereign counsel and most gracious will and purpose of God the Father that the quickening and saving efficacy of the most precious death of his Son should extend to all the elect, for bestowing upon them alone the gift of justifying faith, thereby to bring them infallibly to salvation; that is, it was the will of God that Christ by the blood of the cross, whereby he confirmed the new covenant, should effectually redeem out of every people, tribe, nation, and language, all those, and those only, who were from eternity chosen to salvation and given to him by the Father; that he should confer upon them faith, which, together with all the other saving gifts of the Holy Spirit, he purchased for them by his death; should purge them from all sin,

both original and actual, whether committed before or after believing; and having faithfully preserved them even to the end, should at last bring them, free from every spot and blemish, to the enjoyment of glory in his own presence forever.

ARTICLE 9
This purpose, proceeding from everlasting love towards the elect, has from the beginning of the world to this day been powerfully accomplished, and will henceforward still continue to be accomplished, notwithstanding all the ineffectual opposition of the gates of hell; so that the elect in due time may be gathered together into one, and that there never may be wanting a Church composed of believers, the foundation of which is laid in the blood of Christ; which may steadfastly love and faithfully serve him as its Savior (who, as a bridegroom for his bride, laid down his life for them upon the cross); and which may celebrate his praises here and through all eternity.

REJECTION OF ERRORS

The true doctrine having been explained, the Synod rejects the errors of those:

PARAGRAPH 1
Who teach: That God the Father has ordained his Son to the death of the cross without a certain and definite decree to save any, so that the necessity, profitableness, and worth of what Christ merited by his death might have existed, and might remain in all its parts complete, perfect, and intact, even if the merited redemption had never in fact been applied to any person.

For this doctrine tends to the despising of the wisdom of the Father and of the merits of Jesus Christ, and is contrary to Scripture. For thus says our Savior: *I lay down my life for the sheep, and I know them* (John 10:15, 27). And the prophet Isaiah says concerning the Savior: *When thou shalt make his soul an offering for sin, he shall see* his *seed, he shall prolong his days, and the pleasure of Jehovah shall prosper in his hand*

(Is. 53:10). Finally, this contradicts the article of faith according to which we believe the catholic Christian Church.

PARAGRAPH 2
Who teach: That it was not the purpose of the death of Christ that he should confirm the new covenant of grace through his blood, but only that he should acquire for the Father the mere right to establish with man such a covenant as he might please, whether of grace or of works.

For this is repugnant to Scripture which teaches that *Christ hath become the surety and mediator of a better, that is, the new covenant,* and that *a testament is of force where there hath been death* (Heb. 7:22; 9:15, 17).

PARAGRAPH 3
Who teach: That Christ by his satisfaction merited neither salvation itself for anyone, nor faith, whereby this satisfaction of Christ unto salvation is effectually appropriated; but that he merited for the Father only the authority or the perfect will to deal again with man, and to prescribe new conditions as he might desire, obedience to which, however, depended on the free will of man, so that it therefore might have come to pass that either none or all should fulfill these conditions.

For these adjudge too contemptuously of the death of Christ, in no wise acknowledge the most important fruit or benefit thereby gained, and bring again out of hell the Pelagian error.

PARAGRAPH 4
Who teach: That the new covenant of grace, which God the Father, through the mediation of the death of Christ, made with man, does not herein consist that we by faith, in as much as it accepts the merits of Christ, are justified before God and saved, but in the fact that God, having revoked the demand of perfect obedience of faith, regards faith itself and the obedience of faith, although imperfect, as the perfect obedience of the law, and does esteem it worthy of the reward of eternal life through grace.

For these contradict the Scriptures: *Being justified freely by his grace through the redemption that is in Christ Jesus; whom God set forth to be a propitiation, through faith, in his blood* (Rom. 3:24, 25). And these proclaim, as did the wicked Socinus, a new and strange justification of man before God, against the consensus of the whole Church.

PARAGRAPH 5
Who teach: That all men have been accepted unto the state of reconciliation and unto the grace of the covenant, so that no one is worthy of condemnation on account of original sin, and that no one shall be condemned because of it, but that all are free from the guilt of original sin.

For this opinion is repugnant to Scripture which teaches that we are *by nature children of wrath* (Eph. 2:3).

PARAGRAPH 6
Who use the difference between meriting and appropriating, to the end that they may instill into the minds of the imprudent and inexperienced this teaching that God, as far as he is concerned, has been minded to apply to all equally the benefits gained by the death of Christ; but that, while some obtain the pardon of sin and eternal life, and others do not, this difference depends on their own free will, which joins itself to the grace that is offered without exception, and that it is not dependent on the special gift of mercy, which powerfully works in them, that they rather than others should appropriate unto themselves this grace.

For these, while they feign that they present this distinction in a sound sense, seek to instil into the people the destructive poison of the Pelagian errors.

PARAGRAPH 7
Who teach: That Christ neither could die, nor needed to die, and also did not die, for those whom God loved in the highest degree and elected to eternal life, since these do not need the death of Christ.

For they contradict the apostle, who declares: *Christ loved me, and gave himself up for me* (Gal. 2:20). Likewise: *Who shall lay anything to the charge of God's elect? It is God that justifieth; who is he that condemneth? It is Christ Jesus that died* (Rom. 8:33, 34), namely, for them; and the Savior who says: *I lay down my life for the sheep* (John 10:15). And: *This is my commandment, that ye love one another, even as I have loved you. Greater love hath no man than this, that a man lay down his life for his friends* (John 15:12, 13).

THIRD AND FOURTH HEADS OF DOCTRINE – The Corruption of Man, His Conversion to God, and the Manner Thereof

ARTICLE 1
Man was originally formed after the image of God. His understanding was adorned with a true and saving knowledge of his Creator, and of spiritual things; his heart and will were upright, all his affections pure, and the whole man was holy. But, revolting from God by the instigation of the devil and by his own free will, he forfeited these excellent gifts; and in the place thereof became involved in blindness of mind, horrible darkness, vanity, and perverseness of judgment; became wicked, rebellious, and obdurate in heart and will, and impure in his affections.

ARTICLE 2
Man after the fall begot children in his own likeness. A corrupt stock produced a corrupt offspring. Hence all the posterity of Adam, Christ only excepted, have derived corruption from their original parent, not by imitation, as the Pelagians of old asserted, but by the propagation of a vicious nature, in consequence of the just judgment of God.

ARTICLE 3
Therefore all men are conceived in sin, and are by nature children of wrath, incapable of saving good, prone to evil, dead in sin, and in bondage thereto; and without the regenerating grace of the Holy Spirit, they are neither able nor willing to return to God, to reform the depravity of their nature, or to dispose themselves to reformation.

ARTICLE 4

There remain, however, in man since the fall, the glimmerings of natural light, whereby he retains some knowledge of God, of natural things, and of the difference between good and evil, and shows some regard for virtue and for good outward behavior. But so far is this light of nature from being sufficient to bring him to a saving knowledge of God and to true conversion that he is incapable of using it aright even in things natural and civil. Nay further, this light, such as it is, man in various ways renders wholly polluted, and hinders in unrighteousness, by doing which he becomes inexcusable before God.

ARTICLE 5

In the same light are we to consider the law of the Decalogue, delivered by God to his peculiar people, the Jews, by the hands of Moses. For though it reveals the greatness of sin, and more and more convinces man thereof, yet, as it neither points out a remedy nor imparts strength to extricate him from this misery, but, being weak through the flesh, leaves the transgressor under the curse, man cannot by this law obtain saving grace.

ARTICLE 6

What, therefore, neither the light of nature nor the law could do, that God performs by the operation of the Holy Spirit through the word or ministry of reconciliation; which is the glad tidings concerning the Messiah, by means whereof it has pleased God to save such as believe, as well under the Old as under the New Testament.

ARTICLE 7

This mystery of his will God revealed to but a small number under the Old Testament; under the New Testament (the distinction between various peoples having been removed) he reveals it to many. The cause of this dispensation is not to be ascribed to the superior worth of one nation above another, nor to their better use of the light of nature, but results wholly from the sovereign good pleasure and unmerited love of God.

Hence they to whom so great and so gracious a blessing is communicated, above their desert, or rather notwithstanding their demerits, are bound to acknowledge it with humble and grateful hearts, and with the apostle to adore, but in no wise curiously to pry into, the severity and justice of God's judgments displayed in others to whom this grace is not given.

ARTICLE 8
As many as are called by the gospel are unfeignedly called. For God has most earnestly and truly declared in his Word what is acceptable to him, namely, that those who are called should come unto him. He also seriously promises rest of soul and eternal life to all who come to him and believe.

ARTICLE 9
It is not the fault of the gospel, nor of Christ offered therein, nor of God, who calls men by the gospel and confers upon them various gifts, that those who are called by the ministry of the Word refuse to come and be converted. The fault lies in themselves; some of whom when called, regardless of their danger, reject the Word of life; others, though they receive it, suffer it not to make a lasting impression on their heart; therefore, their joy, arising only from a temporary faith, soon vanishes, and they fall away; while others choke the seed of the Word by perplexing cares and the pleasures of this world, and produce no fruit. This our Savior teaches in the parable of the sower (Matt. 13).

ARTICLE 10
But that others who are called by the gospel obey the call and are converted is not to be ascribed to the proper exercise of free will, whereby one distinguishes himself above others equally furnished with grace sufficient for faith and conversion (as the proud heresy of Pelagius maintains); but it must be wholly ascribed to God, who, as he has chosen his own from eternity in Christ, so he calls them effectually in time, confers upon them faith and repentance, rescues them from the power of darkness,

and translates them into the kingdom of his own Son; that they may show forth the praises of him who has called them out of darkness into his marvelous light, and may glory not in themselves but in the Lord, according to the testimony of the apostles in various places.

ARTICLE 11
But when God accomplishes his good pleasure in the elect, or works in them true conversion, he not only causes the gospel to be externally preached to them, and powerfully illuminates their minds by his Holy Spirit, that they may rightly understand and discern the things of the Spirit of God; but by the efficacy of the same regenerating Spirit he pervades the inmost recesses of man; he opens the closed and softens the hardened heart, and circumcises that which was uncircumcised; infuses new qualities into the will, which, though heretofore dead, he quickens; from being evil, disobedient, and refractory, he renders it good, obedient, and pliable; actuates and strengthens it, that like a good tree, it may bring forth the fruits of good actions.

ARTICLE 12
And this is that regeneration so highly extolled in Scripture, that renewal, new creation, resurrection from the dead, making alive, which God works in us without our aid. But this is in no wise effected merely by the external preaching of the gospel, by moral suasion, or such a mode of operation that, after God has performed his part, it still remains in the power of man to be regenerated or not, to be converted or to continue unconverted; but it is evidently a supernatural work, most powerful, and at the same time most delightful, astonishing, mysterious, and ineffable; not inferior in efficacy to creation or the resurrection from the dead, as the Scripture inspired by the Author of this work declares; so that all in whose heart God works in this marvelous manner are certainly, infallibly, and effectually regenerated, and do actually believe. Whereupon the will thus renewed is not only actuated and influenced by God, but in

consequence of this influence becomes itself active. Wherefore also man himself is rightly said to believe and repent by virtue of that grace received.

ARTICLE 13
The manner of this operation cannot be fully comprehended by believers in this life. Nevertheless, they are satisfied to know and experience that by this grace of God they are enabled to believe with the heart and to love their Savior.

ARTICLE 14
Faith is therefore to be considered as the gift of God, not on account of its being offered by God to man, to be accepted or rejected at his pleasure, but because it is in reality conferred upon him, breathed and infused into him; nor even because God bestows the power or ability to believe, and then expects that man should by the exercise of his own free will consent to the terms of salvation and actually believe in Christ, but because he who works in man both to will and to work, and indeed all things in all, produces both the will to believe and the act of believing also.

ARTICLE 15
God is under no obligation to confer this grace upon any; for how can he be indebted to one who had no previous gifts to bestow as a foundation for such recompense? Nay, how can he be indebted to one who has nothing of his own but sin and falsehood? He, therefore, who becomes the subject of this grace owes eternal gratitude to God, and gives him thanks forever. Whoever is not made partaker thereof is either altogether regardless of these spiritual gifts and satisfied with his own condition, or is in no apprehension of danger, and vainly boasts the possession of that which he has not. Further, with respect to those who outwardly profess their faith and amend their lives, we are bound, after the example of the apostle, to judge and speak of them in the most favorable manner; for the secret recesses of the heart

are unknown to us. And as to others who have not yet been called, it is our duty to pray for them to God, who calls the things that are not as if they were. But we are in no wise to conduct ourselves towards them with haughtiness, as if we had made ourselves to differ.

ARTICLE 16
But as man by the fall did not cease to be a creature endowed with understanding and will, nor did sin which pervaded the whole race of mankind deprive him of the human nature, but brought upon him depravity and spiritual death; so also this grace of regeneration does not treat men as senseless stocks and blocks, nor take away their will and its properties, or do violence thereto; but it spiritually quickens, heals, corrects, and at the same time sweetly and powerfully bends it, that where carnal rebellion and resistance formerly prevailed, a ready and sincere spiritual obedience begins to reign; in which the true and spiritual restoration and freedom of our will consist. Wherefore, unless the admirable Author of every good work so deal with us, man can have no hope of being able to rise from his fall by his own free will, by which, in a state of innocence, he plunged himself into ruin.

ARTICLE 17
As the almighty operation of God whereby he brings forth and supports this our natural life does not exclude but require the use of means by which God, of his infinite mercy and goodness, has chosen to exert his influence, so also the aforementioned supernatural operation of God by which we are regenerated in no wise excludes or subverts the use of the gospel, which the most wise God has ordained to be the seed of regeneration and food of the soul. Wherefore, as the apostles and the teachers who succeeded them piously instructed the people concerning this grace of God, to his glory and to the abasement of all pride, and in the meantime, however, neglected not to keep them, by the holy admonitions of the gospel, under the influence of the Word,

the sacraments, and ecclesiastical discipline; so even now it should be far from those who give or receive instruction in the Church to presume to tempt God by separating what he of his good pleasure has most intimately joined together. For grace is conferred by means of admonitions; and the more readily we perform our duty, the more clearly this favor of God, working in us, usually manifests itself, and the more directly his work is advanced; to whom alone all the glory, both for the means and for their saving fruit and efficacy, is forever due. Amen.

REJECTION OF ERRORS

The true doctrine having been explained, the Synod rejects the errors of those:

PARAGRAPH 1
Who teach: That it cannot properly be said that original sin in itself suffices to condemn the whole human race or to deserve temporal and eternal punishment.

For these contradict the apostle, who declares: *Therefore, as through one man sin entered into the world, and death through sin; and so death passed unto all men, for that all sinned* (Rom. 5:12). And: *The judgment came of one unto condemnation* (Rom. 5:16). And: *The wages of sin is death* (Rom. 6:23).

PARAGRAPH 2
Who teach: That the spiritual gifts or the good qualities and virtues, such as goodness, holiness, righteousness, could not belong to the will of man when he was first created, and that these, therefore, cannot have been separated therefrom in the fall.

For such is contrary to the description of the image of God which the apostle gives in Ephesians 4:24, where he declares that it consists in righteousness and holiness, which undoubtedly belong to the will.

PARAGRAPH 3
Who teach: That in spiritual death the spiritual gifts are not separate from the will of man, since the will in itself has never

been corrupted, but only hindered through the darkness of the understanding and the irregularity of the affections; and that, these hindrances having been removed, the will can then bring into operation its native powers, that is, that the will of itself is able to will and to choose, or not to will and not to choose, all manner of good which may be presented to it.

This is an innovation and an error, and tends to elevate the powers of the free will, contrary to the declaration of the prophet: *The heart is deceitful above all things, and it is exceedingly corrupt* (Jer. 17:9); and of the apostle: *Among whom* (sons of disobedience) *we also all once lived in the lusts of our flesh, doing the desires of the flesh and of the mind* (Eph. 2:3).

PARAGRAPH 4
Who teach: That the unregenerate man is not really nor utterly dead in sin, nor destitute of all powers unto spiritual good, but that he can yet hunger and thirst after righteousness and life, and offer the sacrifice of a contrite and broken spirit, which is pleasing to God.

For these things are contrary to the express testimony of Scripture: *Ye were dead through your trespasses and sins* (Eph. 2:1, 5). And: *Every imagination of the thoughts of his heart was only evil continually* (Gen. 6:5; 8:21). Moreover, to hunger and thirst after deliverance from misery and after life, and to offer unto God the sacrifice of a broken spirit, is peculiar to the regenerate and those that are called blessed (Ps. 51:17; Matt. 5:6).

PARAGRAPH 5
Who teach: That the corrupt and natural man can so well use the common grace (by which they understand the light of nature), or the gifts still left him after the fall, that he can gradually gain by their good use a greater, that is, the evangelical or saving grace, and salvation itself; and that in this way God on his part shows himself ready to reveal Christ unto all men, since he applies to all sufficiently and efficiently the means necessary to conversion.

For both the experience of all ages and the Scriptures testify that this is untrue. *He showeth his word unto Jacob, his statutes and his ordinances unto Israel. He hath not dealt so with any nation; and as for his ordinances, they have not known them* (Ps. 147:19, 20). *Who in the generations gone by suffered all the nations to walk in their own way* (Acts 14:16). And: *And they* (Paul and his companions) *having been forbidden of the Holy Spirit to speak the word in Asia, when they were come over against Mysia, they assayed to go into Bithynia, and the Spirit of Jesus suffered them not* (Acts 16:6, 7).

PARAGRAPH 6
Who teach: That in the true conversion of man no new qualities, powers, or gifts can be infused by God into the will, and that therefore faith, through which we are first converted and because of which we are called believers, is not a quality or gift infused by God but only an act of man, and that it cannot be said to be a gift, except in respect of the power to attain to this faith.

For thereby they contradict the Holy Scriptures, which declare that God infuses new qualities of faith, of obedience, and of the consciousness of his love into our hearts: *I will put my law in their inward parts, and in their heart will I write it* (Jer. 31:33). And: *I will pour water upon him that is thirsty, and streams upon the dry ground; I will pour my Spirit upon thy seed* (Is. 44:3). And: *The love of God hath been shed abroad in our hearts through the Holy Spirit which was given unto us* (Rom. 5:5). This is also repugnant to the constant practice of the Church, which prays by the mouth of the prophet thus: *Turn thou me, and I shall be turned* (Jer. 31:18).

PARAGRAPH 7
Who teach: That the grace whereby we are converted to God is only a gentle advising, or (as others explain it) that this is the noblest manner of working in the conversion of man, and that this manner of working, which consists in advising, is most in harmony with man's nature; and that there is no reason why this

advising grace alone should not be sufficient to make the natural man spiritual; indeed, that God does not produce the consent of the will except through this manner of advising; and that the power of the divine working, whereby it surpasses the working of Satan, consists in this that God promises eternal, while Satan promises only temporal goods.

But this is altogether Pelagian and contrary to the whole Scripture, which, besides this, teaches yet another and far more powerful and divine manner of the Holy Spirit's working in the conversion of man, as in Ezekiel: *A new heart also will I give you, and a new spirit will I put within you; and I will take away the stony heart out of your flesh, and I will give you a heart of flesh* (Ezek. 36:26).

PARAGRAPH 8

Who teach: That God in the regeneration of man does not use such powers of his omnipotence as potently and infallibly bend man's will to faith and conversion; but that all the works of grace having been accomplished, which God employs to convert man, man may yet so resist God and the Holy Spirit, when God intends man's regeneration and wills to regenerate him, and indeed that man often does so resist that he prevents entirely his regeneration, and that it therefore remains in man's power to be regenerated or not.

For this is nothing less than the denial of all the efficiency of God's grace in our conversion, and the subjecting of the working of Almighty God to the will of man, which is contrary to the apostles, who teach that *we believe according to the working of the strength of his might* (Eph. 1:19); and that *God fulfills every desire of goodness and* every *work of faith with power* (2 Thess. 1:11); and that *his divine power hath granted unto us all things that pertain unto life and godliness* (2 Peter 1:3).

PARAGRAPH 9

Who teach: That grace and free will are partial causes which together work the beginning of conversion, and that grace, in order of working, does not precede the working of the will; that is, that God does not efficiently help the will of man unto conversion until the will of man moves and determines to do this.

For the ancient Church has long ago condemned this doctrine of the Pelagians according to the words of the apostle: *So then it is not of him that willeth, nor of him that runneth, but of God that hath mercy* (Rom. 9:16). Likewise: *For who maketh thee to differ? and what hast thou that thou didst not receive?* (1 Cor. 4:7). And: *For it is God who worketh in you both to will and to work, for his good pleasure* (Phil. 2:13).

FIFTH HEAD OF DOCTRINE –
The Perserverance of the Saints

ARTICLE 1
Those whom God, according to his purpose, calls to the communion of his Son, our Lord Jesus Christ, and regenerates by the Holy Spirit, he also delivers from the dominion and slavery of sin, though in this life he does not deliver them altogether from the body of sin and from the infirmities of the flesh.

ARTICLE 2
Hence spring forth the daily sins of infirmity, and blemishes cleave even to the best works of the saints. These are to them a perpetual reason to humiliate themselves before God and to flee for refuge to Christ crucified; to mortify the flesh more and more by the spirit of prayer and by holy exercises of piety; and to press forward to the goal of perfection, until at length, delivered from this body of death, they shall reign with the Lamb of God in heaven.

ARTICLE 3
By reason of these remains of indwelling sin, and also because of the temptations of the world and of Satan, those who are converted could not persevere in that grace if left to their own strength. But God is faithful, who, having conferred grace, mercifully confirms and powerfully preserves them therein, even to the end.

ARTICLE 4
Although the weakness of the flesh cannot prevail against the power of God, who confirms and preserves true believers in a state of grace, yet converts are not always so influenced and actuated by the Spirit of God as not in some particular instances sinfully to deviate from the guidance of divine grace, so as to be seduced by and to comply with the lusts of the flesh; they must, therefore, be constant in watching and prayer, that they may not be led into temptation. When these are neglected, they are not only liable to be drawn into great and heinous sins by the flesh, the world, and Satan, but sometimes by the righteous permission of God actually are drawn into these evils. This, the lamentable fall of David, Peter, and other saints described in Holy Scripture, demonstrates.

ARTICLE 5
By such enormous sins, however, they very highly offend God, incur a deadly guilt, grieve the Holy Spirit, interrupt the exercise of faith, very grievously wound their consciences, and sometimes for a while lose the sense of God's favor, until, when they change their course by serious repentance, the light of God's fatherly countenance again shines upon them.

ARTICLE 6
But God, who is rich in mercy, according to his unchangeable purpose of election, does not wholly withdraw the Holy Spirit from his own people even in their grievous falls; nor suffers them to proceed so far as to lose the grace of adoption and forfeit the state of justification, or to commit the sin unto death or against the Holy Spirit; nor does he permit them to be totally deserted, and to plunge themselves into everlasting destruction.

ARTICLE 7
For in the first place, in these falls he preserves in them the incorruptible seed of regeneration from perishing or being totally lost; and again, by his Word and Spirit he certainly and effectually renews them to repentance, to a sincere and godly

sorrow for their sins, that they may seek and obtain remission in the blood of the Mediator, may again experience the favor of a reconciled God, through faith adore his mercies, and henceforward more diligently work out their own salvation with fear and trembling.

ARTICLE 8
Thus it is not in consequence of their own merits or strength, but of God's free mercy, that they neither totally fall from faith and grace nor continue and perish finally in their backslidings; which, with respect to themselves is not only possible, but would undoubtedly happen; but with respect to God, it is utterly impossible, since his counsel cannot be changed nor his promise fail; neither can the call according to his purpose be revoked, nor the merit, intercession, and preservation of Christ be rendered ineffectual, nor the sealing of the Holy Spirit be frustrated or obliterated.

ARTICLE 9
Of this preservation of the elect to salvation and of their perseverance in the faith, true believers themselves may and do obtain assurance according to the measure of their faith, whereby they surely believe that they are and ever will continue true and living members of the Church, and that they have the forgiveness of sins and life eternal.

ARTICLE 10
This assurance, however, is not produced by any peculiar revelation contrary to or independent of the Word of God, but springs from faith in God's promises, which he has most abundantly revealed in his Word for our comfort; from the testimony of the Holy Spirit, witnessing with our spirit that we are children and heirs of God (Rom. 8:16); and lastly, from a serious and holy desire to preserve a good conscience and to perform good works. And if the elect of God were deprived of this solid comfort that they shall finally obtain the victory, and of this infallible pledge of eternal glory, they would be of all men the most miserable.

ARTICLE 11

The Scripture moreover testifies that believers in this life have to struggle with various carnal doubts, and that under grievous temptations they do not always feel this full assurance of faith and certainty of persevering. But God, who is the Father of all consolation, does not suffer them to be tempted above that they are able, but will with the temptation make also the way of escape, that they may be able to endure it (1 Cor. 10:13), and by the Holy Spirit again inspires them with the comfortable assurance of persevering.

ARTICLE 12

This certainty of perseverance, however, is so far from exciting in believers a spirit of pride, or of rendering them carnally secure, that on the contrary it is the real source of humility, filial reverence, true piety, patience in every tribulation, fervent prayers, constancy in suffering and in confessing the truth, and of solid rejoicing in God; so that the consideration of this benefit should serve as an incentive to the serious and constant practice of gratitude and good works, as appears from the testimonies of Scripture and the examples of the saints.

ARTICLE 13

Neither does renewed confidence of persevering produce licentiousness or a disregard of piety in those who are recovered from backsliding; but it renders them much more careful and solicitous to continue in the ways of the Lord, which he has ordained, that they who walk therein may keep the assurance of persevering; lest, on account of their abuse of his fatherly kindness, God should turn away his gracious countenance from them (to behold which is to the godly dearer than life, and the withdrawal of which is more bitter than death) and they in consequence thereof should fall into more grievous torments of conscience.

ARTICLE 14
And as it has pleased God, by the preaching of the gospel, to begin this work of grace in us, so he preserves, continues, and perfects it by the hearing and reading of his Word, by meditation thereon, and by the exhortations, threatenings, and promises thereof, and by the use of the sacraments.

ARTICLE 15
The carnal mind is unable to comprehend this doctrine of the perseverance of the saints and the certainty thereof, which God has most abundantly revealed in his Word, for the glory of his Name and the consolation of pious souls, and which he impresses upon the hearts of the believers. Satan abhors it, the world ridicules it, the ignorant and hypocritical abuse it, and the heretics oppose it. But the bride of Christ has always most tenderly loved and constantly defended it as an inestimable treasure; and God, against whom neither counsel nor strength can prevail, will dispose her so to continue to the end. Now to this one God, Father, Son, and Holy Spirit, be honor and glory forever. Amen.

REJECTION OF ERRORS

The true doctrine having been explained, the Synod rejects the errors of those:

PARAGRAPH 1
Who teach: That the perseverance of the true believers is not a fruit of election, or a gift of God gained by the death of Christ, but a condition of the new covenant, which (as they declare) man before his decisive election and justification must fulfill through his free will.

For the Holy Scripture testifies that this follows out of election, and is given the elect in virtue of the death, the resurrection, and intercession of Christ: *But the election obtained it, and the rest were hardened* (Rom. 11:7). Likewise: *He that spared not his own Son, but delivered him up for us all, how shall he not also with him freely give us all things? Who shall lay anything to the charge of God's elect? It is God that justifieth; who is he that condemneth? It is Christ Jesus that died, yea rather, that was raised from the dead, who is at the right hand of God, who also maketh intercession for us. Who shall separate us from the love of Christ?* (Rom. 8:32–35).

PARAGRAPH 2
Who teach: That God does indeed provide the believer with sufficient powers to persevere, and is ever ready to preserve these in him if he will do his duty; but that, though all things which are necessary to persevere in faith and which God will use to preserve faith are made use of, even then it ever depends on the pleasure of the will whether it will persevere or not.

For this idea contains an outspoken Pelagianism, and while it would make men free, it makes them robbers of God's honor, contrary to the prevailing agreement of the evangelical doctrine, which takes from man all cause of boasting, and ascribes all the praise for this favor to the grace of God alone; and contrary to the apostle, who declares that it is God, *who shall also confirm you unto the end,* that ye *be unreprovable in the day of our Lord Jesus Christ* (1 Cor. 1:8).

PARAGRAPH 3
Who teach: That the true believers and regenerate not only can fall from justifying faith and likewise from grace and salvation wholly and to the end, but indeed often do fall from this and are lost forever.

For this conception makes powerless the grace, justification, regeneration, and continued preservation by Christ, contrary to the expressed words of the apostle Paul: *That, while we were yet sinners, Christ died for us. Much more then, being now justified by his blood, shall we be saved from the wrath* of God *through him* (Rom. 5:8, 9). And contrary to the apostle John: *Whosoever is begotten of God doeth no sin, because his seed abideth in him; and he can not sin, because he is begotten of God*

(1 John 3:9). And also contrary to the words of Jesus Christ: *I give unto them eternal life; and they shall never perish, and no one shall snatch them out of My hand. My Father, who hath given them to me, is greater than all; and no one is able to snatch them out of the Father's hand* (John 10:28, 29).

PARAGRAPH 4
Who teach: That true believers and regenerate can sin the sin unto death or against the Holy Spirit.

Since the same apostle John, after having spoken in the fifth chapter of his first epistle, verse 16 and 17, of those who sin unto death and having forbidden to pray for them, immediately adds to this in verse 18: *We know that whosoever is begotten of God sinneth not* (meaning a sin of that character), *but he that was begotten of God keepeth himself, and the evil one toucheth him not* (1 John 5:18).

PARAGRAPH 5
Who teach: That without a special revelation we can have no certainty of future perseverance in this life.

For by this doctrine the sure comfort of the true believers is taken away in this life, and the doubts of the papist are again introduced into the Church, while the Holy Scriptures constantly deduce this assurance, not from a special and extraordinary revelation, but from the marks proper to the children of God and from the very constant promises of God. So especially the apostle Paul: *No creature shall be able to separate us from the love of God, which is in Christ Jesus our Lord* (Rom. 8:39). And John declares: *And he that keepeth his commandments abideth in him, and he in him. And hereby we know that he abideth in us, by the Spirit which he gave us* (1 John 3:24).

PARAGRAPH 6
Who teach: That the doctrine of the certainty of perseverance and of salvation from its own character and nature is a cause of indolence and is injurious to godliness, good morals, prayers, and other holy exercises, but that on the contrary it is praiseworthy to doubt.

For these show that they do not know the power of divine grace and the working of the indwelling Holy Spirit. And they contradict the apostle John, who teaches the opposite with express words in his first epistle: *Beloved, now are we children of God, and it is not yet made manifest what we shall be. We know that, if he shall be manifested, we shall be like him; for we shall see him even as he is. And every one that hath this hope* set *on him purifieth himself, even as he is pure* (1 John 3:2, 3). Furthermore, these are contradicted by the example of the saints, both of the Old and the New Testament, who though they were assured of their perseverance and salvation, were nevertheless constant in prayers and other exercises of godliness.

PARAGRAPH 7
Who teach: That the faith of those who believe for a time does not differ from justifying and saving faith except only in duration.

For Christ himself, in Matt. 13:20, Luke 8:13, and in other places, evidently notes, besides this duration, a threefold difference between those who believe only for a time and true believers, when he declares that the former receive the seed in stony ground, but the latter in the good ground or heart; that the former are without root, but the latter have a firm root; that the former are without fruit, but that the latter bring forth their fruit in various measure, with constancy and steadfastness.

PARAGRAPH 8
Who teach: That it is not absurd that one having lost his first regeneration is again and even often born anew.

For these deny by this doctrine the incorruptibleness of the seed of God, whereby we are born again; contrary to the testimony of the apostle Peter: *Having been begotten again, not of corruptible seed, but of incorruptible* (1 Peter 1:23).

PARAGRAPH 9
Who teach: That Christ has in no place prayed that believers should infallibly continue in faith.

For they contradict Christ himself, who says: *I made supplication for thee* (Simon), *that thy faith fail not* (Luke 22:32), and the evangelist John, who declares that Christ has not prayed for the apostles only, but also for those who through their word would believe: *Holy Father, keep them in thy name*, and: *I pray not that thou shouldest take them from the world, but that thou shouldest keep them from the evil one* (John 17:11, 15, 20).

CONCLUSION
And this is the perspicuous, simple, and ingenuous declaration of the orthodox doctrine respecting the five articles which have been controverted in the Belgic Churches; and the rejection of the errors, with which they have for some time been troubled. This doctrine the Synod judges to be drawn from the Word of God, and to be agreeable to the confession of the Reformed Churches. Whence it clearly appears that some, whom such conduct by no means became, have violated all truth, equity, and charity, in wishing to persuade the public:

> *That the doctrine of the Reformed Churches concerning predestination, and the points annexed to it, by its own genius and necessary tendency, leads off the minds of men from all piety and religion; that it is an opiate administered by the flesh and the devil; and the stronghold of Satan, where he lies in wait for all, and from which he wounds multitudes, and mortally strikes through many with the darts both of despair and security; that it makes God the author of sin, unjust, tyrannical, hypocritical; that it is nothing more than an interpolated Stoicism, Manicheism, Libertinism, Turcism; that it renders men carnally secure, since they are persuaded by it that nothing can hinder the salvation of the elect, let them live as they please; and, therefore, that they may safely perpetrate every species of the most atrocious crimes; and that, if the reprobate should even perform truly all the works of the saints, their obedience would not in the least contribute to their salvation; that the same doctrine teaches that God, by a mere arbitrary act of his will, without the least respect or view to any sin, has predestinated the greatest part of the world to eternal damnation, and has created them for this very purpose; that in*

the same manner in which the election is the fountain and cause of faith and good works, reprobation is the cause of unbelief and impiety; that many children of the faithful are torn, guiltless, from their mothers' breasts, and tyrannically plunged into hell: so that neither baptism nor the prayers of the Church at their baptism can at all profit them; and many other things of the same kind which the Reformed Churches not only do not acknowledge, but even detest with their whole soul.

Wherefore, this Synod of Dort, in the name of the Lord, conjures as many as piously call upon the name of our Savior Jesus Christ to judge of the faith of the Reformed Churches, not from the calumnies which on every side are heaped upon it, nor from the private expressions of a few among ancient and modern teachers, often dishonestly quoted, or corrupted and wrested to a meaning quite foreign to their intention; but from the public confessions of the Churches themselves, and from this declaration of the orthodox doctrine, confirmed by the unanimous consent of all and each of the members of the whole Synod. Moreover, the Synod warns calumniators themselves to consider the terrible judgment of God which awaits them, for bearing false witness against the confessions of so many Churches; for distressing the consciences of the weak; and for laboring to render suspected the society of the truly faithful.

Finally, this Synod exhorts all their brethren in the gospel of Christ to conduct themselves piously and religiously in handling this doctrine, both in the universities and churches; to direct it, as well in discourse as in writing, to the glory of the Divine name, to holiness of life, and to the consolation of afflicted souls; to regulate, by the Scripture, according to the analogy of faith, not only their sentiments, but also their language, and to abstain from all those phrases which exceed the limits necessary to be observed in ascertaining the genuine sense of the Holy Scriptures, and may furnish insolent sophists with a just pretext for violently assailing, or even vilifying, the doctrine of the Reformed Churches.

May Jesus Christ, the Son of God, who, seated at the Father's right hand, gives gifts to men, sanctify us in the truth; bring to the truth those who err; shut the mouths of the calumniators of sound doctrine, and endue the faithful ministers of his Word with the spirit of wisdom and discretion, that all their discourses may tend to the glory of God, and the edification of those who hear them. Amen.

INDEX

'ad 'olam 137
à Lasco 40, 236, 238, 241
Alva 30, 31, 233
Amsterdam consistory 74
Amyraut 240
Anabaptists 25, 26, 27, 32, 33, 233, 235
"analogy of being" 220
Andreae 235
Annotata ad Vetus Testamentum 132
Antibarbarus biblicus 131
Apocrypha 63, 127, 128
Aristotelian 80, 216, 220
Augustine 162, 205
autotheos 48
Barth 14, 15, 195–198, 200–204, 206, 226–228
Baudartius 125, 128, 129
Bavinck 48, 138, 216
Belgic Confession 31, 34, 42, 45, 46, 47, 73–75, 145, 152, 154, 164, 201, 217, 218, 233
Bellarmine 65, 240
Berkhof H. 205
Berkhof L. 211
Berkouwer 78, 116, 117, 198, 202–206, 208, 209, 212
Beza 45, 47, 57, 64, 66, 67, 74, 77, 126, 146, 218, 235–237
biblical humanism 40
Bijencorf 240
Boer 208
Boettner 211
Bogerman 57–59, 60, 126, 128–130, 141, 151, 235, 254
Bolsec 77
Brethren of the Common Life 23
Bruly 233
Bucer 25, 241

Bucerus 125, 128, 129
Bullinger 26, 40, 165, 242
Calvin 13, 14, 15, 26, 27, 40, 53, 66, 77, 82, 90, 109, 111, 118, 133, 142, 146, 154, 162, 165, 170, 183, 184, 190–194, 195–199, 203, 204, 208, 216–218, 223, 224, 228, 230, 233, 235–237, 242, 261
Castellio 43, 77, 146, 235
catechesis 37
Catechism of Geneva 208
Charles the Bold 20
Charles II 17
Charles V 20, 21, 28, 29, 233
church order 31, 32, 34, 36, 37, 152, 239
Collatio Hagiensis 52, 54, 75
Compendium 238
Confession of the Schools 208
Confession of 1967 226, 228
conventicles 25, 29
Coolhaes 41, 42, 44, 77
Coornhert 41, 74, 77, 145, 146, 235, 238, 240
Cornelii 128
Council of Blood 30
Council of Trent 29, 76, 225
Count Edzard 233
Counter Remonstrance 47, 52, 75, 234, 238, 247, 248, 254
Cranmer 239, 241
Cunningham 49, 76–78, 155
Curcellaeus 49, 77
Czar Peter 141
Daane 198
Dammannus 58, 236, 253
Dathenus 233, 236
de Brès 233
Decalogue 84, 286
decretum absolutum 196–199, 202
de la Grange 233
Delft, conference at 75, 146, 148, 234
Deodatus 256

deposed/deposition 11, 34, 51, 148, 260
de Sales 235
Descartes 69
Deus nudus 197, 198
Deux Aes Bible 124
Diestel 132
Doleerende 51
Drusius 57, 125, 129, 131, 236
Duifhuis 41–44, 66, 237
Dyrkinus 123, 124
Egmont 29, 31
Eighty Years' War 22, 233
ekloge 206, 209
Elector Frederick 236, 251
Emden, Synod of 42, 124, 233, 240
Episcopius 48, 49, 59–61, 63, 67, 75–77, 154, 237, 259
Erasmus 40, 74, 77, 238
Erastian 43, 44, 237, 238
Faukelius 58, 128, 129, 237, 238, 254
foreign delegates 63, 68, 73, 150, 151, 255–257, 269
Forma ac Ratio 239
Forms of Unity 42, 47, 145, 152
Formula of Concord 196
Frederik Hendrik 67, 68
French Confession 208
Gansfort 25
Gomarus 47, 48, 61–69, 75, 127, 132, 146, 147, 234, 238, 255
Gouda Catechism 147, 234
Granvelle 28–29
gravamen 206
Groen van Prinsterer 39, 50
Grotius 49–51, 75, 132–134, 137, 138, 142, 234, 238, 240
Gutenberg 23
Hague, Synod of the 32, 42, 124, 234
Hales 47
Heidelberg Catechism 14, 34, 42, 46, 48, 73–75, 114, 145, 147, 150, 154, 217, 218, 233, 236
Heiligerlee 30

Hendry 227
Herberts 41–44
hermeneutics 132, 133
historiography 39, 40
Hoen 25
Holy Office 29
Holy Roman Empire 19
Hommius 47, 52, 58, 75, 129, 236, 238, 253
Hoorn 31, 44, 51, 259
iconoclasm 30, 233
image of God 43, 83, 108, 221, 223, 248, 285, 291
infralapsarians 47, 48, 53, 66, 90, 187, 188, 199, 213
Inquisition 22, 29, 30, 31, 33
Institutes 53, 111, 170, 183, 192, 233
interrelatedness of doctrines 80, 102
James I 66, 69, 255
Jesuits 33, 77, 239, 240
Joris 26
Junius 146
Kant 225–227
Kerckelycke Historie 39, 243
Kierkegaard 227, 228
King James Version 126
Klare Wijn 228
Koster 23
Kraus 133, 134
Kuchlinus 146
Kuenen 133
Laud 50
League of Arras 31
Leicester 234
liber vitae 196
Liesveldt Bible 121–123, 233
Limborch 48
Lubbertus 59, 61, 64–66, 70, 237, 239
Luther 23–26, 40, 77, 121–125, 133, 154, 216, 217, 221, 233
Lutherans 25, 26, 32, 64, 131, 154, 228, 235, 236, 257
Lydius 146, 239, 251, 253

Index

311

Maccovius 59, 239
Magdeburg edition 123
Margaret of Parma 28
Marloratus 124
Marnix 124, 125, 239
Martinius 63, 256
Matthias 31
Maurice 35, 51, 67, 68, 75, 149, 234, 241, 242
Melanchthon 40
Middelburg, Synod of 32, 34, 42, 234
ministers, training of 37, 151
missions 37, 109, 169, 240
More 40
"natural light" 84, 156, 286
Newman 225
Nicole 46, 48
oath of Synod 79
Oecolampadius 25, 26
Oldenbarnevelt 33, 35, 44, 49–51, 75, 234, 247
order of Canons 81
Pacification of Ghent 31, 234
Pastor 26
Pastoral Letter 201
Pelagianism 41, 49, 77, 154, 283–285, 294, 295, 300
perfectionism 48
"permissive decree" 109
Philip II 21, 22, 28–30, 233, 234
Pietersma 208
Piscator 125, 240
Piscator Bible 125
Plancius 45, 75, 146, 240, 247
Platt 80, 154
Polman 52–56, 206–208, 212
precursors 41–43
predestinatio gemina 52
Proof of the Power of Godliness 69
"pure" church 26
Puritan influences 69

"quinquarticular controversy" 147
rationalism 48, 219
reconciliation 12, 85, 99, 102, 135, 159, 167, 244, 249, 263, 264, 284, 286
"Rederijkerskamers" 23
Reformed Church in America 114, 269
Reformed churches ("Gereformeerd") 202
refugee congregations 62, 233, 236, 239, 241
Remonstrance 47, 48, 52, 67, 75, 80, 147, 148, 154, 183, 191, 218, 222, 234, 243–245, 247
Renaissance 19
Resolution for Peace 50, 234
Ridderbos 205
Rivetus 132, 240
Rode 25
Rolandus 58, 128, 241, 253
Romanticism 40
Ruysbroec 23
Sacramentarians 25, 33
Sadoleto 40
Schaff 36, 77, 147, 243, 269
schism 26, 34, 44, 50, 62, 149
Scriptura sola and *tota* 170
Semi-Pelagianism 40, 43, 73, 74, 81, 196, 208
Sententia Remonstrantium ("Opinions") 13, 76, 81, 97, 145, 261
"Sharp Resolution" 50, 51, 234
Sheol 139
Simons 26, 27
Snecanus 41, 42
Socinianism 45, 49, 69, 77, 135, 154, 239
"soul" 139
speculum electionis 196–198
Stadholders 21
Staten-Bijbel 124, 130, 131, 133, 134, 136, 137, 139–142
States-General 11, 58, 69, 70, 234, 251, 252
Stelling 141
Sturm 62

Index

subordinationism 48
supralapsarianism 47, 48, 53, 64, 75, 90, 188, 199, 213, 239
syllogismus practicus 203
synergism 154, 204, 207, 208
Synopsis Purioris 241, 242
Taffin 146
tertium genus 40
theological students 152
theologoumenon 55
Triglandius 39, 45, 51, 55, 241, 243, 248, 253
Trijpmaker 25
"unfeigned" call 85, 161, 162, 208, 287
Union of Utrecht 31, 234
Ursinus 62, 64, 242
Utenhove 122, 123, 241
Uytenbogaert 39, 46, 48, 49, 66–70, 75, 146, 234, 241, 243, 247
Vander Borre 146
Van Til 15, 197, 215
van Wingen 122–124
Vatican 224–226, 228
Venator 41–42, 44
virgin birth 140
Voetius 68, 69, 228, 241, 253
Vorstius 63, 65–67, 69, 70, 154, 241
waardgelders 35
Walaeus 129, 242, 255
Waldensians 23, 235
Wesel, Convent of 31, 233, 236, 240
Westminster Confession 114, 183–194, 211, 226–230
Wiggerts 41–44
William Louis 51
William of Orange 28–31, 33, 234, 236, 239
William III 17
Woelderink 199, 200
Zanchius 146, 242
Zwingli 25, 26, 154

ENDNOTES

Chapter 1 – The Rise of the Reformed Churches in the Netherlands
1. Conditions in the Netherlands at the beginning of the fifteenth century are described esp. by P. J. Blok: *A History of the People of the Netherlands*, 3 vol. (New York: 1899–1900) and the well-known work of John L. Motley: *The Rise of the Dutch Republic*, 3 vol. (London-New York: 1856), on which accounts many church historians have leaned heavily also J. Reitsma: *Geschiedenis van de Hervorming en de Hervormde Kerk der Nederlanden*, 4th ed. (Utrecht, 1933), pp. 1–72 on the social, educational and religious conditions of the people.
2. On the aspirations of the French kings to control the dutch ports, cf. Henry S. Lucas; *The Renaissance and the Reformation* (New York, 1934), pp. 461–464.
3. On the significant role played by Charles V, cf. G. R. Elton: *Reformation Europe 1517-1559*, pp. 35–52, 239–267.
4. From the beginning of his reign Charles V was determined to stamp out heresy. However, as Preserved Smith relates in his *The Age of the Reformation* (New York, 1920), pp. 242, 243, many people "kept Luther's opinions" but without openly breaking with the Roman Catholic Church and organizing themselves as Protestant churches. The first edict against heresy dates from 1520, published the next year.
5. This is true even of the formidable Edict of 1550, which besides forbidding the reading and possessing of religious books not approved, the holding of services outside of the church, etc., went so far as to decree:

> Moreover we forbid all lay persons to converse or dispute concerning the Holy Scriptures, openly or secretly, especially on any doubtful or difficult matters, or to read, teach, or expound the Scriptures, unless they have duly studied theology and been approved by some renowned university . . .
>
> That such perturbators of the general quiet are to be executed, to wit: the men with the sword and the women to be buried alive, if they do not persist in their errors; if they do persist in them, then they are to be executed with fire; all their property in both cases being confiscated to the crown.

quoted by Raymond P. Stearns; *Pageant of Europe: Sources and Selections from the Renaissance to the Present Day* (New York, 1947), p. 166. This was the Edict, however, which was renewed and vigorously enforced by Philip II five years later.
6. On Philip II cf. Wm. H. Prescott: *History of the Reign of Philip II*, 3 vol. (New York, 1855–1858), esp. vol II, bk. 2; also Motley, *op. cit.*, vol. 1, p. 422, 531, on Philip's duplicity in dealing with the Netherlands and the documentary evidence for this which is found in his letter to the papal nuncio.
7. The dates of this war, often called the Dutch Revolt, are 1568 to 1648, when the Peace of Westphalia achieved a balance of power in Europe and marked the end of the fierce wars of religion that had devastated the continent for more than a

century. A twelve year truce between Spain and the Netherlands was signed in 1609, but this peace was an uneasy one. During that period the Arminian controversy reached its crisis and was resolved at the Synod of Dort. For the first period of this war cf. Pieter Geyl: *The Revolt in the Netherlands 1559–1609*, (London, 1932).

8. Reitsma, *op. cit.*, pp. 17, 18 raises the question concerning Waldensian influences in the Netherlands. Mention is made of "Vaudois" in a few records; also of those who follow Wycliffe and Hus.

9. Reitsma, *op. cit.*, pp. 29–54; Maurice G. Hansen: *The Reformed Church in the Netherlands* (New York, 1884), pp. 17–22; Albert Hyma: *The Christian Renaissance: A History of the Devotio Moderna* (Grand Rapids, 1924) and *The Brethren of the Common Life* (Grand Rapids).

10. On Ruysbroec, cf. Reitsma, *op. cit.*, pp. 22–25.

11. D. H. Kromminga: *The Christian Reformed Tradition* (Grand Rapids, 1943), p. 7.

12. That reorganization of the Roman Catholic hierarchy in the Netherlands was greeted with fear and rage has been widely acknowledged. Stearns, *op. cit.*, p. 166, stresses fear of the inquisition, since

> . . . by a bull of May 18, 1559, Paul IV created three new archbishoprics, fifteen new bishops, and nine prebends to each new bishop, 'who were to assist him in the matter of inquisition throughout his bishopric, two of whom were themselves to be inquisitors.' This clerical force, backed by Spanish soldiers, was an efficient body to root out heresy . . .

Smith, *op. cit.* p. 252, takes the position that this was also intended as "the nationalization of the church," to which Reitsma, *op. cit.*, pp. 135–138, adds that the common people and nobility alike saw in this a violation of their ancient privileges and rights as well as an economic threat. The clergy selected were men of poor spiritual caliber, spending more time on finances than on revitalizing the faith.

13. On the significance of the many Bible translations published in the Netherlands in these first years, cf. De Hoop Scheffer: *Geschiedenis der Kerkhervorming* pp. 256–282. The first English translation of the New Testament by William Tyndale was also published at Antwerp, for which the translator was burned at the stake in Vilvoorde in 1536.

14. A Eekhof: *De Avondmaalsbrief van Cornelis Hoen* (1528), (The Hague, 1917).

15. All historians agree on the immense influence of the early Anabaptists in the Netherlands. On whether the movement was inherently revolutionary and violent, however, there is wide disagreement. A sympathetic and admittedly biased view is presented by L. Verduin; *The Reformers and their Stepchildren* (Grand Rapids, 1964). Elton, *op. cit.*, p. 103, presents as his evaluation in the light of the facts cited,

> During the heyday of Anabaptism it appeared to contemporaries that there were now three religions to choose from: the popish, the reformed, and the sectarian. It has sometimes been argued that the effective elimination of that third choice wrecked the prospects of early toleration and liberty for the private conscience. This is to mistake the true nature of Anabaptism. Since it always embodied a conviction of sole salvation for a particular group of believers, and

often also the chiliastic dreams of salvation realized in the destruction of the wicked with the establishment of Christ's kingdom on earth, it was in its essence markedly more intolerant than the institutional Church. Its victory, where it occurred, led to terror; and that was in the nature of things . . . The Anabaptism of the early Reformation—no matter what pious and respectable sects may look back upon it as an ancestor—was a violent phenomenon born out of irrational and psychologically unbalanced dreams, resting on the denial of reason and the elevation of that belief in direct inspiration which enables men to do as they please . . .

A balanced but thorough evaluation is given by J. J. Westerbeek van Eerten in his popularly written *Anabaptisme en Calvinisme* (Kampen, 1905), esp. pp. 104–108.

16. The question of Calvin's influence in the Netherlands is by no means a purely academic one. Many historians who sympathized with the ideals and ideas of the Arminians have vigorously propounded the notion that the Dutch reformation was of a unique kind, represented by Erasmus and especially the "Sacramentarians" whose influence was throttled by disciples of Calvin after 1560. If this is true, then the Reformed faith was superimposed from without and at a late date. The proponents of this theory insist that Bullinger and not Calvin was the theologian early appealed to. However, on all major points these two were agreed and had close contact with each other. Calvin also signed the *Consensus Tigurinis* (1549) which he helped to prepare with Bullinger. Cf. Westerbeek van Eerten, *op cit.*, p. 201. Note also Pierre Brully's work in southern Netherlands as early as 1544, Reitsma, *op. cit.*, p. 119ff.

17. A. A. van Schelven: *De Nederduitsche Vluchtelingen-kerken der 16de Eeuw* (The Hague, 1909), which deals with the several emigrations from 1544 through 1576 in great detail, also on Calvin's influence and his relation to Bullinger and à Lasco, p. 316ff.

18. On Calvin's view cf. *Institutes*, 2 vol. (Grand Rapids, 1949) Bk IV ch. 20, esp. xxxi, vol. 1, p. 804, which does not allow for opposition to tyrants by private persons but appeals to the lesser magistrates "appointed for the protection of the people and the moderation of the power of kings." His views were much expanded by Francois Hotman (1524–1590): Franco-gallia (1573); Theodore Beza; *On the Right of the Magistrates on their subjects* (1574) which defended the position that even tyrannicide was justifiable when all other means of restraint had been tried in vain; and esp. the influential tract by the anonymous "Brutus" entitled, *Vindiciae contra Tyrannos* (1579) which has been ascribed to either Hubert Languet (1518–1582) or Phillip du Plessis Mornay (1549–1623), both influential French Huguenots.

19. George P. Fisher; *The History of the Reformation,* (New York, 1873) p. 289.

20. On the economic distress which stimulated the early emigrations of 1540 to 1546, cf. van Schelven, *op. cit.*, pp. 13–16, who mentions that in seven parishes of Bruges there were no less than 7696 poor, and the later and even larger emigrations of 1566–1570 under Alva, *op. cit.*, p. 25ff.

21. The iconoclastic movement of 1566 was not entirely a Protestant movement, although it resulted in a hardening of the division between Roman Catholic and Protestant. Nearly all the Protestant clergy had earlier warned stringently against

the "chanteries," realizing that these might lead to inciting the people to violence and bring upon their heads the vengeance of the king and his soldiers. In the movement of Aug. 1566 the mobs, however, did not loot in the hope of personal gain. An eyewitness account of what took place in the Cathedral of Notre Dame in Brussels is provided by the letter of Richard Clough, English representative in that city, to Sir Thomas Gresham, dated Aug. 21, 1566. After commenting that it began with a few "boys and rascals," he adds how thousands continued the work.

> So that, after I saw that all should be quiet, I, with above 10 thousand more, went into the churches to see what stir was there; and coming into our Lady Church, it looked like a hell, where were 1000 torches burning, and such a noise! as if heaven and earth had gone together, with falling of Images and beating down of costly works; in such sort, that the spoil was so great that a man could not well pass through the church . . . Yet they that this did, never looked towards any spoil, but broke all in pieces, and let it lie under foot . . . and before it was 3 of the clock in the morning, they had done their work, and all (were) home again, as if there had been nothing done: so that they spoiled this night between 25 and 30 churches.

quoted by Stearns, *op. cit.*, p. 167.

22. On the number of Protestant martyrs in the Netherlands estimates vary widely. Grotius, writing less than a century later, puts this at 100,000; Edward Gibbon asserts that "the number of Protestants who were executed by the Spaniards in a single province and a single reign, far exceeded that of the primitive martyrs in the space of three centuries and of the Roman empire." Motley, *op. cit.*, vol. II, p. 504, also puts the number high. Reitsma, *op. cit.*, p. 160 considers all these estimates much too high, even 18,000 under Alva as too high, mentioning that contemporaries speak of six to eight thousand cruelly executed during Alva's few years. But besides those publicly tried and executed for heresy, there were thousands put to death by the soldiery who at the instigation of king and inquisition sought to suppress the Reformed faith which during these years swept the entire southern Netherlands.

23. For the significance of the Union of Utrecht in the light of William of Orange's policy of religious toleration for all, as well as for the consequences of the League of Arras for the future of Calvinism in southern Netherlands, cf. Lucas, *op. cit.*, pp. 681, 682.

24. Biesterveld, P., and *Kuyper, H. H.: Kerkelijk Handboekje* (Kampen, 1905) contains all the church orders in effect from 1568 (Wesel) through Dordrecht (1618–19) with an introductory essay and supplementary decisions of the synods. This material is invaluable for an understanding of the confessional commitment of the Reformed churches as well as for their devotion from the beginning to the presbyterian-synodical polity against which the Arminians early began to agitate.

25. It is uncertain when the public worship of the Roman Catholics was prohibited. At the first assembly of the States of Holland, 1572, William of Orange through Marnix proposed that both Reformed and Roman Catholics should receive the right to worship publicly. Before the Synod of Dort met in 1574, however, this right was withdrawn from the Roman Catholics by the government largely

Endnotes

for political and military reasons. Cf. Reitsma, *op. cit.*, p. 170 ff. Meanwhile the government insisted on a measure of direct control in the ecclesiastical affairs of the Reformed, which is reflected in the church order adopted at Dort in 1574. This entangling alliance is defended by Reitsma and others who incline to defend the right of the Arminians in later decades to remain in the Reformed churches. It cannot be denied, however, that the concessions made in that and later church orders were forced by the government and always were protested by ecclesiastical leaders.

26. The church order adopted by this Synod was highly favorable to the Reformed who insisted on the church's right and duty to manage its own internal affairs. That it received approval at first from the States of Holland and could be widely introduced in the land must be ascribed in large measure to the favor which Robert Dudley, Earl of Leicester (1531–1588), showed to the Reformed when he was invested for a brief season with the government of the country. On Leicester, cf. *Encyclopedia Britannica* 14th ed., vol. 13, pp. 888–889; also article by Sidney Lee in *Dictionary of National Biography* (1888). After his fall from power, the States-General revoked their earlier approval, again fearing that the churches had too much independent power, and attempted to foist on them a church order prepared by a committee appointed by the government in 1591. Because of ecclesiastical opposition this could not be introduced. Cf. Reitsma, *op. cit.*, pp. 205–211.

27. Johan van Oldenbarnevelt, Holland's greatest statesman during the thirty years after 1586 and "raadspensionaris" of the States of Holland, played a significant role in the events leading up to Dort. He championed "states' rights" against a strongly centralized government under the Prince of Orange and authorized the "Scherpe Resolutie" of 1617 which pushed the nation to the brink of civil war and for which he was tried for treason and executed. A generally sympathetic description of him and his position is given by Reitsma, *op. cit.*, p. 245, 259, 271–279. For a detailed study cf. G. Groen van Prinsterer: *Maurice en Oldenbarnevelt* (Utrecht, 1875).

28. Philip Schaff, *op. cit.*, vol. I, pp. 514, 515.

Chapter 2 – The Background of the Arminian Controversy (1586–1618)

1. Letter to Bullinger, dated October 1, 1560.
2. In his *Verschooninghe van de Roomsche Afgoderye* (Excuse of Roman idolatry), answered by Calvin in his "Response a un certain Hollandois" (Answer to a certain Dutchman), *Corpus Reformatorum* vol. IX, p. 593. Coornhert was also the editor of a Dutch translation of the works of Calvin's opponent, Castello.
3. J. C. Triglandius: *Kerckelijcke Geschiedenissen* (1650), p. 281.
4. C. M. Vander Kemp: *De Eere der Nederlandsche Hervormde Kerk gehandhaafd* (1830), vol. p. 105.
5. Details of this story are found in W. to Water: *Tweede eeuw-getijde van de geloofsbelijdenisse der gereformeerde kerken van Nederlant* (1762), p. 75 ff. 11.
6. *Acta der Provinciale en Particuliere Synoden*, ed. Reitsma and Van Veen (1892), vol. I, p. 167.
7. *Ibid.*, vol. II, p. 18.
8. *Acta van de Nederlandsche Synodes der 16de Eeuw*, ed. F. L. Rutgers (1889), pp. 56, 57.
9. L. H. Wagenaar: *Van Strijd en Overwinning* (1909), p. 18.

10. Vender Kemp, *op. cit.*, pp. 190–103.
11. J. Hania: *Wernerus Helmichius* (1895), p. 195.
12. Triglandius, *op. cit.*, p. 241.
13. W. Geesink: *Calvinisten in Holland* (1887), p. 62.
14. "The safest faith is to know nothing." This motto is inscribed above the entrance of his great grandfather's house in Amersfoort; cf. D. H. Krommings: *The Christian Reformed Tradition* (1943), p. 29.
15. Coolhaes' biography has been written by H. C. Rogge: C. J. *Coolhaes, de voorlooper van Arminius en de Remonstranten* (1856, 1858), 2 vol.
16. Trigiandius, *op. cit.*, p. 283. A list of works on Arminius and Arminianism is found in the article by Roger Nicole on "Arminianism" in *The Encyclopedia of Christianity* (1964) vol. I, p. 411.
17. In terms of our time: "being a complete liberal."
18. His motto was "Bona conscientia Paradises" ("A good conscience is a Paradise"); cf. B. Glasius: *Geschiedenis der Nationale Synode* (1860), vol. I, p. 156.
19. *Encyclopedia of Christianity*, vol. I, p. 411.
20. After the draft of a declaration of principles entitled "Remonstrantie." The carefully chosen words of this Remonstrance approach orthodoxy as closely as possible.
21. P. J. Wijminga: *Festus Hommius* (1899), pp. 108, 109.
22. The twentieth century Groenewegen speaks of "the anti-confessional principle of the Remonstrants" in *De Remonstranten*, ed. G. J. Heeling (1919), p. 72.
23. John Hales: *Golden Remains* (1653), p. 433.
24. This distinction concerns the (dogmatic) order of the decree of God. Both supra- and infralapsarians taught that God's predestination preceded any human decision. But the difficult problem of the place of sin in the decree divided them. Both schools taught that God (actively) permitted sin and that he is not the author of sin; but the supralapsarians referred election and reprobation to the *Homo labilis* (man who can fall, man *before* the fall); the infralapsarians to the election and reprobation of the *homo lapsus* (fallen man).
25. K. Dijk: *De strijd over Infra en Supra-lapsarisme in de Gereformeerde Kerken van Nederland* (1012), pp. 91–97.
26. H. Bavinck: *Gereformeerde Dogmatiek*, 4th edit. (1928), vol. II, p. 330.
27. "of himself God"
28. Cf. *Encyclopedia of Christianity*, vol. I, p. 411. John Wesley was a consistent Arminian in his perfectionism.
29. William Cunningham: *Historical Theology*, 4th edit. (1960), vol II, pp. 375, 376.
30. Wijminga, *op. cit.*, p. 89.
31. Grotius: *Epistolae*, no. 966 (1687); quoted by J. Huizinga: Men and Ideas (1959), p. 337.
32. G. Groen van Prinsterer: *Maurice en Barnevelt* (1875), p. 130.
33. "complaining," i.e. in mourning because of injustices done against them.
34. *Ex Auditu Verbi*, Theological Essays presented to Prof. Dr. G. C. Berkouwer (1965), pp. 176–193.
35. Polman translates: "are not born" (Lat. *creantur*).
36. Vander Kemp, *Geschiedenis Nationale Synode* (1861), vol. II p. 19.
37. Wijminga, *op. cit.*, p. 113.
38. Triglandius, *op. cit.*, p. 557.

39. "Theologoumenon" is a theological opinion. Bavinck explains in his Dogmatics that according to Augustine and all Reformed theologians both Christ and the church are included in the decree of predestination. He continues

> There was difference of opinion, however, on the question whether Christ must be considered the object of predestination only or also of election. There were some like Calvin, Gomarus, Marck, De Moor, who said that Christ was appointed Mediator to bring salvation to his own; in that case the predestination of Christ as Mediator was logically preceded by the election of men. But others like Zanchius, Polanus and the Synopsis considered Christ also as object of election, because he was appointed to be not only Mediator but also Head of the church. In that case the election of Christ logically preceded that of the church. Cf. *Gereformeerde Dogmatiek*, vol. II, p. 367; also Polman: *Onze Nederlandsche Geloofsbelijdenis*, Vol. II p. 233–235.

40. Wijminga, *op. cit.*, pp. 105–111.

Chapter 3 – Leading Figures at the Synod of Dort

1. I wish to acknowledge my indebtedness to my colleague Professor Merle Meeter of the English Department, who spent considerable time in doing basic research for this chapter.
2. Maurice G. Hansen, *The Reformed Church in the Netherlands* (1884), p. 142.
3. *Acta der Nationale Synode te Dordrecht 1618–1619*, p. 9.
4. Hansen, *op. cit.*, pp. 158ff.
5. A. Kuyper Jr., *Johannes Maccovius* (Leiden, 1899), pp. 82–100.
6. Anton H. Haentjes, *Simon Episcopius* (Leiden, 1899), pp. 43ff.
7. *Acta*, pp. 15ff.
8. Haentjes, *op. cit.*, p. 44.
9. *Acta*, p. 60.
10. *Ibid.*
11. *Acta*, p. 68.
12. Cornelis Vander Woude, *Sibrandus Lubbertus* (Kampen, J. H. Kok. 1963), pp. 181–184.
13. G. P. Van Itterzon, *Franciscus Gomarus* ('s Gravenhage, M. Nijhof, 1930), pp. 102–106.
14. *Ibid.*, p. 379.
15. *Acta*, p. 248.
16. Van der Woude, *op. cit.*, p. 599.
17. *Acta*, p. 206.
18. Van der Woude, *op. cit.*, p. 576.
19. Haentjes, *op. cit.*, pp. 41ff.
20. P. Geyl, *The Netherlands in the Seventeenth Century, I* (New York, Barnes and Noble, 1961), p. 216. Regretably, C. Steenblok, *Gijsbert Voetius, Zijn leven en worken,* published in the Netherlands in 1942 could not be consulted.
21. Van der Woude, *op. cit.*, pp. 157.
22. *Ibid.*

Chapter 4 – The Doctrinal Delieverances of Dort

1. Arminius (1560–1609) was born in the year in which Melanchthon died, and he died in the year in which the Pilgrim fathers arrived in Leiden.

2. Dr. Fairbairn summarizes Arminius' views thus: "He held that it (the Calvinistic doctrine) made God the author of sin, that it restricted his grace, that it left multitudes outside without hope, that it condemned for believing the truth, namely that for them no salvation was either intended or provided in Christ, and it gave absolutely false security to those who believed themselves to be the elect of God." (Encyclopedia Brittanica. (Chicago: The University of Chicago, 1945), Vol. II, p. 386).

3. W. Cunningham, *Historical Theology* (Edinburgh: T. & T. Clark, 1870), Vol. II, pp. 374ff.

4. *Ibid.*, pp. 375ff.

5. P. Schaff, *The Creeds of Christendom*, 6th ed. (New York: Harper & Brothers Publishers, 1919). Vol. I, p. 509.

6. *Op. cit.*, II, p. 377.

7. *Ibid.*, p. 378.

8. "Vragen Rondom De Belijdenis," *Gereformeerd Theologisch Tijdschrift*, 63e jrg. Afl. 1 (1 Feb. 1963), p. 11. Berkouwer refers to Canons I, 8, 9, 18.

9. *Encyclopedia of Religion and Ethics*, ed. by James Hastings. (New York: Charles Scribners, 1962) Vol. I, pp. 811ff.

10. *Ibid.*, p. 812.

11. *The Articles of the Synod of Dort, Trs. by T Scott. Introductory Essay by S. Miller.* (Philadelphia: Presbyterian Board of Publication, 1856), p. 27.

12. Conclusion of the Canons of Dort.

13. Cf. the Form of Subscription in use in the Christian Reformed Church which had its origin at the Synod of Dort: "We the undersigned . . . do hereby, sincerely and in good conscience before the Lord, declare by this our subscription that we heartily believe and are persuaded that all the articles and points of doctrine contained in the Confession and Catechism of the Reformed Churches, together with the explanation of some points of the aforesaid doctrine made by the National Synod of Dordrecht, 1618–'19, do fully agree with the Word of God." Psalter Hymnal, Centennial Edition. *Doctrinal Standards and Liturgy of the Christian Reformed Church* (Grand Rapids: CRC Publishing House, 1959), p. 71. The Confession referred to is the Belgic Confession and the catechism meant is the Heidelberg Catechism.

14. P. Schaff, *op. cit.*, Vol. III, p. 549.

15. *Encyclopedia of Religion and Ethics*, Vol. I, p. 812. footnotes.

16. E.g., T. F. Torrance states that classical Calvinism as expounded by the Synod of Dort and the Westminster Assembly is "an amalgam of Aristotelian logic and the Reformed faith." Introduction to Robert Bruce, *The Mystery of the Lord's Supper*, p. 32.

17. Cf. F. H. Klooster, Calvin's Doctrine of Predestination, (Grand Rapids: Calvin Theological Seminary Monograph Series: III, 1961), pp. 8ff.

18. In what follows the positive articles in the Canons will simply be referred to thus (I, 1). The negative parts of the Canons, the Rejection of Errors, will be cited thus (I, par. 1) etc. The text quoted is from the official version of the CRC, see note 13 above.

19. Cf. *Acts of the Christian Reformed Church*, 1924.

20. *Institutes*, III, 21 ff. Cf. F. H. Klooster, *op. cit.*, pp. 8ff.

21. For a summary exposition of these views, see L. Berkhof, *Systematic*

Theology, (Grand Rapids; Wm B. Eerdmans Pub. Co., (1941) 2nd revised & enlarged edition., pp. 118 ff. For an extensive study of these doctrines see K. Dijk, *De strijd over Infra- en Supra lapsarisme in de Gereformeerde Kerken van Nederland* (Kampen: J. H. Kok, 1912) pp. 299.

22. Italics added. Cf. A. A. Hoekema, "Needed: A New Translation of the Canons of Dort," *Calvin Theological Journal,* Vol. 3, No. 1 (April 1968), pp. 41–47.

23. Cf. also the Heidelberg Catechism, Q. 10–18 and the Belgic Confession, Art. 16–20.

24. Cf. the recent controversy in the Christian Reformed Church concerning the atonement and the love of God. For summary and literature cf. Acts of Synod, 1967, pp. 486–607.

25. Note the repeated references throughout the Canons to both original sin as well as all our other sins. Note that this is also what is meant when the Canons say that we are under condemnation also for original sin and not just for the sin of unbelief, I, 15. Cf. II, par. 5.

26. It would conflict with the explicit teaching of the Canons if one were to take the reference in this article to unbelief as "not owing to any defect or insufficiency in the sacrifice offered by Christ upon the cross" to mean that it was a sacrifice which actually expiated the sins of all. That is not the implication of the Canons here. They are simply explaining that the entire responsibility and causality of sin lies wholly in man and not in God.

27. Cf. L. Berkhof, *Systematic Theology* (Grand Rapids: Wm. B. Eerdmans, 1941), pp. 78 ff., 105.

28. The Apostles Creed is mentioned (II, par. 1). Reference is made to the "prevailing agreement of evangelical doctrine" in V. par. 2. The Socinian error is referred to in II, par. 4 and Pelagius is mentioned in I, par. 4; II, par. 3, 6; III/IV, par. 7, 9; V, par. 2. Cf. also specific errors referred to in the Conclusion of the Canons.

29. *Op. cit.,* pp. 12–18, especially.

30. *Ibid.,* p. 17.

31. J. Murray, *The Epistle to the Romans, Vol. II* (Grand Rapids: Wm. B. Eerdmans, 1965), p. 18.

32. *Ibid.,* p. 24.

33. *Eternal Predestination,* p. 36 (C. O. VIII, 265).

34. III, xxi, 1(0. S. IV, 368).

35. III, xxi, 1(0. S. IV, 369).

36. Conclusion of the Canons of Dort.

Chapter 5 – The Synod and Bible Translation

1. This survey is based on C. C. de Bruin's *De Statenbijbel en Zijn Voorgangers* (Leiden: A. W. Sijthoff, 1937), pp. 211–173; cf. also S. van der Woude, "Dutch Versions" in *The Cambridge History of the Bible.* (Cambridge: The University Press, 1963), pp. 122–125; and J. C. Rullmann, "De *Staten-Bijbel*" in *De Dordtsche Synode van 1618-1619* (Gereformeerd Traktaatgenootschap "Filippus." 1918), pp. 137–145.

2. In a note on Colossians 1:2 one reads: "Grace, that is forgiveness of sins through Christ; peace, that is that we know within ourselves that we surely believe to be saved by Christ." A note on 1 Peter 2:5 reads: "To be built upon the stone is to put all our hope upon Christ."

3. The London refugee congregation was very influential for the development of the Reformed church on the mainland. Cf. Marten Woudstra, *De Hollandsche VreemdelingenGemeente to London* (diss), (Groningen: J. B. Wolters, 1908), pp. 92 ff. This work contains specimens of Utenhove's metrical psalms.

4. Cf. S. Van der Woude, *op. cit.* p. 124, who states that the "J. D." who translated the New Testament was "probably" Dyrkinus. De Bruin, *op. cit.*, p. 236, is more sure about "J. D.'s" identity.

5. Marnix was a nobleman, writer, diplomat, city-magistrate and philogian. He is the author of the Dutch national anthem. He carried a Hebrew Bible with him on all his wanderings, cf. C. D. Busken Huet: *Het Land Van Rembrandt*, 2nd ed., (Haarlem: H. D. Tjeenk Willink, 1886), Vol. II, 1. p. 11.

6. Marnix' opinion about the *Deux Aes Bible* was expressed in a letter to his friend, the well-known Franeker orientalist J. Drusius.

7. Bogerman, 1576–1637, a native of Friesland and much attached to his native province, was a minister of the Reformed church at Leeuwarden. He had studied at Oxford, Cambridge, Zürich and Geneva (Beza!) and had received his linguistic training from the learned Drusius at Franeker.

8. Giovanni Diodati, (1576–1649) was born in Geneva of *emigre* parents. He played a leading part in the defense of the orthodox position at the Synod of Dort and participated in the formulation of the Canons. His Bible translation is still being used in Italy: cf. *Cambridge History of the Bible*, p. 112; and *Die Religion in Geschichte and Gegenwart*, (Tubingen: J. C. B. Mohr, 1958), Vol. II, Co. 199, 200.

9. An edition of the *Staten-Bijbel* in the present writer's possession contains the apocrypha, preceded by a lengthy "Warning To The Readers." The following points are mentioned whereby one may discern between canonical and non-canonical books. The canonical books of the Old Testament (1) are written by prophets (cf. Rom 16:26); (2) they are written in the Hebrew language; (3) they are contained in the canon of the Jewish or Israelite church (*Kercke*), since Jesus and the apostles never accused the Jews of having tampered with Scripture as such; (4) they contain nothing against holiness and truth.

10. Cf. H. J. Kraus, *Geschichte der Historisch-Kritischen Erforschung des Alten Testaments* (Neukirchen: Buchhandlung des Erziehungvereiss, 1956), p. 3; cf. also Herman Bavinck, *Gereformeerde Dogmatiek* (Kampen: J. H. Kok, 1928), 4e druk, p. 192; 2e druk, p. 219.

11. Cf. *Ludwig Diestel, Geschichte des Alten Testaments in der Christlichen Kirche* (Jena: Mauke's Verlag, 1869), p. 420 and *Realencyclopaedie für Protestantische Theologie und Kirche* ed. Albert Hauck (Leipzig: J. C. Hinrichs'sche Buchhandlung, 1901), s. v. Drusius.

12. Drusius had studied in Louvain and Cambridge. In 1572 he became a professor at Oxford, in 1577 at Leiden (Hebrew, Syriac and Chaldee) and in 1585 at Franeker. He was "an orientalist of European fame."

13. *Op. cit.*, p. 380; cf. p. 351.

14. Cf. L. Diestel, *op. cit.*, p. 422.

15. *Idem*, p. 431.

16. Cf. H. J. Kraus, *op. cit.*, p. 48

17. Grotius did not consider the Old Testament to be binding for the Christian. He believed that for the greater part it contained nothing but the civil right for the Hebrews (cf. *Die Religion in Geschichte and Gegenwart*, Vol. II, col. 1885, s. v. Grotius.)

18. Cf. H. J. Kraus, *idem*.

19. Cf. Avery Dulles, S. J. in *The Bible and Modern Scholarship* (Nashville: Abingdon Press, 1965), ed. J. Ph. Hyatt, p. 211: "The rigorous demands of historical method, *which can be practiced by men of all shades of belief and disbelief* (italics supplied), help one and all to enter more authentically into what Karl Barth has aptly termed "the strange new world of the Bible."

20. Cf. F. Mendenhall, in the volume cited above, p. 31.

21. Mendenhall remarks, somewhat pathetically it would seem, that in his opinion there is no academic method to the understanding of the mind of the Ultimate Author of the Bible, *idem*, p. 36; cf. also John Bright, *The Authority of the Old Testament* (Philadelphia, Westminster Press, 1967), p. 94; for a critique of Professor Bright's position from a Reformed perspective cf. John Stek, "The Modern Problem of the Old Testament in the Light of Reformed Perspective," *Calvin Theological Journal*, Vol. II, 2, Nov. 1967, p. 202–225.

22. On the possibility of subjectivism, also within evangelical circles, cf. the review of *Jesus of Nazareth, Savior and Lord*, by Daniel P. Fuller in *Journal of the American Academy of Religion*, Vol. XXXV, nr. 2, June 1967, p. 177.

23. On the interrelatedness of these movements and their influence on contemporary biblical criticism cf. H. Bavinck, *op. cit.*, Vol. I, p. On the Arminian influence on the contemporary scene; also H. J. Kraus, *op. cit.* p. 47.

24. This view is common to Protestants and modern Roman Catholics alike; (cf. Bruce Vawter, C. M. "Messianic Prophecies in Apologetics," in *Studies in Salvation History*, ed. C. Luke Salm, F. S. C., (Englewood Cliffs, Prentice Hall, 1964), pp. 68–80. Modern hermeneutics prefers to speak of the "views," "expectations," "hopes" of the writers of the Bible who are said to have shared the "aspirations of their people." All that Jesus does upon this view is to "realize" the "best hopes" of the prophets; he no longer fulfills "Scripture."

Chapter 6 – Preaching and the Synod of Dort

1. An exception to this in Reformed creedal statements is the Second Helvetic Confession, written by Bullinger (1562) and published in Latin (1566). It is printed in full in Philip Schaff: *Creeds of Christendom* (4th ed.), vol. III, pp. 234–306 (Latin), pp. 831–909 (English). Cf. ch. xiii, xiv, and esp. xviii.

2. Biesterveld, P., and Kuyper, H.H.: *Kerkelijk Handboekje* (Kampen, 1905), The preamble to the Articles of Wesel (1568) acknowledges a unity in doctrine as requisite for ecclesiastical fellowship, p.1; only such men are to be called and ordained to the office of minister of the Word as acknowledge the doctrine of Confession and Catechism, pp. 7, 8; cf. also on this matter the *Acta* of the Synod of Emden (1571), art. 2, p. 35; Dordrecht (1574) art. XIV, p. 66; art. XXII, p. 69; art. XXXII, p. 71; etc.

3. On the preaching of Arminius as occasion for the conflict, cf. *Acta ofte Handelinghe des Nationalen Synodi . . . tot Dordrecht, Anno 1618 ende 1619* (Dordrecht, 1621) "Voor-Reden aende Ghereformeerde Kercken Christi"; also L. Wagenaar: *Van Strijd en Overwinning* (Utrecht, 1909), pp. 39–40; J. Reitsma: *Geschiedenis van de Hervorming en de Hervormde Kerk der Nederlanden*, 4th ed. (Utrecht, 1933), pp. 245–247. Reitsma dates the initial conflict the year after Arminius was ordained, thus 1591. The 27 theses that occasioned much of the opposition to Arminius' appointment as professor in 1602 date from his discussions with Junius in 1597.

4. The issues involved are set forth in the gravamen of Classis Dordrecht to the provincial Synod of South Holland, 1604, demonstrating the serious proportions of the conflict evident in the churches.

> "Dewijle de mare gaet dat inde Academie ende Kercke van Leyden
> eenige verschillen geresen zijn, aengaende de leere der Gereformeerde
> Kercken, so heeft de Classis noodigh geacht, dat de Synodus

beraetslage over de middelen, daer mede op het bequaemeste ende spoedigste dese verschillen bijgeleght mogen worden, op dat alle scheurigen ende ergernissen, die daer uyt souden connen ontstaen bij tyts geweyrt ende de eenigheyt der Gerformeerde Kercken tegen de lasterigen der vijanden bewaert worde." *Acta*, p.iii.

5. This brief manual of 45 questions and answers was prepared by the ministers of Gouda, all inclined to Arminius' position. He had been consulted by them at the time of preparation. It was published without seeking the approval of the particular Synod. Title in Dutch: "Corte onderwysinghe der kinderen in de Christelijcke religie." It was attacked by Donteclock and thereupon defended by Corvinus, giving rise to dispute and dissension with respect to the value of the Heidelberg Catechism and the proper means and method of instructing children in the faith. Cf. Vander Tuuk, H. Edema: *Johannes Bogerman* (Groningen, 1868), pp. 90–93; and Uytenbogaert: *Kerckelijke Historie* (Amsterdam, 1646), vol III, pp. 168–204, for the Arminian argumentation and evaluation.

6. For the Remonstrance cf. Appendix C, p. 243.

7. Schaff, *op. cit.*, vol. I, p. 509.

8. One of the chief reasons why the controversy continued to smolder so long must be found in interference in ecclesiastical affairs by the government, which aimed at peace in the churches at all costs. Thus in 1608 the States of Holland placed a temporary ban on the holding of provincial synods, which was made permanent the next year. This explains to a large extent why during ensuing years the consistory of the Amsterdam church played its significant role in attempting to maintain some measure of contact among the churches. When the controversy spread to other provinces the States of Gelderland also suspended meetings of provincial Synod from 1612 through 1618. Cf. Reitsma, *op. cit.*, p. 255.

9. On difficulties experienced by the Reformed, schisms, etc., cf. Wagenaar, *op. cit.*, pp. 146–148; 175–211; also, J. Faber et al: *De Schat van Christus' Bruid* (Goes, 1965) pp. 46–53 which treats especially the experiences at the Hague where Uytenbogaert was strongly entrenched.

10. On the role played by the Amsterdam consistory cf. F. L. Rutgers: *Het Kerkverband der Nederlandsche Gereformeerde Kerken, gelijk dat gekend wordt uit de handelingen van den Amsterdamschen Kerkeraad in den aanvang der 17de Eeuw* (Amsterdam 1882).

11. For details on the Synod, its agenda, method of working, etc., cf. H. Kaajan: *De Dordtsche Synode van 1618 and 1619*. (Amsterdam 1918). Materials dealt with the opening sessions are analyzed and evaluated in H. Kaajan: *De Pro-Acta den Dordtsche Synode in 1618* (Rotterdam, 1618), and a similar study of even greater proportions on the closing sessions, after the foreign delegates had finished their work, is found in H. H. Kuyper: *De Post-Acta, een historische studie* (Amsterdam, 1899).

12. The language used at Synod was Latin. This quotation is from the report given by the foreign delegates of Hesse: "Conciones catecheticas debere esse quam brevissimas et ad captum rudiorum maxime accomodatas." It reproduces the emphasis of the decision as found in the *Acta Contracta*.

13. The background and development of synodical discussion on the issue of preparing men for the gospel ministry is thoroughly discussed by Kaajan: *De Pro-Acta*, pp. 260–303.

14. Cf. Biesterveld en Kuyper, *op. cit.*, "Kercken-Ordeninghe; ghestelt in den Nationalen Synod . . . in de jaren 1618 ende 1619," pp. 225–250; with the matters decided relative to the churches and their government in the 155th to the 180th sessions, pp. 251–296.

15. *Ibid.*, pp. 273, 274. This matter was dealt with in the 171st, 172nd, and 173rd sessions.

16. All quotations are taken from the official translation used in the Christian Reformed Church, found in Psalter Hymnal (Grand Rapids, 1959), pp. 44–66.

17. James Hastings (ed.): *Encyclopedia of Religion and Ethics*, art. on "Arminianism" by Frederic Platt, vol. I, p. 811ff. To the quotation cited in the article may be added the following.

> "The Calvinistic conception of justice was based altogether on the supremacy or rights of God; Arminianism so construed justice as to place over against him (ital. ours) the rights of man . . . The Creator owed something to the creatures he had fashioned, because of the manner of his fashioning; and these obligations did not cease because the first man had sinned . . ." We can hardly agree with his judgment, however, that "Its (i.e. Arminianism's) doctrine of man probably differentiates it more definitely from Calvinism than its doctrine of God." These two are so intimately bound up with each other, that a change of emphasis in the one involves a change with the respect to the other.

18. William Cunningham: *Historical Theology* (Edinburgh, 1870), vol II, pp. 374ff.

Chapter 8 – Calvin, Dort and Westminster—A Comparative Study

1. Space will not permit us to adduce the teaching of Calvin on this subject. A cursory reading of the *Institutes*, Book III, Chapters xxi–xxiii and of his *Commentary on the Epistle to the Romans*, Chapter 9 will show that this same insistence is sustained and pervasive. Cf. my *Calvin on Scripture and Divine Sovereignty* (Grand Rapids, 1960), pp. 56–64.

2. Cf. Calvin: *Institutes*, III xxiv, 1–4.

3. Calvin frequently uses the term "reprobation." Cf. citations given above.

4. *Comm. ad* Rom. 9:30 and 9:11 respectively.

5. *Ibid. ad* 9:30 (E.T., 1960), p. 216.

6. Cf. also *Inst.*, III, xxiii, 3, 8, 9, and 10.

7. Cf. Calvin: *Inst.*, III, xxi, 1 and 2; xxiii, 5, 12, 13 and 14.

8. *Inst.* I, xvii, 5 (E. T., 1960), p. 217.

9. *Comm. ad* Eph. 1:4. Cf. *Inst.*, III, xxii, 1 and 2; *De Aeterna Dei Praedestinatione, in Opera* (Brunswick, 1870), VIII, coll. 318ff.

Chapter 9 – Recent Reformed Criticisms of the Canons

1. Karl Barth, *Church Dogmatics*, 11, 2, pp. 3–506.

2. *Op. cit.*, 17/18.

3. Calvin, *Institutes*, 111, xxiv, 5.

4. Formula of Concord, Ep. XI, 7.

5. C. D., II, 2, 67.

6. *Op. cit.*, 69.

7. *Op. cit.*, 1/11.

8. *Op. cit.*, 11 2/3.
9. *Op. cit.*, 332.
10. C. Van Til, *Christianity and Barthianism*, 1962, 166.
11. J. Daane, in a review of Van Til's book, in *The Reformed Journal*, Jan. 1963, 29.
12. G. C. Berkouwer, *Divine Election*, 1960, 155/6.
13. *Op. cit.*, 156. Cf. also 57 ff. (Calvin on the "absolute power" of God); 105ff. and 139ff. (Christ, the mirror of election). Unfortunately this cannot be said of all later theologians. E.g., L. Boettner, *The Reformed Doctrine of Predestination*, 1932, completely omits a discussion of the "in Christ"-dimension of election. Although we are convinced that the author himself would utterly reject the *decretum absolutum-idea*, it cannot be denied that his presentation often gives the impression of speaking of a *Deus nudus*.
14. *Erratum—missing note.*
15. We use this term, not in the way of the Arminians at Dort (this has always been rightly criticized, because they saw the divine election as "motivated" by Christ's act, cf. Berkouwer, *op. cit.*, 134f), but in the way it was used by the English delegates at Dort, viz., that from all eternity God appointed Christ as the Head of the elect and the elect themselves as members of Christ. Cf. *Acts*, as republished in the nineteenth century by J. H. Donner and S. A. van den Hoorn, 342.
16. The judgments of the various groups of delegates vary at this point. Some very clearly state that our election was "in Christ," e.g., the English and the Genevan delegates, cf. *Acts*, 342, 385. Others mention Christ as executor only; e.g., the delegates from Switzerland (375), Nassau (368, 382), Bremen (394) and Emden (399, 409). The reason for this emphasis of Christ as executor lies no doubt in the fact that the Arminians explained the phrase "election in Christ" in the sense of a "*fides praevisa*," viz., he chose us as *being* in Christ. Hence the Swiss delegates declare: "But although the election refers to Christ, the Mediator, in whom we are all elected unto salvation and grace, yet God chose us, not as being in him before we were elected, but in order that we should be in him and saved by him" (*Acta*, 375). It is to be regretted that these theologians were led by this fear of misinterpretation by the Arminians, and therefore were unable to do full justice to the "in Christ" of Eph. 1:4. The official Canons, however, cannot be said to have succumbed to this fear. Read 1. 7.
17. J. G. Woelderink, *De Uitverkiezing*. 1951, 19.
18. Cf. *op. cit.*, 23, 25, 26, 76.
19. Cf. *op. cit.*, 19, 21, 22, 23, 26.
20. *Op. cit.*, 21.
21. *Op. cit.*, 43ff. One of Woelderink's criticisms of the Canons is that they almost completely ignore the O. T. (*op. cit.*, 8). This criticism is valid and explains the one-sided emphasis on individual election in the Canons.
22. *Op. cit.*, 49.
23. *Op. cit.*, 35, 45ff., 49, 58ff.
24. He does discuss it on p. 57, but by distinguishing between predestination and election he virtually separates the expression "before the foundation of the world" from the election.
25. *Op. cit.*, 46, 53. Cf. also his view that believers can fall away completely and definitely, 53ff.
26. *Op. cit.*, 70ff.

27. De Uitverkiezing, Richtlijnen voor de behandeling van de leer der uitverkiezing, aanvaard door de Generale Synode der Nederlands Hervormde Kerk, 1960, 13.
28. Op. cit., 14.
29. Op. cit., 15ff., 26ff.
30. Op. cit., 18; cf. 35.
31. Erratum—missing note.
32. Op. cit., 35ff.
33. Op. cit., 39.
34. Op. cit., 39. Cf. Canons III–IV, II and 17.
35. Op. cit., 39f. Cf. Canons I, 12, 13, 16; III–IV, 13.
36. Op. cit., 40. Cf. Canons 1, 7, 10, 15.
37. Op. cit., 40ff. The O. T. is hardly quoted. Many quotations from the N. T. are based on a wrong interpretation (Matt. 10:25, in I, 18 and Matt. 11:25, in Rejection of Errors I, 8; Acts 15:18 and Eph. 1:11 in I, 6). In I, 15, dealing with the decree of reprobation, no Scripture proof is given at all!
38. G. C. Berkouwer, *Divine Election*, 1960, 145ff.
39. Op. cit., 161.
40. Op. cit., 279ff.
41. Op. cit., 180.
42. Op. cit., 181.
43. Op. cit., 181. The last words of this sentence in the English translation are incorrect. They should not read: "the *Praescientia* of determinism" but "*praescientis (i.e.,* indeterminism) or determinism." Cf. the Dutch edition, 212.
44. Cf. op. cit., 20, where they are mentioned for the first time.
45. Op. cit., 183.
46. Op. cit., 185.
47. Op. cit., 187. But read also 189, where Berkouwer points out that time and again Calvin breaks through this scheme of a twofold *causa* and confesses that "the real cause of sin is not the counsel of God, but man's sin." On p. 190 Berkouwer adds: "Dort's criticism of the *eodem modo* finds its *preludium* in Calvin."
48. Op. cit., 188; cf. 189, 200, 215ff.
49. Cf. Dutch edition, 237.
50. Erratum—missing note.
51. Op. cit., 204.
52. Op. cit., 204/5.
53. H. Berkhof, *In de Waagschaal*, X1, 24.
54. H. N. Ridderbos, *Gereformeerd Weekblad*, X1, 33.
55. G. C. Berkouwer, "Vragen rondom de belijdenis," *Geref Theol. Tijdschrift*, LXIII, pp. 1–41.
56. Art. cit., 14.
57. Art. cit., 11.
58. Art. cit., 16.
59. A.D.R. Polman, "De leer der verwerping van eeuwigheid op de Haagse conferentie van 1611," in *Ex Auditu Verbi*, Festschrift for G. C. Berkouwer, 1965, 193.
60. Op. cit., 189–190. Cf. also Polman in several articles in *Gereformeerd Weekblad*, XVII, 10, XVIII, 2 and, in particular, in XIX, 4.
61. Polman, "Waar is the banier?" II, in *Gereformeerd Weekblad*, XIX, 4, p. 26.

62. H. R. Boer, "The Doctrine of Reprobation and the Preaching of the Gospel." *The Reformed Journal*, March, 1965; *Ibid.*, "Reprobation in Modern Reformed Theologians," April, 1955. H. Pietersma, "Predestination," Dec. 1966, Jan., Feb., May–June and Nov., 1967.
63. The same is true of Pietersma. In his articles, however, we again find the tendency to "actualize" election. He formulates predestination as "God's entering into history to deal with men in a new way," viz., in Jesus Christ. In his statements the pre-temporal aspect ("before the foundation of the world'), (Eph. 1:4; cf. 1 Tim. 1:9) is not done full justice.
64. G. C. Berkouwer, *Divine Election*, 195.
65. A.D.R. Polman, in *Ex Auditu Verbi*, 183; cf. 188.
66. *Ibid.*, *Gereformeerd Weekblad*, XIX, 5. p. 34.
67. Cf. *Ibid.*, in *Ex Auditu Verbi*, 179, 184, 185; Woelderink, *op. cit.*, 79.
68. Polman, *op. cit.*, 177.
69. *Ibid.*, *op. cit.*, 183.
70. *Erratum—missing note.*
71. *Acta*, 385.
72. *Erratum—missing note.*
73. L. Berkhof, *Systematic Theology*, 1953, 117/8.
74. L. Boettner, *op. cit.*, 104. For other examples, see H. R. Boer, "Reprobation in Modern Reformed Theologians," *The Reformed Journal*, April, 1965.
75. Cf. G. C. Berkouwer, art. cit., 16/17.
76. Cf. *Herderlijk Schrijven*, 30ff.
77. Polman, *Gereformeerd Weekblad*, XVII, 10. Underlining by us.
78. Cf. Polman, *Ibid.*, XIX, 5.
79. Polman, *Ibid.*, XVII, 10.
80. Cf. *Herderlijk Schrijven*, 18/19.
81. *Ibid.*, 19.

Chapter 10 – The Significance of Dort for Today
1. Johann Adam Möhler, *Symbolism*, tr. by James Burton Robertson (London: Gibbings and Co., 1894), p. 90.
2. *Ibid.*, p. 191.
3. *Ibid.*, p. 91.
4. *Ibid.*, p. 117.
5. *Ibid.*, pp. 117–118.
6. *Ibid.*, p. 103.
7. *Ibid.*, p. 129.
8. *Ibid.*, p. 190.
9. *Ibid.*, p. 175.
10. *The Documents of Vatican II*, gen. ed. Walter M. Abbott, S. J.; trans. ed. Very Rev. Magr. Joseph Gallagher (New York: Guild Press, 1966), p. 710.
11. *Ibid.*, p. 717.
12. *Ibid.*
13. George S. Hendry, *The Westminster Confession for Today* (Richmond: John Knox, 1960), p. 21.
14. *Ibid.*, p. 22.
15. George S. Hendry, *The Holy Spirit in Christian Theology* (Philadelphia: Westminster Press, 1956), p. 101.

Endnotes

16. Karl Barth, *Kirchliche Dogmatik*, II:2, p. 119; Eng. tr. p. 111.
17. *Ibid.*
18. *Klare Wijn* ('s-Gravenhage: Boekencentrum, n.v., 1967).
19. Cf. *Ibid.*, p. 32.
20. *Ibid.*, p. 34.
21. *Ibid.*, p. 35.
22. *Ibid.*, p. 71.
23. *Ibid.*, p. 77.
24. *Ibid.*, p. 82–83.
25. *Ibid.*, p. 102.
26. *Ibid.*, p. 107.
27. *Ibid.*, p. 113.
28. *Ibid.*, p. 117.

For documentation on references to Karl Barth and to the Confession of 1967 see the writer's *Christianity and Barthianism* and The Confession of 1967.

Notes

Notes

Notes

Notes